MAKE IT WITH MADEMOISELLE

By the Editors of Mademoiselle Magazine

Created by
the editors and staff of
MADEMOISELLE
Coordinator:
Dona Guimarães
Book and Cover Design:
Susan Niles
Technical Consultant:
Jo Springer
Illustrations:
Jackie McKee, Cheryl Lickona
Photographs:
George Barkentin, Andre Carrara, Tom
Clayton, Patrick DeMarchelier, Arthur
Elgort, Ishimuro, David McCabe,
Duane Michals, Darnell Mitchell,
Deborah Turbeville, Albert Watson

MAKE IT WITH MADEMOISELLE

By the Editors of Mademoiselle Magazine

Harmony Books

New York

Publisher: Bruce Harris
Executive Editor: Linda Sunshine
Editor: Pamela Riddle
Production: Gene Conner, Murray Schwartz
Typesetter: Ruth Hochbaum, B.P.E. Graphics,
Spring Valley, NY

Published simultaneously in Canada by General Publishing
Company Limited
Printed in the United States of America

Library of Congress Cataloging in Publication Data
Main entry under title:

Make it with Mademoiselle.

Includes index.
1. Textile crafts.   2. House furnishings.
3. Fashion.   I. Mademoiselle.
TT699.M34   1977   746   76-50108
ISBN 0-517-52864-9
ISBN 0-517-52865-7 pbk.

TABLE OF CONTENTS

SCARVING IT

TART UP A "T" AND SNAZZ UP A SHIRT

BUY IT AND BETTER IT

SHEETS ALL OVER

SCRAPBOOK: MAKING THE BEST OF BITS

SOURCES

Matmakers place mat kits are available from:
Fabrications
146 East 56th Street
New York, NY 10022
at $3.00 per kit postpaid

Trade names for some of the materials called for are:
Polyester quilting fleece—Thermolam
Nylon tape fastener—Velcro
Fusible web—Stitch Witchery
Fusible stiffening—Fusible Pellon
Iron-on fabric—Bondex
Window shade laminating kit—Lam-eze

Useful information you may need. If you have trouble finding a particular yarn, the following manufacturers will be able to recommend a source close to you.

American Thread
High Ridge Park
Stamford, CT 06905

Brunswick Worsted Mills
230 Fifth Avenue
New York, NY 10001

Bucilla
30-20 Thomson Avenue
Long Island City, NY 11101

Coats & Clark
72 Cummings Point Road
Stamford, CT 06904

Columbia Minerva
Consumer Service Dept.
P.O. Box 500
Robesonia, PA 19551

Emile Bernat & Sons
230 Fifth Avenue
New York, NY 10001

Lion Brand Yarn
1270 Broadway
New York, NY 10001

Malina Yarn
1071 Avenue of the Americas
New York, NY 10018

Reynolds Yarn International Creations
P.O. Box 55
Great Neck, NY 11023

Spinnerin
230 Fifth Avenue
New York, NY 10001

Tahki Imports, Ltd.
836 Palisade Avenue
Teaneck, NJ 07666

INTRODUCTION

There are two good reasons for doing-it-yourself. The first is to save money; the second is to make something unique, that reflects your personal style. Up till now the how-to guides available could demonstrate the former but did very little to provide the latter. And that's where Mademoiselle comes in—because only in the pages of Mademoiselle can you find clothes, accessories and home decorating ideas with this snap and dash.

Everything here was devised and done by the Editors of Mademoiselle. There's not a professional seamstress or wallpaper hanger among us which is why we've made the directions so quick and easy. If we can follow them, so can you. We're as aware of penny-pinching as is anyone which is the reason nothing in this book demands a lot of coin. Most of all, however, we're involved with style—it's our business— and that's what we think these pages have. But we're not saying that these are the *only* ways a sweater or a shirt or a room should look. These ideas and instructions will serve as a jumping-off point for your own ideas about colors and fabrics. We're giving you the basics—how-tos and tips we've gained from experience. Use them to make your wardrobe and your home absolutely and uniquely yours.

—The Editors of Mademoiselle

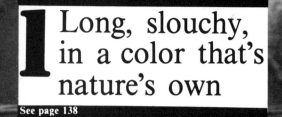

1 Long, slouchy, in a color that's nature's own

See page 138

MAKE IT A NATURAL

KNITTING AND CROCHETING

What you really want is fashion

If you're going to take the time and trouble to get out the knitting needles, the crochet hook and some yarn and get to work, you want the result to be considerably more than the kind of sweater or top you could buy just about anywhere. You want something special, something with snap and dash ... exactly what's coming up when you turn the page. Most of what's here is easy to make, a lot of what's here is quick to make — and everything here is fashion. Take it — and make it — from *Mademoiselle*.

All directions for this chapter begin on page 135.

 means you knit it

 means you crochet it

2 A quick
little crewneck
See page 138

3 Hooded, belted,
crunchy as cereal
See page 139

NATURALS

14

4 A long lean
line of ribs

See page 139

5 A pull of a vest
See page 140

MAKE IT RED! MAKE IT MEMORABLE!

16

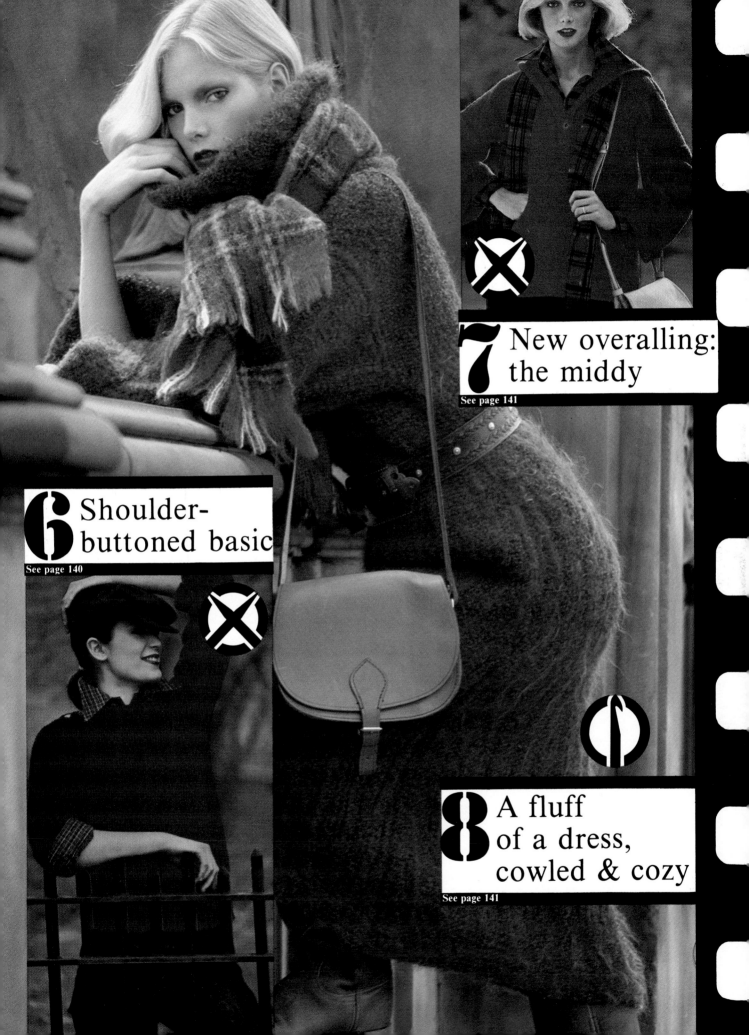

7 New overalling:
the middy

See page 141

6 Shoulder-
buttoned basic

See page 140

8 A fluff
of a dress,
cowled & cozy

See page 141

9 Drop-shouldered boatneck & brimmed hat
See page 142

10 Tweedy, hooded sweaterjack & big beret
See page 143

BEAUTIFUL BUNDLING: BIG,

11 Hooded, cabled, handy as a parka & baby cap

See page 144

HANDSOME & WARM AS TOAST

12 Chunky, crunchy
sweaterjack & cap

See page 145

BEAUTIFUL BUNDLING:
MOTTLED AND MARVELOUS

13 "Tweed" cardigan margined with satin-stitch

See page 146

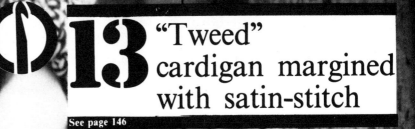

14 Sweaterjack & cap —terribly tweedy

See page 147

21

15 Brilliant Peruvian geometrics on a pull-vest and cap

See page 147

22

16
Icelandia—a long, wrappy cardigan trekked with zigzags

See page 150

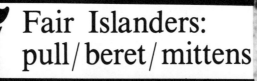

17
Fair Islanders: pull / beret / mittens

See page 151

PRIMAL THEMES

18 Tibetan cardigan & cap

See page 152

19 Guatemalan brights on black; Cardigan & small beret

See page 153

PRIMA THEMES

21 Guatemalan brights on black; Smock & big beret

See page 155

20 Pleasant peasantry: a striated tie-vest

See page 154

25

23 South American striping
See page 156

22 Romantic & lacy
See page 155

26

24 Celtic warmth

See page 157

SUMMER & WINTER SHAWLING

25 Haltered, sexy

See page 157

WORLD CLASSIC: THE TURTLENECK

28 Tennis warm-up

See page 159

WINDBREAKS

29 Color-rimmed singlet & babybag

See page 160

SAILOR SWEATERS

30 Striped boatneck

See page 161

THE PERFECTION OF POINTELLE

32 Tiny tie-on halter

See page 162

34 Tiny tank
See page 163

31 A long &
lacy smock
See page 162

33 Eyeletted
baby-pull
See page 163

See page 164

35 Barebacked, with a shrug of shawl

OPENWORK: BARE & BEAUTIF

For how to do these headwraps turn to page 44.

36 Small sexies: Halter
See page 165

37 Small sexies: Skivvy
See page 165

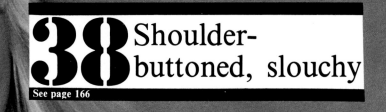

38 Shoulder-buttoned, slouchy

See page 166

39 Stringy carry-all

See page 167

GREAT FEELINGS: MARVELOUS TEXTURES

40 Stringy tote

See page 167

41 Long pull & scarf

See page 168

42 Boat-necked, easy

See page 168

PATRICK DEMARCHELIER

1 Drawstring scarfskirts

2 The shiek's
kaffiyeh

3 Small, snug
Chinoiserie

4 Peasant
headwrapping

SCARVING IT

Fashion editors, like magicians, can do miracles with scarves. A twist here, a knot there, the occasional pin and they can turn them into headwraps, beach gear (even a swimsuit), summer saronging...just about anything and everything. And if you follow the directions here and following, pick up their tricks and tips, so can you.

① Drawstring scarfskirts

How to make a scarfskirt
You'll need two 27″ or 36″ scarves per skirt—border scarves are particularly snappy for these. You'll also need 1¼ yds., ¾″ contrasting ribbon or twill tape. 1. With right sides of 2 scarves together, sew ⅝″ side seams. 2. Press seams open. 3. Turn top edge under 1″ to form casing. Stitch along top and bottom edges of casing. 4. Make a buttonhole in center front of casing and insert ribbon or tape for drawstring.
These skirts are at their best if low-slung, pick up extra dash if, as we did (middle row, left), you tie a contrasting 27″ scarf diagonally over one hip or wrap your waist several times with a long, skinny scarf.

② The shiek's kaffiyeh

Use a 36″ cotton or wool challis scarf. 1. Fold scarf into triangle, place center of long edge low on forehead and wrap around head. 2. Cross ends in back *under* the point. 3. Bring ends around front of neck, cross again. 4. Tie ends at back of neck *over* the point. 5. Take a second 36″ scarf and do the same over the first one.

③&④ Chinoiserie & peasant

Both of these are the same as #6 on the next page, but that *Chinoiserie* takes a 27″ scarf with #5 (next page) added over it. The *Peasant* takes a 36″ scarf for the base. Use a 14″ x 60″ rectangle for the twist and tuck a flower in one side.

Headwraps: How to really tie-one-on

5 Headwrapping's a great way to hide a pincurl (or hair that missed its last shampoo) as well as being a marvelous finish for a look. This double twist takes two cotton squares, 26" x 26" each. Fold each into a triangle, then roll them into long narrow tubes. Twist together very loosely, center on forehead (low over brow) and tie in back of head, tucking ends under.

6 Start with a small (22" x 22") cotton square, triangled, centered low over forehead and tied under its tail. Roll ends under to hide. Add on a cotton rectangle (14" x 60" here) twisted into a narrow rope. Center it over forehead, cross in back and tie, off center, up front in a bow.

⑦ We used a tablecloth-sized (42″ x 42″) thin cotton gauze scarf for this one. It's triangled, centered low on the forehead with the ends knotted once in back under the tail and once again over it. Each end is then tightly twisted, brought around to the front and crossed over the other end, and both finally tied in back under the tail.

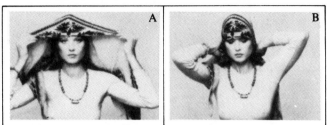

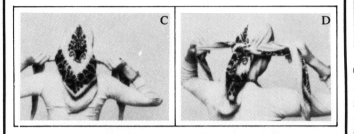

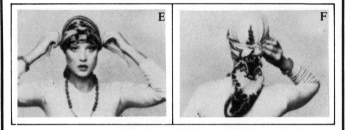

⑧ Triangle a small (24″ x 24″) cotton and tie it on very low, as shown, over the eyebrows. Let the tail fly free in back.

⑨ To fancy #8, tuck the tail under the knotted ends and roll under to hide. Take a second 24″ x 24″ square, triangle it, roll into a tube and twist. Center over forehead, tie in back and tuck ends under toward the front. Tuck your hair under as well—it's smoother.

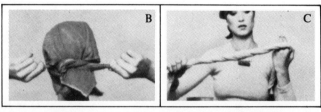

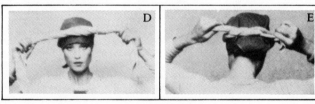

The universal headwrap

⑩ How to do it:

The universal headwrap

This is the single most useful headwrap to know about. It's one of the simplest, yet manages to look quite different each time you vary the size/shape/pattern of scarf you're using. It can be a square or long and narrow, but it *has* to be big enough to wrap around your head and have enough length to twist and tie. (See sketch below for the basic idea and take off from there.) The two below show variants. The head, left, is wrapped in a 45″ square of sheer cotton; the right in a 14″ x 60″ thin wool scarf.

Using a square, fold opposite corners together to form a triangle. (This step is unnecessary if you're using an oblong.) Place center of long side low on forehead, cross the two side tails behind head and twist into ropes (view A). Wind ropes in front and tuck the ends into each other. Tuck the back triangle flap over the rolled ropes (view B). Using a long narrow scarf, you'll get an open-crown turban effect.

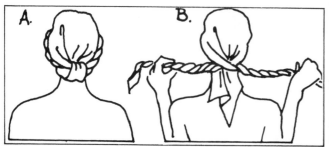

⑪ A headwrap hairdo

You can also use the right scarf to come up with the right hairdo. If you've got short to shoulder-length hair try this trick for a great look. Wash your hair, towel-dry it well and spray with setting lotion. Set your hair in flat pincurls, using thinner strands than you would for a dryer set. Use crossed hairpins rather than bobbypins so they'll lie flatter under the scarf.

Tie a 36″ cotton scarf in The Universal Headwrap around your head. Make it really tight as that's what gives the pincurls their staying power. Be careful not to disarrange them. Your head should be dry within 3 hours. If when you take off the scarf your hair's still a little damp, run a blow dryer over your head, then unpin and brush out.

Scarf toppings

There's a lot more to scarf toppings than a rectangle tied on like a long bandage. A few folds, loops, twists and knots and you get a lot of elegant variations on a theme.

(12) Halter bra

You need two 36″ squares. Fold one of them to wrap around the bosom and tie in back. Fold and roll the other to pull through the center and tie around the neck.

(13) Front knotted halter bra

Same idea as #12 but front-knotted. For turban, use one square triangled and tied to cover the head; roll two long ones around that and knot in the back.

(14) Crisscross halter

Use a 6′ rectangle, loop it around neck, cross in front and tie in back.

(15) African halter

Use a 6′ long cotton rectangle and loop around neck and under arms to cross in back, then bring around in front to tie.

12

13   14   15

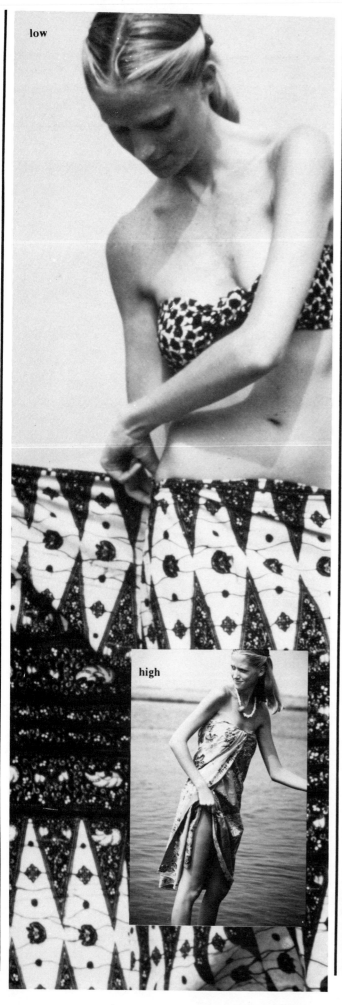

Giant scarf = beach pareu

The pareu is one of the simplest swimsuit coverups. It works best when made out of cotton and looks best when done in the gloriously flamboyant florals of its origin—the tropics. Classically the pareu is a length of fabric 35″ x 72″. If, however, you want a pareu that goes from bosom to almost ankle, 45″ x 72″ is better.

(16) On the beach, wear it high, wear it low

1. Place your giant scarf at the bustline or hipline so that the ends are front and center. Pull it so that you have a short piece and a long piece. 2. Take the corner of the short piece and a section of the top edge of the long piece and make a tight double-knot. 3. Tuck in the double-knot. You should have about 20″ of scarf left. Fold this twice, forming a panel and tuck top behind knot.

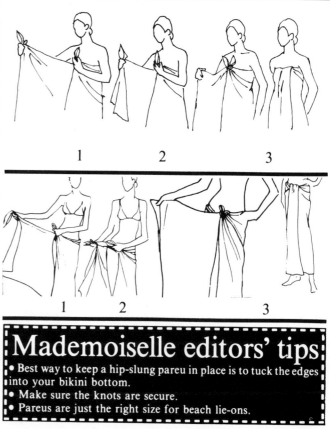

1   2   3

1   2   3

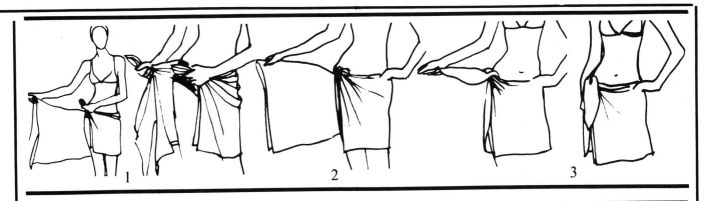

(17) The short pareu ⬆

1. Fold the pareu in half lengthwise and put it around your hips, the fold at the top with the opening at one side, one end long, one short. 2. Make a knot with the short piece and a section of the folded edge of the long one. 3. Take the remaining section, pass it under the knot and pull about 12 inches through. Fan it out.

(18) The halter wrap ⬇

1. Hold the scarf around your back with the two ends stretching out in front of you. 2. Still holding the scarf out stiffly, cross the two pieces tightly, twist the ends, (2A) then knot behind your neck (3).

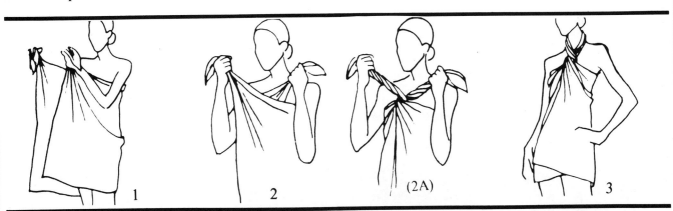

(19) The one-shoulder wrap ⬇

1. Hold the scarf in front of you, placing one of the corners at your right shoulder. 2. Pull the scarf under your left arm and around the back. Make it straight and tight. 3. Pull the scarf under the bust and under the left arm again. Tie it tightly on the right shoulder.

(20) Men's easy pareu ⬇

1. Fold the scarf lengthwise. 2. Wrap around the waist taking a corner of the short side and a small section of the long side to make a knot at the hip. 3. Make a double fold of the remaining fabric. 4. Tuck the outside part of the fold under the knot.

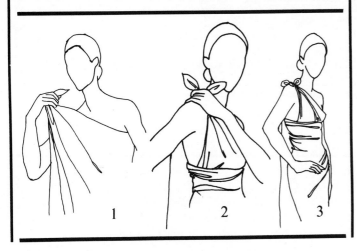

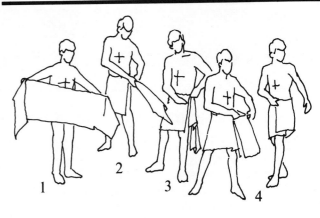

Great ways to work a scarf

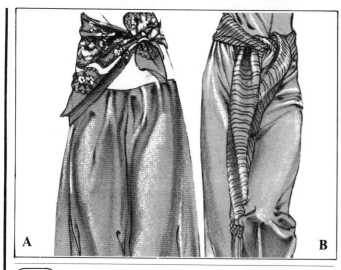

A   B

21 Let it go to your hips

A Gypsy hips—Take a square scarf, preferably a peasanty floral, triangle it once and knot at the hip.
B Hip sashing—Pull a superlong 7-footer taut around the hips and tie dead center. (Wool and cotton scarves are the best to use around the hips. They'll hold position better than scarves in a slipsy fabric.)

B

A

22 Use a scarf long and narrow

A Using a wool 7-footer, drape it around the neck, making sure it's centered, crisscross in front and tie loosely in back. Great for smockdresses.
B Twist two long (6'-7') chiffon scarves into ropes and knot together at the side of the hips. Best over narrow dresses or dropped-waistline skirts.

A   B

23 Use a man's scarf

Men's scarves are a good working size (12" x 50" or 60") and if they're wooly (as they often are) they're clingy.
A To make an obi-wrap, fold the scarf in half lengthwise and loop it dead center. For extra security, use a safety pin under the top flap.
B Cowling a scarf's a good way to fill in the neckline of a coat. Fold the scarf in half lengthwise, loop around the neck at the front leaving the ends at the back. Cross the ends, bring around to the front and tuck them in among the folds. This one takes a little practice for correct cowling.

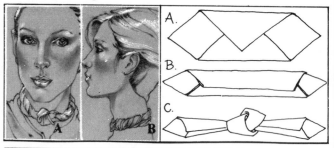

A   B   A.   B.   C.

24 The scarf as choker

A Using a 22" square fold it as in diagrams A and B. Tie a knot at the center (C). Tie in back keeping the big knot in front and tuck in the ends.
B Using an 18" cotton square (a man's handkerchief's about the right size) slightly dampened, fold as in diagrams A and B, then twist tightly into a thin rope. Tie in front and hide the ends underneath.

Scarves make a day at the beach

Your initial investment is six scarves. Out of them you'll get a bikini (it takes four) and a beach bag (that takes the other two) big enough to haul a hat, a towel, your sunshades and sun stuff.

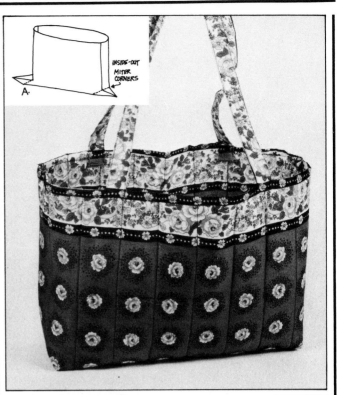

25 The scarf bikini

You'll need 4 22″ scarves, preferably soft cotton.
Top:
Fold two of the scarves into oblongs and tie one end of each together. Center this knot between the breasts and tie the other ends firmly in back. Tuck in back ends. (As with any other scarf top, this one goes better if the scarves are slightly dampened when tied.)

Bottom:
1. Fold two scarves into triangles as in Diagram 1.
2. Place the triangle points of both scarves together, as in Diagram 2, overlapping the two from point to point.
3. Sew the points together to form the crotch.
4. Tie firmly at the hips.

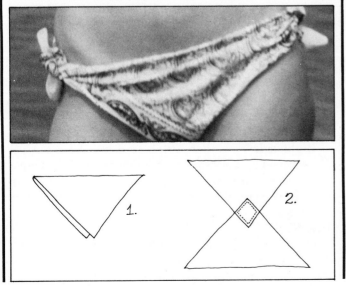

26 Quilted scarf bag

Materials: 2 border-print cotton scarves, each a 26″ square. ⅝ yard of polyester quilting fleece. Thread.

1. Cut 3″ off each side of both scarves (the width of the border here), so that each scarf now measures 20″ x 26″. Save scraps.

2. Cut piece of quilting fleece 20″ x 26″. Sandwich fleece between wrong sides of the 2 scarves. Pin around edges and through center to keep from slipping.

3. Quilt the three layers together by stitching parallel rows the length of the fabric (from border to border), with the rows about 2″ apart. Or quilt any design.

4. Stitch top and bottom edges of layers together by stitching along hem.

5. Fold, right sides together, bringing two border ends together. Stitch raw edges in ⅝″ seam. Stitch again ¼″ inside seam. Trim close to stitching.

6. Miter the bottom inside corners by bringing seam to center to form a triangle. Stitch across triangle about 2″ from the apex (corner of the bag). (Diagram A)

7. Make handles for bag from 2 long border strips cut from scarves. Turn in long edges of each strip ½″ toward wrong sides and press. Fold each strip in half lengthwise and press. Cut pieces of quilting fleece length and width (about 1″) of strips. Sandwich quilting fleece inside each strip, stitch along long edges.

8. Center handles on sides of bag. Lap edges of handles 1″ inside edge of bag. Stitch securely.

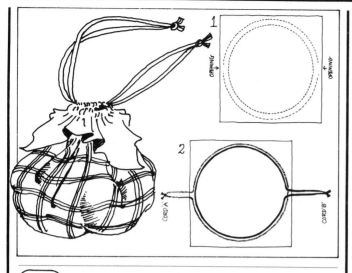

27 Run up a purse

You'll need 2, 20″ square scarves; 2, 1 yard lengths of cord.

1. Place scarves wrong sides together.
2. Make a casing by stitching parallel rows around edges (Diagram 1) skirting the corners. Leave the opposite sides of the casing open.
3. Insert a cord into the casing (Diagram 2) for drawstring, making a complete circuit. Knot the ends together. Insert the other cord in opposite opening and make a complete circuit of casing. Knot ends.
4. Pull cords to form purse. Tuck corners of lining scarf inside. N.B.: This purse is completely reversible.

28 Make a picture

The idea here is to handle the scarf as an artist would a canvas, making sure it is absolutely even and flat against the stretcher. By using this artist's technique, you're sure of having a smooth scarf picture. (Incidentally, flimsy fabrics, when stretched, show every wrinkle.) And we'd suggest you use a scarf with a big central motif.

1. Measure the scarf.
2. Buy 4 artist's canvas stretchers, available at art supply stores. They are sold in all standard sizes. Buy the stretchers about 2″ shorter in each dimension than the scarf measures. (E.g., for a 27″ square, buy four 25″ stretchers; for a 12″ x 24″ scarf, buy two 10″ stretchers and two 22″ stretchers.)

3. Assemble the stretchers, gluing if desired. To make sure frame is correctly aligned, put it into a door frame and tap the corners until stretcher frame is flush with door frame.
4. Lay out the scarf flat on the floor, right side down, and center the stretcher over it.
5. Fold the scarf over the stretcher and, using decorative upholstery tacks, tack at center of top.
6. Repeat at bottom, again tacking in center. Pull firm, but not tight.
7. Do the same to both sides.
8. Stand the frame up and begin tacking all the way around, working from centers out and following the same sequence as before, alternating sides so that you are always placing a tack directly opposite the previous one. Place tacks about 1″ apart.
9. Hang by setting on two nails hammered into the wall.

29 Pick a pillow

...any pillow: the size and shape depends on the scarf or scarves you choose to make it with. Square or sausage-y, silk or cotton, whipped up out of men's handkerchiefs or French provincial scarves—the range is enormous.

SQUARE PILLOW

Size: About 18 inches square.

You'll need: Two 18 inch square scarves or 1 scarf and an 18 inch square of similar fabric—cotton for a cotton scarf, silk for a silk scarf. And an 18 inch square pillow form.

Right sides together, stitch together the 2 scarves (or scarf and fabric) around outside edges, leaving 8 inches open in center of one side. Clip corners, turn and press. Insert the pillow form and slipstitch opening.

BOLSTER

Size: 15 inches long, 5 inches in diameter.

You'll need: ½ yard muslin. Kapok or polyester stuffing. 24 inch square scarf. 1 yard silky cord.

For bolster form: From muslin cut 2 circles 6 inches in diameter and a rectangle 16 x 18 inches. Stitch 16 inch sides of rectangle together with ½ inch seam, leaving 4 inches open in center. Stitch ends of the tube just formed around each circle with ½ inch seams. Clip seams around circles. Turn, stuff firmly and slipstitch opening.

For bolster cover: Cut scarf to 19 inches, centering design. Leave other 2 sides uncut. Place uncut sides together, wrong side out, and join with ½ inch seam. Make narrow hems on raw edges. Press, turn. Slip in bolster form, having an even amount of extra scarf on each end. Gather ends and fasten each with half of the cord.

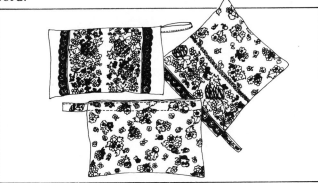

30 Make up 3 make-up bags

You'll need: 2 matching border print scarves (30 inches square). Oblong scarves can be used but size and number of bags you can make may vary. 2 yards fusible web. 3 packages nylon tape fastener.

1. Cut 3 paper pattern rectangles 9 x 11, 10 x 12, 8 x 16 inches.

2. Place fusible web between wrong sides of 2 scarves. Follow directions included with fusible web to fuse scarves together. Second scarf becomes self liner for bags.

3. Now lay out all of the paper patterns on the scarf, trying all three patterns together to make the best use of the fabric and the borders. (You may have to piece a border together.) When you've worked it out, pin the patterns down and cut them out.

4. Overcast all 4 sides of each bag using zigzag stitch on machine.

5. Fold rectangles in half crosswise. Cut nylon tape fastener for ends (opposite the fold), making pieces ½ inch narrower than ends. On right side of each end sew the nylon tape fastener strips according to package directions.

6. Turn nylon tape fastener edge to wrong side and stitch second edge of strip. Repeat for other side. Nylon tape fastener is now in position for concealed opening.

7. Make a 3 inch tab of scrap fabric. Fold tab in half.

8. Place right sides of bags together. Place ends of tab near top edge sandwiched between nylon tape fastener. Sew ½ inch side seams, catching tab in place.

9. Turn bags right side out. Press open edges together to close.

ASBESTOS MAT

31 Scarf a shade

You'll need: A cotton scarf of a suitable size for your lampshade. An asbestos hot mat (from a housewares department).

If your old or unattractive shade has a finial, remove it by unscrewing. Just lay the asbestos mat on the lampshade and drape the scarf in place.

Warning: Since the fibers of delicate scarves will not withstand the heat of a lamp, use only a sturdy cotton scarf. *Be sure* to use an asbestos mat large enough to cover top of shade.

32 Wrap a package

Wrapping gifts in scarves is a nice idea...a present-within-a-present. Relatively inexpensive gifts become more important—and impressive when the wrappings are also a keepable gift. It's important to wrap your scarf-packages so that the scarf isn't damaged, so use transparent tape or a rubber band to secure them.

A. Center package on scarf and wrap in the usual way, fastening as necessary with tape.

B. Center package on scarf, gather corners and form "pouf" on top by fastening gathers with a rubber band. You can finish off with a bid of ribbon or chunky yarn tied around the rubber band.

C. For a Japanese scarf wrap, center package on scarf and draw 2 opposite corners to top. Take 2 remaining corners and use them to tie around the first 2 corners.

1. LACE & RIBBON CHARMERS

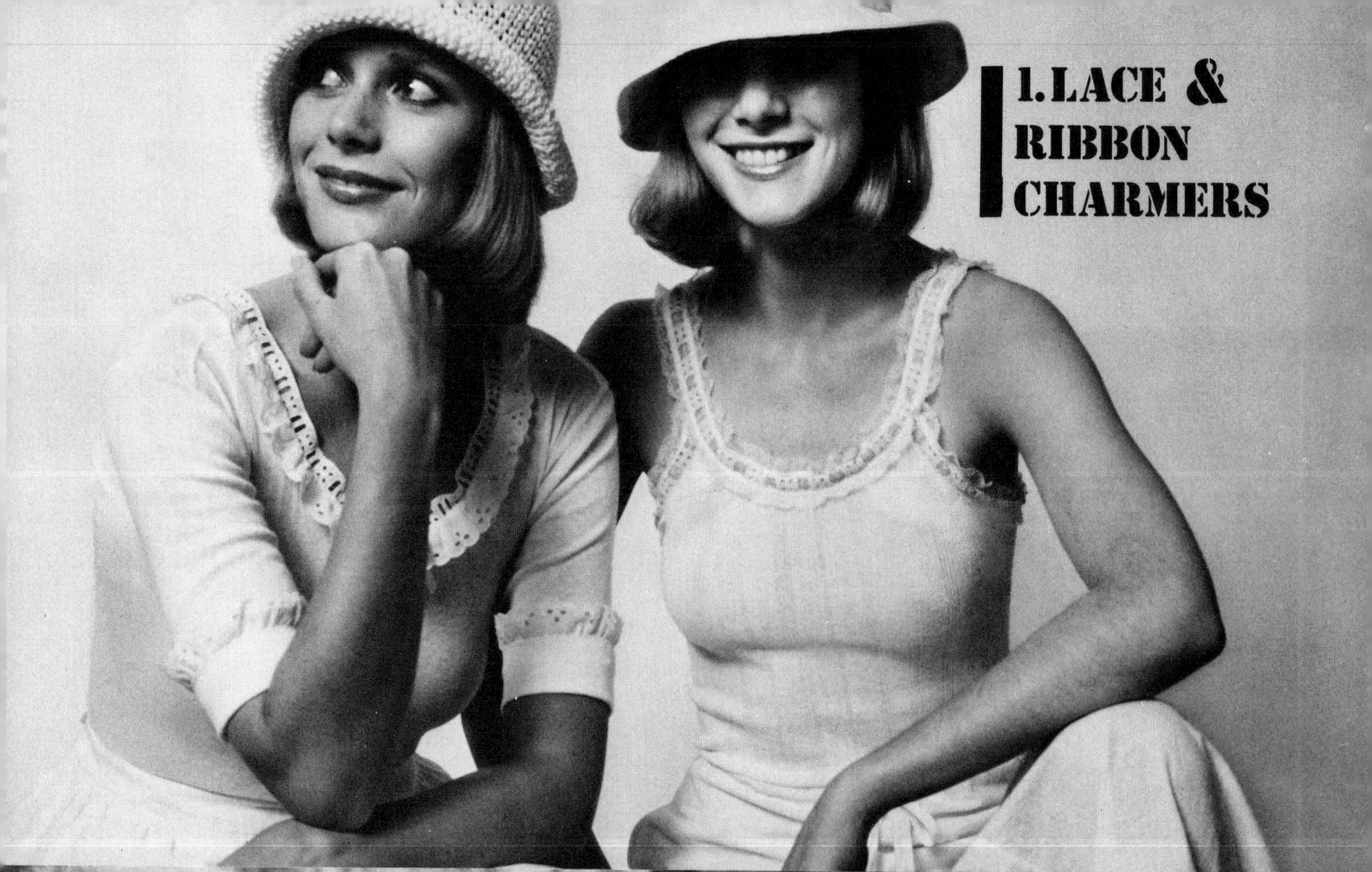

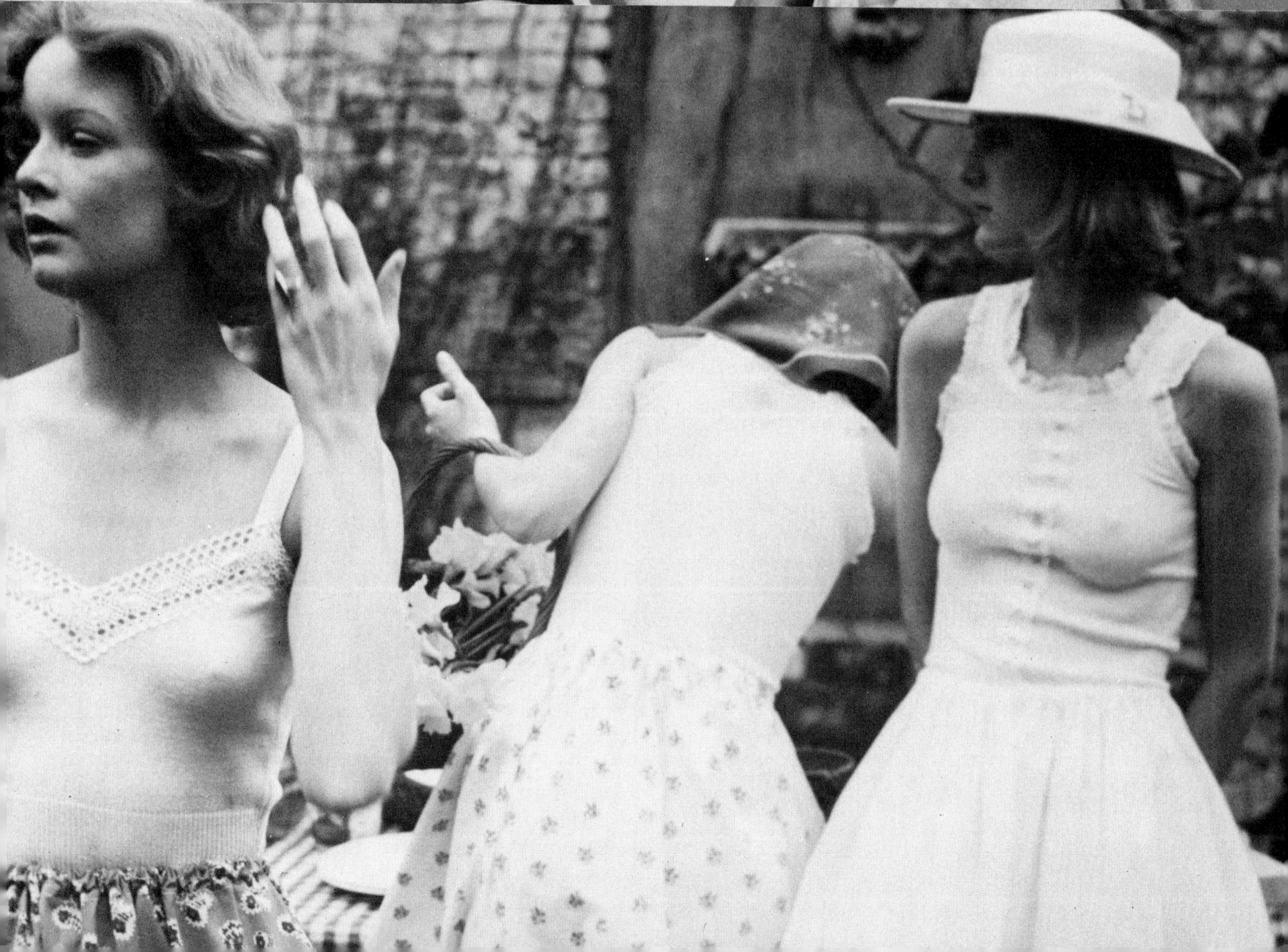

TART UP A T &
SNAZZ UP A SHIRT

Plain to fancy: that's the way to go with a T-shirt

A T-shirt, bare or sleeved, is the fashion equivalent of a plain sheet of paper: it doesn't mean much till you start writing on it. The kind of writing we're talking about is done with embroidery or frills of lace, special crayons or appliques. It's the same way with shirts. The little extra you put on is what makes them special. What you can't do is overspend: all these trimmings-up are pennies from your pocket.

1. Lace & Ribbon Charmers

Since some T-shirts are finished with sizing—a starch-like substance—it is better to wash them before applying trims. It also takes care of shrinkage.

Measure the area to be trimmed, allowing 2 inches for finishing ends. Buy that amount.

Since T-shirt fabric is stretchy, do not stretch when applying trims. To take care of this problem, you might first make a simple hand running stitch along the edge you plan to trim. Fasten firmly.

When applying trims, do any under layers first. For example, on the right hand tank, upper picture, you would do the underarms first, then overlap the neck trim over the underarm trim.

Since most trims are woven, they won't have the "give" to fit neatly around a curved edge. To take care of this, ease them around the curve. Or you might even put a row of shirring along the outer edge of the trim to help in easing it around a curve.

EASY APPLIQUES

One of the easiest ways to tart up a T is via applique, either the sew-on or iron-on kind. You can do a scenic, initials or, if you've got one, a message to the world.

PATTERNS: Almost any design can be appliqued to a T-shirt. The alphabet on these pages is a good one to use if you want words. Or try the little Tuscan village shown here. Just remember—the fewer sharp points, the easier it is to applique. Fine lines must be done in embroidery or with a waterproof felt-tipped pen.

To enlarge a design (or make it smaller) draw a grid of ¼ inch squares horizontally and vertically over the entire surface. Follow directions on this page, making your new grid of ½ inch squares for a design **twice** as large. Use 8 to the inch graph paper for a design **half** as large. Or use the scale desired.

Cut heavy paper patterns of each piece of the design. Place on wrong side of fabric—calico, percale, broadcloth or any smooth cotton is fine—and draw around patterns, leaving ½ inch between pieces.

SETTING PIECES: Cut out pieces, leaving ¼ inch around all edges. Press under seam allowance. Clip seam allowance on curves and slash at corners. Baste seam allowance.

Trace entire design on T-shirt, using dressmakers' carbon paper. Pin each piece in its appropriate place on design. Baste. **Note:** if pieces overlap, the under one does not need to have raw edges turned under.

APPLIQUEING, Blind Method: Use blind hemming or slipstitch to anchor pieces. **Blanket Stitch Method:** for a decorative way of applying pieces, use blanket stitch (see page 126) around entire edge. Make stitches as close as necessary to hold pieces firmly in place.

PRETEND APPLIQUE: A quick method of applying pieces is to bond them to the fabric. Just use pieces cut from bonding fabric (comes in packages), following the directions on the package. Or use regular applique fabrics (no seam allowances needed) and fusible web from a notions or fabric department. Bond with an iron following directions with the web or the bonding fabric.

HOW TO ENLARGE A DESIGN OR DIAGRAM

Sometimes a design or diagram that you want to use is not in scale for your project. In order to get it to the right scale you must graph it. Often designs printed in books will be smaller than normal and have to be enlarged. To enlarge them, follow these steps:

1. On a large sheet of paper carefully mark out the squares indicated on the diagram. If it says, "Each square = ½ inch square" mark out ½ inch squares—or if "Each square = 1 inch square" mark out 1 inch squares.

2. Now copy whatever is in any given square to the corresponding square on your graph.

3. Smooth out all your lines and you're ready to use the pattern.

2. THREE WAYS TO PUT YOUR MARK ON A T

HOW TO COLOR WITH A CRAYON... OR A NEEDLE

Working with a crayon

You'll need: T-shirt (must be synthetic if permanent color is desired). Crayola Craft Fabric Crayons.

1. See General Directions on page 63 for how to "Paint or Color on Just About Anything."

2. Trace design and copy on white paper. Using the crayons, color in design. Brush off any loose specks of crayon.

3. Lay a pad of newspapers on ironing board. Top with clean white paper. Also insert several sheets of paper between the front and the back of T-shirt. Lay shirt on pad on ironing board.

4. Position paper design face down on T-shirt.

5. Use a cotton setting on iron (but watch carefully that you do not scorch the T). Iron with a steady pressure over entire design until its image becomes slightly visible through back of paper. Do not move iron excessively or design may blur.

6. Remove paper carefully. Design may be used again if it is re-crayoned.

Note: T-shirt may be machine washed with cool water and a gentle cycle but do not use the drier.

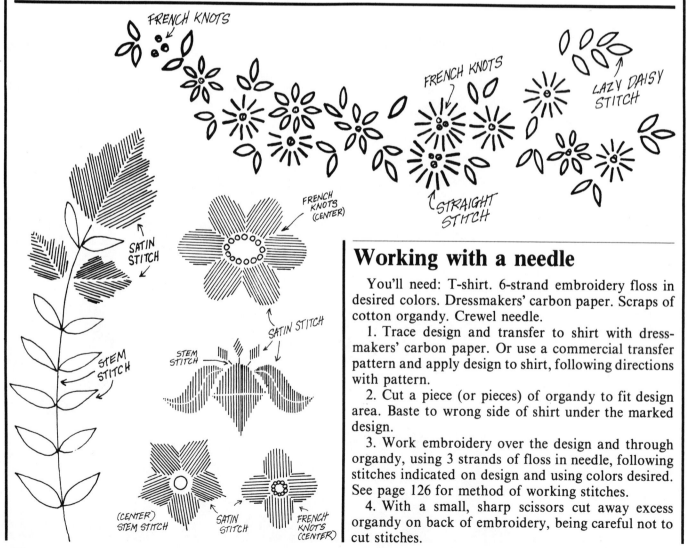

Working with a needle

You'll need: T-shirt. 6-strand embroidery floss in desired colors. Dressmakers' carbon paper. Scraps of cotton organdy. Crewel needle.

1. Trace design and transfer to shirt with dressmakers' carbon paper. Or use a commercial transfer pattern and apply design to shirt, following directions with pattern.

2. Cut a piece (or pieces) of organdy to fit design area. Baste to wrong side of shirt under the marked design.

3. Work embroidery over the design and through organdy, using 3 strands of floss in needle, following stitches indicated on design and using colors desired. See page 126 for method of working stitches.

4. With a small, sharp scissors cut away excess organdy on back of embroidery, being careful not to cut stitches.

3. CRAYONS MADE THESE FLOWERS

4. AND NEEDLEWORK MADE THESE

57

5. BREW UP A BATCH O

Burnt Orange
¼ tsp. Golden Yellow
¼ tsp. Orange
¼ tsp. Chestnut Brown
¼ tsp. Dark Brown

Plum
1 tsp. Wine
¼ tsp. Charcoal Gray
¼ tsp. Cocoa Brown

Mulled Green
½ tsp. Dark Green
½ tsp. Charcoal Gray

F T'S & SKIRTS

...Using dyes you'll mix (don't take them straight) for haunting, offbeat shades like these.

Blue Smoke
½ tsp. (heaping) Navy Blue
½ tsp. (less than level) Charcoal Gray

Mocha
½ tsp. (heaping) Pink
½ tsp. (less than level) Dark Brown

Directions: next page.

6. SNAZZ A SHIRT WITH STITCHING

Take a simple shirt, hand-embroider or machine stitch around the shoulders, collars and cuffs, and you've got something special. Contrast colors are best on solid colored shirts; with printed ones, pick up one of the colors in the pattern. Many variations are possible with stitched edges. Several rimming rows of plain machine stitching in a slightly darker color can zip up a little-nothing shirt. Zigzag machines are marvelous for this—try a dark shirt edged all around with several bright stitching rows.

Stitching up a shirt

For machine stitching

You'll need: Ready-made shirt, preferably Western-cut. Silver or gold thread. Regular polyester thread—gray for silver, yellow for gold. Dressmakers' carbon paper.

1. Plan design by drawing yoke area—front and back. Work out front design of straight lines, diamonds or squares and let them connect up with a similar or contrasting design on back.
2. Transfer design with dressmakers' carbon paper.
3. Using metallic thread in the needle, regular thread in the bobbin, stitch design with a straight stitch (not too fine). If you have a zigzag stitch machine, try a satin stitch on the back—or take advantage of the fancy stitches on your machine.

For hand-embroidering

You'll need: Ready-made shirt. 6-strand embroidery floss. Crewel needle.

1. Since you will be working this design freehand, use shirt edges as guide lines. Double rows of track stitching on shirts are useful for this.

FEATHERSTITCHING

1. With 3 strands of floss in needle, work feather-stitch along edges and down seams.
2. If you plan to roll back your cuffs, it's a nice touch to do the decorative stitching on the insides of the cuff.

BUTTONHOLE STITCHING

1. Since the buttonhole stitch works best only around edges, work with 3 strands of floss around collar, cuffs and all outer edges.

See stitch diagram, page 126, for both stitches.

BUTTON HOLE STITCH

FEATHER STITCH

How to dye knitted and woven fabrics

1. Home dyes will work on all washable fabrics except glass and mineral fibers, some polyesters and acrylics.

2. If garment is likely to shrink or stretch, measure or trace outline before washing. Do this for T-shirts.

3. Wash article; do not dry.

DYE AMOUNTS

Dye packages hold about 3 tablespoons dye each of which is dissolved in 3 gallons of water. If you are making your own color combination, remember proportions. For example, if you are making the Blue Smoke color, where the recipe is ½ tsp (heaping) Navy Blue and ½ tsp (less than level) Charcoal Gray, you have a total dye amount of about 1 tablespoon. This amount should be dissolved in about 1 gallon of water. (3 scant teaspoons equal 1 tablespoon.) This amount will dye one T-shirt. Double the recipe for dyeing a skirt, and triple the recipe if you are dyeing the skirt and T together.

It's a good idea to measure how much water your sink holds before you start.

SINK METHOD:

1. Pull on a pair of rubber gloves. Put dye powder into a strainer that you have lined with a layer of paper towels.

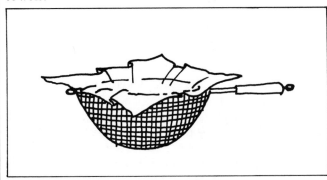

2. Hold strainer under the tap while you fill kitchen sink ¾ full with hottest water possible. Swish your hands around in sink to help everything dissolve. (Any undissolved particles will spot your finished garment.)

3. Put thoroughly clean and wet unfolded garment into sink and leave it until it's a darker shade than you want it to be—it will dry several shades lighter. You can always re-dye it if it doesn't come out dark enough (or un-dye it with dye remover if it's all wrong). You can even change the shade by adding a little more of one color or another the second time around.

4. Rinse thoroughly under cold running water.

5. Dip garment into a solution of ½ cup of white vinegar to a sinkful of cold water to help keep color fast.

6. Roll article in an old clean towel and squeeze out (the dyed garment can stain) excess water. Do not wring or twist. Let dry until slightly damp; press. Or block to the measurements you traced out and let dry thoroughly.

STOVE METHOD:

1, 2, 3 as above as under **How to dye knitted and woven fabrics**.

4. Dissolve dye solution in small amount of water. Strain solution into a large pan of simmering water on the stove.

5. Place clean, wet unfolded garment in dye bath and continue to simmer for 30 to 60 minutes. Stir constantly until a shade darker than desired color is obtained. Fabric appears darker when wet.

6. Rinse thoroughly in lukewarm water.

7. Dry as in 6 above.

Note: You can experiment with your own dye recipes by mixing drops of dissolved color together in a bowl and dipping in a paper towel to test the solution. Jot down the proportions you used.

Dyed to match

1. If you are color-matching 2 or more articles—such as the skirt and the T—dye them at the same time. Of course, add together the amount of dye needed for each article. Recipes for dyeing T-shirts are on page 58. Since skirts require double recipes, you will be using 3 times the amount for the 2 pieces together.

2. When you are making a garment, then dyeing it, the fabric can be dyed first. However, since it's easier to handle just the garment rather than a length of fabric, and by dyeing the skirt, you also dye the thread used, it's recommended that you make up the skirt and *then* dye it.

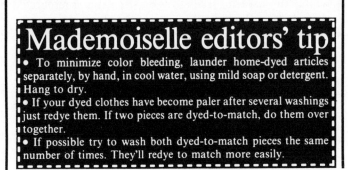

Mademoiselle editors' tip

• To minimize color bleeding, launder home-dyed articles separately, by hand, in cool water, using mild soap or detergent. Hang to dry.

• If your dyed clothes have become paler after several washings just redye them. If two pieces are dyed-to-match, do them over together.

• If possible try to wash both dyed-to-match pieces the same number of times. They'll redye to match more easily.

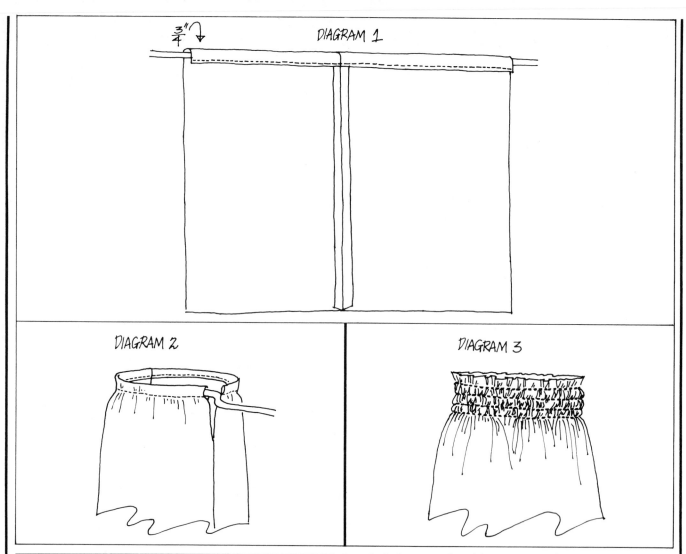

DIAGRAM 1

DIAGRAM 2

DIAGRAM 3

How to make the matching skirts on the previous page

This is an easy, simple skirt to make—it takes about an hour to do. You can make it with either a drawstring or an elasticized waistline. How long the skirt is depends on you. Measure yourself from waist to where you want the skirt to end, add 5 inches for the hem, and double it. Example: waist to knee measures 24 inches plus 5 = 29 inches. You need two times 29 inches or 58 inches of fabric. You should buy 2 yards of fabric to have extra for the drawstrings. If you're making the skirt from a remnant, choose the elasticized waistline—it takes less fabric.

You'll need: 45 inch-wide plain cotton fabric in white or cream. Thread. Elastic and mercerized threads (for elasticized waist skirt only).

WITH DRAWSTRING WAISTLINE

1. For front and back of skirt cut 2 lengths each plus 5 inches. For tie cut 2 strips 3 x 36 inches.

2. Place front and back right sides together. Stitch ⅝ inch seam, joining 2 selvages (Diagram 1). Press seam open.

3. Turn ¼ inch of top edge to wrong side; press. Turn 1 inch of top edge to wrong side; press. Edge-stitch along top and bottom, forming casing.

4. Join opposite side seam, leaving 5 inches open at top for placket. Press seam open.

5. Join the 2 strips along the short ends, making 1 long tie. Right sides together, fold the tie lengthwise. Stitch ½ inch seam; trim. Turn right side out.

6. Place a large safety pin at 1 end of tie and insert tie in casing (Diagram 2). Try on skirt; tie the tie. If it is too long, cut off excess. Turn in both ends and slip-stitch closed.

7. Measure skirt to desired length; hem.

8. To dye: follow instructions on this page.

WITH ELASTICIZED WAISTLINE

1. Same as #1 above but omit tie strips.

2. Same as #2 above but stitch both side seams.

3. Turn ½ inch of top edge to wrong side; press; stitch.

4. Wind bobbin of machine with elastic thread—by hand if necessary. Use mercerized thread for top threading. Use a 10-12 stitch length. Make a test piece to check fullness of stitching. Then on skirt, starting ½ inch below top edge, stitch rows of elastic ¼ inch apart. In stitching the second and all following rows, stretch elastic in preceding rows (Diagram 3). Make as many rows as desired but make at least 4. Draw up to desired tightness. At each end of stitching, tie elastic and needle threads together. Draw knot close to fabric.

5. See #7 above.

PAINT OR COLOR ON JUST ABOUT ANYTHING

Don't say you can't do this because you can't even draw a straight line. That doesn't matter. Designs can be traced or copied, and adding the color, whichever the method—fabric paint, fabric crayon or marking pens—is pretty simple. Follow these directions carefully and you'll be able to paint or color just about anything.

What is anything? Basically we think it's something to put on your (or anyone else's) body. And that's some sort of fabric. Below are a few ground rules that you should know.

1) If you can, try your fabric first to see how it takes color. Use a hidden part of the garment or an inside seam if possible.

2) Any fabric that needs to be dry cleaned (like silks, wools, some synthetics, etc.) should really have good testing before you adventure. Better to steer clear of these unless you are sure. Basically, a washable fabric is the best for coloring.

3) Try to use the smoothest surface possible. Bumpy fabrics or straws can take paint unevenly.

4) Denims and canvases are traditional background fabrics for coloring. However, fabric crayoning and markers do not show up well on very dark denims. Use bleached or medium shaded ones for these methods. Dark denims take well to fabric paints, embroidery or appliques.

5) Knit fabrics (like T-shirts) are stretchy. Always wear them a couple times to get the stretch out of the garment before you begin working on them.

6) Always wash garments before working designs. Most fabrics contain sizing. If you leave it in, some of the color of your design will wash out with the sizing the first time it's laundered.

Summing it up: Fabric paints are the cheapest to use—and probably the most versatile. Marking pens are cheap, and easy for amateurs. Crayons, once you've mastered the technique, are also easy, but sometimes don't come in a wide range of colors. Don't be tempted by drawing inks or ball-point pen ink. They're both quick fades after just one washing.

General Directions

Transfer patterns freehand to your garment. Or work out the exact pattern on tracing paper, then transfer to your garment with dressmakers' carbon paper.

When painting, garments must be protected from colors soaking through from front to back. Shirts can be opened out on a work surface. T-shirts, sleeves and the like must have a piece of cardboard cut to the proper size and inserted between the layers. Be sure to pad the inner surface with newspapers so that the color does not spread and bleed back up to the front.

The same holds true for ironing painted areas. Be sure to place a pad of press cloths between the front and the back.

There are three good ways of coloring fabric: marking pens, fabric paints and fabric crayons.

MARKING PENS:

These pens, which are readily available and come in a wide range of colors, must have permanent ink. Check the label which must read "permanent" or "waterproof."

Pens are more difficult to use when covering large areas or shading colors. They are ideal, however, for doing fine lines, initials and geometric small areas.

Colors may bleed or run slightly. You can escape this to a degree by using colored, rather than white, fabrics—especially in T-shirts. Always start coloring in an area from the center out to the edge. If the color bleeds, you can stop before you reach the edge.

FABRIC PAINT:

Art supply stores and craft shops sell kits of fabric paint. Or buy larger quantities in separate containers. Full instructions come with these paints. When your garment is painted, it may require heat to set the colors. Be sure to protect them with a piece of paper over the design before you apply the iron. And don't forget to iron the wrong side of the design as well as the right side.

FABRIC CRAYONS:

Complete sets of crayons are available for transferring designs to fabric. Full directions are on the box. It's a simple process in which the design is drawn on paper, then transferred to the garment with an iron. Since the design is flopped over in the process, be sure to draw your design in reverse. This is particularly important in transferring letters.

Washing Painted or Colored Garments

The hand coloring process is rarely totally colorfast but good washing techniques help. Wash in cold water by hand, using a mild detergent. Do not use bleach. Do not wring the garment. Lay flat on a towel and let dry. If it is necessary to press the piece, always cover the design with a dry press cloth.

Designs done with fabric crayons can be machine washed with cool water and a gentle cycle.

7 IMAGINATION AND OLD LACE

There's hardly a flea market worth its entry fee that doesn't have a box of old lace. This time don't walk on by. Old lace properly washed, snipped and sewed can bring new snazz to shirts, T's, sweaters, light and bouncy skirts.

Use it for cuffs, collars, panels, edgings—and when you've run out of what's in your closet turn to what's in the linen closet. Think of a lace-hemmed tableskirt, a small lace plump of a pillow. It's never too late for lace.

Applying lace

LACE EDGINGS: SHIRRED:
You'll need: Lace, 2½ times the length of edge to be trimmed.

1. Finish raw edge with a machine zigzag stitch or overcast it.

2. Gather the upper edge of lace to fit the edge of garment. Some laces already have a gathering thread worked into the lace. If not, stitch across lace with a wide stitch and gather.

3. Place gathered edge of lace over the edge of garment on the right side. Sew by hand with a running or backstitch or attach with a small machine zigzag stitch.

4. Overlap ends, turn in raw edge and sew in place.

FLAT (see A):
You'll need: Lace the length of edge to be trimmed plus 3 to 4 inches extra.

1. Prepare edge as in 1 for shirred edging.

2. Lay lace along edge on right side and join as in #3 above.

3. Or lay lace *over* edge with a backing of fabric and sew upper edge as in #3 above.

4. Finish ends as in #4 for shirred edgings.

LACE INSERTIONS (see B):

1. Using tailors' chalk, mark outlines of areas where you want lace on your garment.

2. Pin and baste lace in place.

3. Using a narrow zigzag stitch on your machine, stitch lace in place.

4. Working on the wrong side, carefully cut away fabric from behind the lace. **Note:** The fabric does not always have to be cut away since a pretty color makes an attractive backing for lace.

HANDLING COLLARS AND CUFFS (C, D, E):

1. Some antique lace collars and cuffs are separate items. However you may find lovely old ones as part of a worn blouse or dress. Sometimes these can be cut away, leaving ½ inch of the garment fabric attached. This can be hemmed back for a convenient edge to sew to new T-shirt or blouse.

2. If you have to rip a collar or cuffs from an old garment, do it carefully. A sharp-pointed embroidery scissors or dressmaker's seam ripper will help.

3. If you are going to insert collar or cuffs in a blouse or dress, lay the lace over the garment, baste in place.

Stitch all around. Then cut away the background fabric, being extremely careful not to cut the lace.

Laundering lace

Modern laces made of synthetics need no special care. Just be sure not to press with a hot iron. Fine old laces need special handling.

1. Baste lace to a piece of white fabric—an old sheet will do.

2. Dissolve soap flakes in a large screw-top jar. Place lace in jar and shake vigorously. Let stand, then repeat as many times as necessary to loosen dirt.

3. Rinse thoroughly in jar, changing the water a number of times.

4. Remove lace from cloth and pin out on a towel, using rustproof pins. Let dry.

5. Press the dry lace through a heavy press cloth with a warm iron.

Cleaning lace

If the lace is very old and/or delicate, clean rather than launder it.

1. Roll up lace and place in a large screw-top jar.

2. Fill jar with cleaning fluid. CAUTION: Be sure to work away from all flames and near an open window.

3. Shake the jar until the lace is clean.

4. Pin lace out on a towel, using rustproof pins. Let dry.

Tinting lace

Sometimes you'd like a white lace to have the antique look of old ecru lace.

1. Brew a pot of strong tea. Strength of brew depends on how dark you want the lace to be and the lace's absorbency.

2. Test a small area or a scrap of the lace before dyeing the entire piece.

3. Keep solution simmering over low heat and place lace in pot. When lace is a shade darker than desired color (it dries lighter), remove from pot and squeeze out moisture.

4. Follow step 4 in "Laundering Lace."

5. If you want a deeper color, repeat process or use commercial dye.

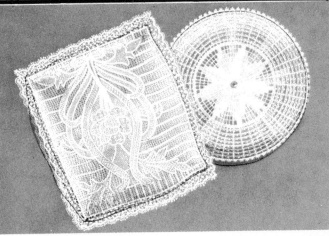

The round lacy pillow began as an antique doily. It was dyed a pale beige and mounted over camel colored silk. The oblong pillow was made of the center panel of an old lace curtain, mounted over pale blue.

Lacy pillows

You'll need: Square or round lace. Ready-made pillow of same size and shape as lace. Or pillow fabric and polyester stuffing.

1. Choose a pillow in solid-color fabric. Paler colors—peach, mauve, light blue—look well with delicate thread lace. High contrast colors like black and red work better with heavier crochet lace.

2. Measure lace. If you are not using a ready-made pillow, cut 2 pieces of fabric to the lace measurements, adding ½ inch seam allowance all around.

3. Right sides together, stitch around edges with ½ inch seams, leaving center of 1 side open. Clip off corners, trim seams, turn right side out. Press.

4. Stuff pillow firmly—especially in the corners. Turn in opening; slipstitch closed.

5. Lay lace over front of pillow and sew with a running stitch all around edges. The lace can easily be removed for washing.

6. If a ruffled lace edge is desired, use lace edging 2½ times the length of the perimeter of pillow. Attach by hand, following steps 2, 3, 4 of "Lace Edgings: Shirred."

Some lace ideas from Mademoiselle's fashion editors....all done with flea market lace leftovers.

A. A roll of pale ivory Val lace went on the edges of this camisole and skirt. Narrower Val outlines neckline and armholes.

B. Lace strips—unmatched ones—inserted in a drawstring cotton skirt (for skirt directions see page 62). The shirt had more lace banding inserted on the diagonal.

C. This high lace collar and front panel was all that was usable in a tattered 1900 blouse. It was cut away from the original blouse and inserted in a modern one.

D. A pale filet collar went down the front of a '20s dress. Detached, it made a collar and lacy cuffs for a T-shirt.

E. This filet collar was originally the back of a '20s dress. Turned frontward, it was sewn on the front of a U-necked T-shirt.

BUY IT & BETTER IT

How to make something marvelous out of something mundane

The idea is this: you start with, say, a pillowslip or a sheet or a plain, ordinary dishcloth, give it a lot of imagination and a little sewing and come up with something entirely new and terrific. Piles of petticoats maybe, like those opposite (see p. 76 for directions), or a flouncy skirt. The coolest, lightest kimono or the warmest, fluffiest poncho. A cache of pillows, a sachet, a nest of notebooks. . . . To start, just turn the page.

◀All these petticoats began as pillowslips!

Directions: page 76.

1 Take a sheet and turn it into a kimono

This is the breeziest kind of warm-weather robing, and it's also a breeze to make. The iron-on motifs are Japanese-y and you can add as few or as many as you like, put them any place that pleases *your* special eye.

Size: One size fits all.

Materials: 81 x 104 inch flat double sheet. Iron-on fabric (we used red and blue).

1. Rip hems from both ends of sheet; press.
2. Fold sheet in half lengthwise; pin in place.
3. Copy all markings in Diagram 1 on your folded sheet.
4. Fold sheet along crosswise fold (Diagram 2), making sure markings are aligned front and back. Cut side seams and sleeves.
5. Open cut-out kimono along crosswise fold. Cut front lengthwise fold for front opening. Cut neck opening.
6. From remaining fabric cut 2 strips—one the length of sheet and 6 inches wide for band around front opening. The other strip 6 x 64 inches for belt.
7. Place kimono right sides together. Stitch ½ inch side seams starting at hem, pivoting at underarms and continuing along sleeves. Clip seams at underarms.
8. To finish front edges of kimono, fold and press longer band lengthwise, wrong side together. Pin center of opened-out band to back center of neck, placing **right** side of band to **wrong** side of neck. Pin band down each front. Stitch with ½ inch seam. Turn under and press ½ inch on other long edge. Turn band to right side of kimono along original fold line. Edge-stitch band to front.
9. On sleeves make 4 inch finished hems. Turn up end of each sleeve for 3 inches to form cuff. Press.
10. Make a 1 inch finished hem on lower edge of kimono. If you're shorter, make the hem deeper.
11. Fold belt piece in half lengthwise, right side together. Make ½ inch seams along ends and long edge, leaving a 5 inch opening. Trim seams, clip corners, turn right side out. Slipstitch opening closed.
12. For designs enlarge chart (each large square equals 1 inch square). To enlarge chart see page 54. Make paper patterns of enlarged designs. Cut designs from iron-on fabric, half in red, half in blue. (You can make about 3 motifs from 1 package.) Use a small, sharp pointed scissors. Scatter motifs as in photograph and around back shoulders; pin in place. Note that some motifs overlap. Try on kimono to check placement of units. Iron on the motifs following directions on the package.

Mademoiselle editors' tip

• Don't limit yourself to a simple white sheet for this one. A kimono run up out of a flower-printed sheet is just as handsome.

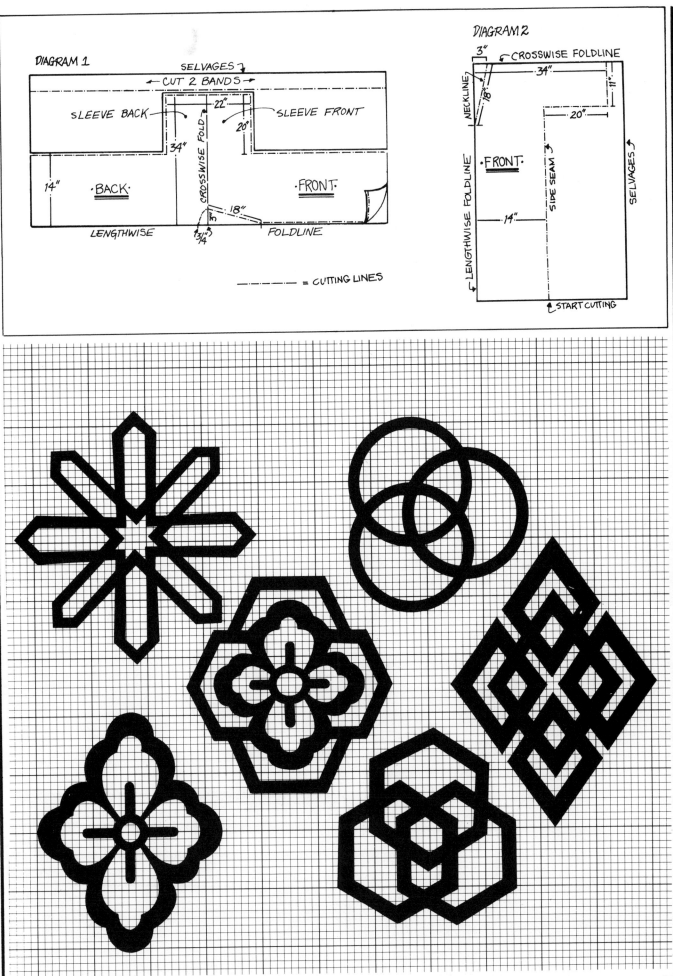

DIAGRAM 1

SELVAGES

← CUT 2 BANDS →

SLEEVE BACK   22"   SLEEVE FRONT

20"

34"   CROSSWISE FOLD

14"   ·BACK·   ·FRONT·

3"   18"

1¾"

LENGTHWISE   FOLDLINE

———·——— = CUTTING LINES

DIAGRAM 2

3"

CROSSWISE FOLDLINE

NECKLINE   34"   11"

18"

20"

·FRONT·

SIDE SEAM

SELVAGES

LENGTHWISE FOLDLINE

14"

↑ START CUTTING

2 Take a blanket—and make it a poncho

Size: 51 inches wide, 41½ inches long.
You'll need: Campers' blanket 62 x 83 inches (from Army/Navy store). Heavy duty thread.

1. Cut off an 11 inch strip down length of blanket.
2. Zigzag stitch cut edge of large piece.
3. In center of large piece cut a 10 inch slit. From center of slit cut 2 more slits, each ½ inch long. Now cut diamond-shaped neck opening (Diagram 1). Zigzag stitch around neck opening. Repeat stitching again for added strength.
4. Cut 30 inch piece from strip. Fold in half crosswise. Zigzag stitch cut side together to form hood (Diagram 2), leaving selvage edge for front of hood. Zigzag stitch lower edge of hood.
5. Turn hood inside out and open out sides so that the seam runs up center back. Zigzag stitch across the point you've formed, 2 inches down from the top. Turn right side out.
6. Pin bottom edge of hood around neck edge of poncho, lining up seam of hood with back point of neck opening. Leave 2 inches of hood edge free on each side. Zigzag stitch in place.

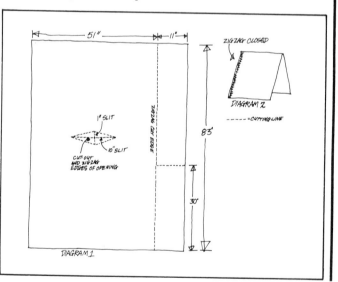

DIAGRAM 1

These were made with placemats

These were made with dishtowels

3 Pillows out of placemats and dishtowels

You can do a lot more with a placemat than put a table setting on it, a lot more with a dishtowel than drying a plate. Both have prints so pretty they deserve more exposure. Be sure to use *new* dishtowels, though—old ones are too limp—and mass them for effect. When you're doing a cheapie like this one, more is definitely more.

Size: About 11 x 17 inches if made from placemats; about 15 x 25 inches if made from dish towels.
You'll need: 2 matching fabric placemats (or 2 matching dish towels). Polyester stuffing. Optional: 1¾ yards trimming for placemats, 2¼ yards for towels.

1. Remove hems from mats (or towels). Press.
2. Place placemats (or towels) right sides together. With ½ inch seams stitch around edges, leaving 4 inches open at center of one side. Trim seams, clip corners, turn. Press.
3. Stuff pillow firmly with polyester stuffing, making sure to work stuffing well into corners.
4. Slipstitch opening closed.
5. If desired, trim with ruffling, twisted cord, even eyelet embroidery ruffling. Cut trim to fit outer edges of pillow plus 1 inch. Slipstitch around edges. Join ends neatly.

4 Dishcloth into delicious sachet

. . .which you can stuff with dried lavender for a linen closet, pot-pourri for a clothes closet, dried artemesia or woodruff to keep the moths away. Or you can fill it full of crushed mint, tie it over a shower nozzle and have the *spritz* of a lifetime.

Size: Bag is 5 inches deep.
You'll need: 1 dishcloth about 13-14 inches square. 2 bright colored shoe laces. About 1 cup packed mint leaves.

1. Fold opposite sides of dishcloth down 1 inch and stitch across, forming casing (Diagram 1). Leave ends of casing open.
2. Fold dishcloth in half, casing to casing, with casings on the outside (Diagram 2). Stitch sides with narrow seams from just below casing to fold.
3. Turn inside out. Flatten dishcloth so side seams run down center and ends of seams form points (Diagram 3). Sew across points about 1½ inches from tip. Turn bag right side out.
4. Insert a shoe lace in each half of casing. Knot ends together.

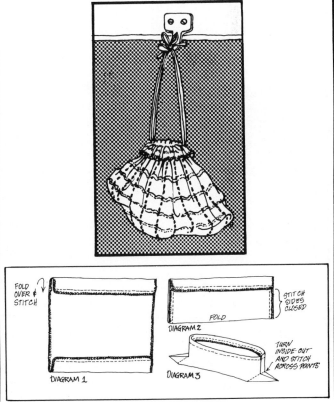

FOLD OVER & STITCH

DIAGRAM 1

FOLD

STITCH SIDES CLOSED

DIAGRAM 2

TURN INSIDE-OUT AND STITCH ACROSS POINTS

DIAGRAM 3

5 Start with one bedspread and you can get enough goodies out of it to knock off your xmas list!

...or you could start with 2 spreads instead of one, that way get some extra borders and have enough left over to turn out a treasure from our Scrapbook (see p. 117).

You'll need: 1 Indian bedspread, twin size, about 72 x 108 inches. 2½ yards multi-purpose quilting fleece. 1 address book (one shown was long and narrow—3 x 12 inches). 1 clipboard. 1 folio cover. 1 can of spray adhesive. 4 placemats by Matmaker (see page 10).

TOTES: For each bag: 1. From bedspread cut front and back 11 x 16½ inches; cut 2 similar lining pieces. Cut gusset 3½ x 37 inches; cut similar lining piece. Cut 2 handles 3 x 14 inches. Cut fleece to size of front, back and gusset and two 1 x 14 inch strips for handles.

2. Sandwich fleece between front and lining, back and its lining, gusset and its lining. Baste. Machine quilt in any simple pattern—straight lines, squares or diamonds. Overcast all edges using wide zigzag stitch. Center fleece down wrong sides of handles. Fold fabric over fleece and turn under raw edge. Stitch through entire thickness down length of handles.

3. With ½ inch seam sew gusset to front, going down one side, across bottom and up other side. Repeat for back.

4. Turn under top edge of tote ¾ inch; stitch.

5. Stitch handles just inside front and back 4 inches from each side seam.

FOLIO COVER: 1. Open out folio cover and measure. Add 1 inch to each dimension. Cut fabric to these measurements for outside cover. Cut lining ½ inch shorter and ½ inch narrower than original measurements.

2. Following directions on spray adhesive can, attach outside of cover to wrong side of fabric, centering it. Draw excess fabric to inside, mitering or pleating extra fabric in corners.

3. Adhere lining to inside of cover, centering it.

Each single spread will make:

2 totes

4. Make any slits for note pads, etc., that might have been on original cover.

CLIPBOARD: 1. If possible, remove the clip mechanism.

2. Measure board and add 1½ inches to each dimension. Cut fabric to these measurements for front cover. Cut back cover ½ inch shorter, ½ inch narrower than original measurements.

3. Following directions on spray adhesive can, attach front of board to center of wrong side of fabric. Draw excess fabric to back, mitering or pleating extra fabric in corners. If you were unable to remove clip, first cut out necessary opening before adhering fabric to board.

4. In same manner adhere back cover to back, centering it.

5. Attach clip mechanism if it was removed.

ADDRESS BOOK: 1. Measure your book opened out and add 1 inch to each dimension. Cut bedspread to these measurements for cover. For lining cut an inside front and an inside back piece, making each ½ inch shorter and ½ inch narrower than actual cover.

2. Following directions on can of spray adhesive, attach opened out book centered on wrong side of cover. Cut away small spaces at top and bottom of spine. Draw excess fabric to inside of book, mitering or pleating in extra fabric at corners.

3. Adhere lining to inside of front and back covers.

PLACEMATS: 1. Make 4 placemats following directions in Matmaker kit. If you are not using a kit, cut 4 mats 13 x 19 inches.

2. Make ¼ inch finished hems, mitering corners.

NAPKINS: 1. Cut 4 pieces of fabric 19 inches square.

2. Make ¼ inch finished hems, mitering corners.

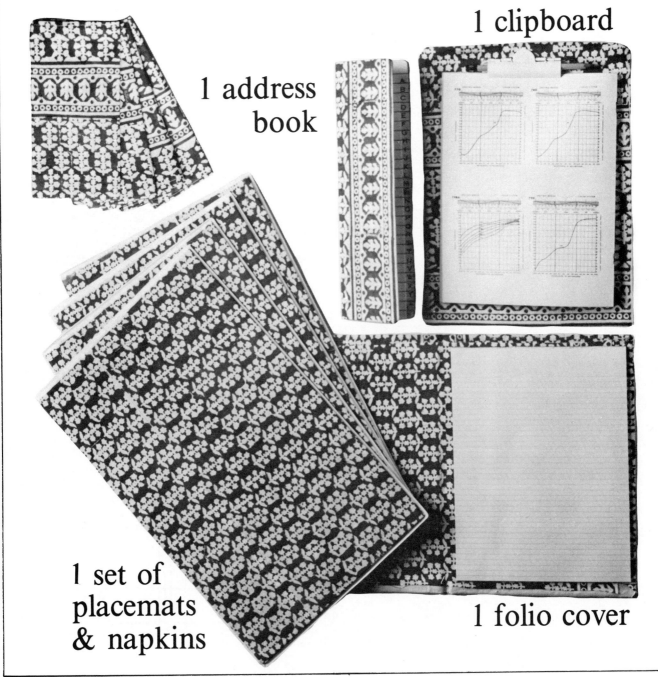

1 address book

1 clipboard

1 set of placemats & napkins

1 folio cover

6 A beach wrap

BEACH WRAP

You'll need: 2 matching bath towels about 26 x 50 inches with finished hems. Eight ⅞ inch buttons. 1¼ yards ¾ inch wide elastic.

1. Place towels right sides together and stitch along one long side to make back seams (see diagram). Press seam open.

2. Place piece wrong side up and fold entire top edge down 1 inch, forming a casing. Stitch casing along top and bottom edges.

3. Put a safety pin on one end of elastic and insert in casing. Try on garment and pin elastic to fit snugly. Cut off excess elastic and sew ends firmly just inside openings.

4. Starting from the top, make 8 machine-stitched buttonholes 3½ inches apart down right front. Sew buttons on left front to line up with buttonholes.

Mademoiselle editors' tip

- Wiggle this down to the waist and you'll have a long beach skirt
- Make this the same color as your bathroom towels and you'll have a quick after-bath blotter

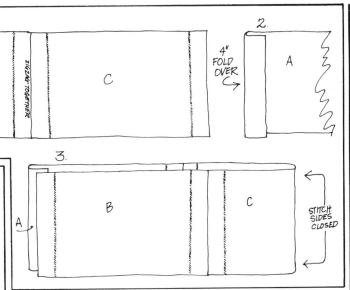

1.

A   B   C

2.
4" FOLD OVER →   A

3.
A   B   C

STITCH SIDES CLOSED

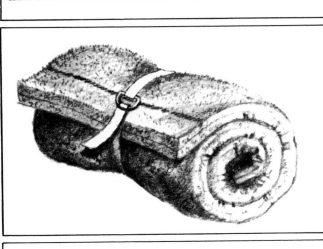

7 An exercise mat

AN EXERCISE MAT

You'll need: 3 bath towels (about 25 x 45 inches) with finished hems. 1 inch thick foam bed pad (mattress topper)—twin size. Small amount nylon tape fastener. A discarded belt.

1. Making small seams, stitch together the 3 towels end to end (Diagram 1).

2. Lay towels right side up as in Diagram 1. Fold end A over for 4 inches (Diagram 2). Fold end C all the way to the left, overlapping end A (Diagram 3).

3. Zigzag stitch long sides together, keeping the stitching on towel selvages. Turn cover right side out.

4. Sew small nylon tape fastener tabs in 3 places inside of flap.

5. For a snug fit cut foam pad ½ inch larger in length and width than finished mat. (Ours was about 24½ x 66½ inches.)

6. Insert pad in cover.

7. Roll mat for storage, securing with belt.

8 An apron

AN APRON

You'll need: 1 hand towel. 1 fingertip towel. 2½ yards cording.

1. Place towel crosswise, right side up. Center fingertip towel on upper edge, letting 7 inches of small towel overlap large towel (Diagram 1).

2. Zigzag stitch along line A-B in Diagram 1.

3. Fold up the 7 inches of small towel. Join side

edges with zigzag stitch, then zigzag stitch down center of pocket, forming 2 compartments (Diagram 2).

4. Sew a cording waist tie cut 32 inches long to each upper corner of large towel. Sew each end of a single cording neck tie cut 22 inches long to upper corners of small towel.

5. Knot ends of all ties to prevent raveling.

6. When wearing apron, wrap ends around to front and tie low, butcher style.

STITCH TOWELS TOGETHER

A   B

7"

DIAGRAM 1

ATTACH CORDING

FOLD FLAP UP AND ZIG ZAG STITCH

DIAGRAM 2

9 Pillowslip into a skirt in one hour

How good this skirt looks depends on the good looks of the pillowslip, so choose carefully. If you want a longish skirt, buy king-size. And if you're planning to pile these on in layers—and you can—make sure one of the layers is white and ruffly. Look for pillowslips with borders, good contrasts for best effect. The trims you'll find in a notions department. (And you'll find directions for the dolled-up T-shirts on p. 53.)

PILLOWSLIP SKIRT
You'll need: 2 pillowslips. ¾ inch wide elastic as long as your waist measurement plus 1 inch. 2½ yards trim (as desired).

1. Open top and side seams of both pillowslips; iron flat.

2. Determine finished skirt length. Add 1¼ inches. Measure this length up from hem edge. Mark evenly for a straight top edge on both pillowslip. Cut off any excess fabric at top.

3. Right sides together, pin side seams, starting at hem and working to top (to be sure hems line up evenly). Stitch ⅝ inch seams; press open.

4. To make casing for elastic, measure 1¼ inches from top; turn in and press. Edgestitch along fold line. Turn in raw edge ¼ inch and edgestitch to garment, leaving a 2 inch opening.

5. Attach safety pin to one end of elastic and use pin to guide elastic through casing, being careful not to twist it. Remove pin. Overlap ends of elastic 1 inch (or enough to fit waist comfortably) and sew ends together securely. Close opening in casing.

Trims: Skirt may be trimmed with rows of wide to skinny rickrack or rows of bright bias tape or peasanty jacquard ribbon. Or try a double row of ruffled eyelet for a tiered flounce. Some pillowslip patterns are edged with galloons (printed borders) which automatically become the hem trim of the skirt. A pretty add-on for these—a fluted ruching border along the bottom. Or add eyelet trim with grosgrain ribbon through the top beading. Or simply sew lovely Cluny lace to the edge of the skirt.

10 Shawl in one hour

Just the thing for a breezy summer night—a thin and pretty fringed shawl made in no time on next to no money.

PILLOWSLIP SHAWL
You'll need: 1 pillowslip. 1½ yards fringe. 1½ yards rickrack.

1. Open side and top seams of pillowslip. Cut off pillowcase hem and iron flat. You now have a fabric rectangle.

2. From rectangle cut a square with sides equal to the original rectangle's shortest side (see Diagram).

3. Right sides together, fold square in half diagonally to form triangle.

4. Stitch open edges together with ¼ inch seam, leaving a 4 inch opening at center of one side. Clip corners, turn. Press. Topstitch short sides.

5. Pin solid edge of fringe along 2 short sides of triangle (on top of fabric) so that fringe extends beyond edge. Stitch a row along top of fringe, another row close to shawl edge.

6. Place rickrack over fringe stitching and stitch in place.

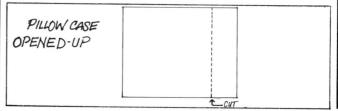

PILLOW CASE OPENED-UP

CUT

27

2A

2E

2F

2C

1

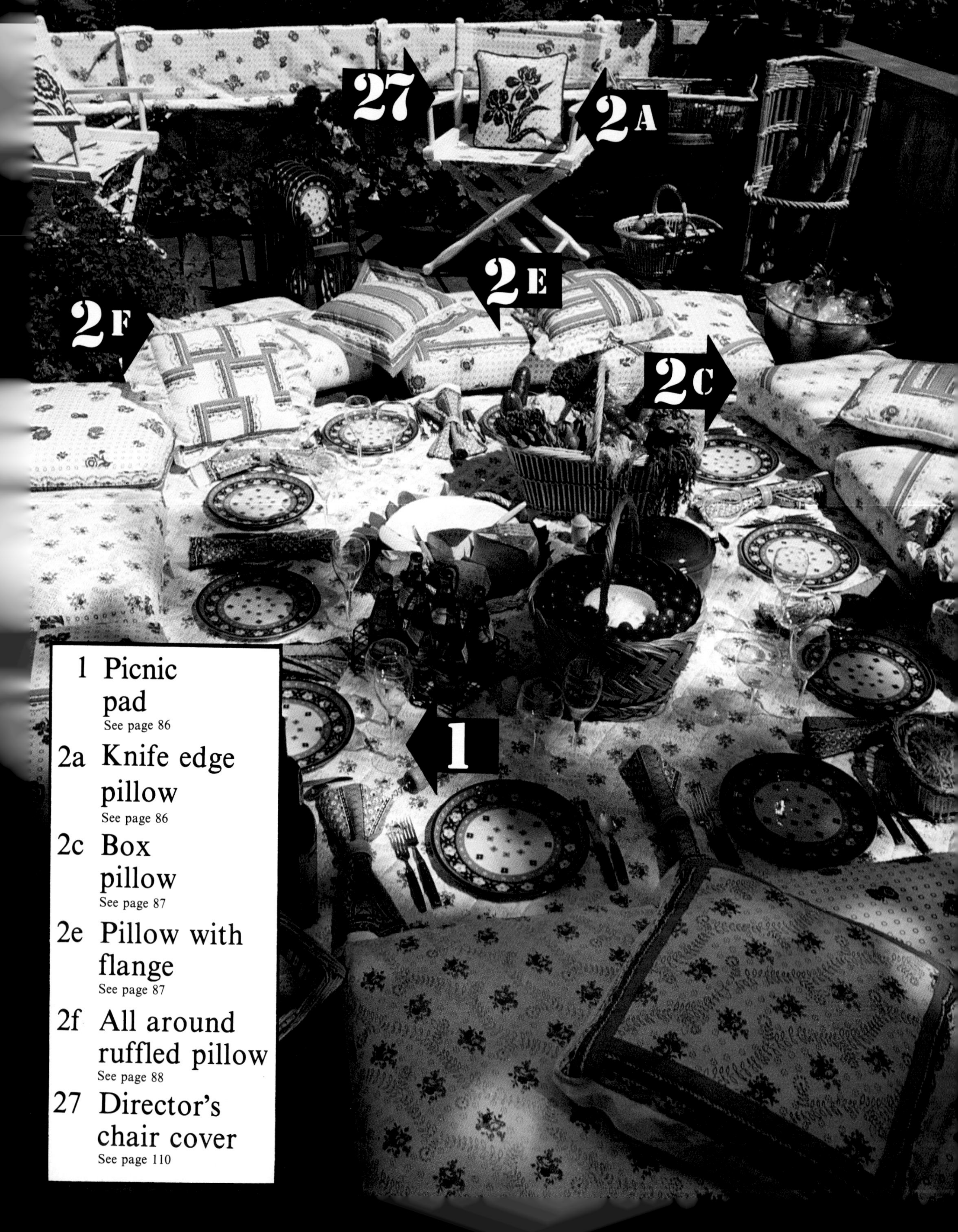

1 Picnic
   pad
   See page 86

2a Knife edge
   pillow
   See page 86

2c Box
   pillow
   See page 87

2e Pillow with
   flange
   See page 87

2f All around
   ruffled pillow
   See page 88

27 Director's
   chair cover
   See page 110

SHEETS ALL OVER

How far can you go with a sheet? As far as you like!

Sheets will do a lot more than make a bed, curtain a window or fabric a wall. They'll save you a pretty penny: with sheets you get the most width for the least money. You also get the most good looks: the range of sheet patterns today is extraordinary. Another good thing: everything on these pages was made by MLLE Editors, not one of whom is a professional seamstress or paperhanger. Which means that you can make them too.

Through this chapter, the numbers on the pictures refer to the direction numbers.

SHEETS ALL OVER

Mademoiselle editors' tip
One pattern keeps this look clean and simple.

3A

10A

2a Knife edge
   pillows
   See page 86

3a Sheets as
   "wallpaper" flat
   See page 89

10a Tailored
    bedskirt
    See page 94

19 Coverlet for
   a platform bed
   See page 107

2A

19

Mademoiselle editors' tip

To clutter up a platform bed is to ruin its stripped-down good looks. Which is why a simple quilted coverlet and piles of pillows are vital here—there's not an extraneous inch of fabric around.

81

13

12

14

SHEETS ALL OVER

25

18

2A

2I

2J

17

2a Knife edge
pillow
See page 86

2i Sheet
border pillow
See page 88

2j Bolster
pillow
See page 89

17 Loft bed
cover
See page 107

18 Quilted
fabric rug
See page 107

25 Sheet
curtain
See Page 109

SHEETS ALL OVER

WHAT YOU GET WHEN YOU BUY...

A list of sizes

PILLOWCASES (before assembling):
Standard	42″ x 36″
Queen	42″ x 40″
King	42″ x 46″

FLAT SHEET SIZES (Before hemming):
Twin	66″-72″ x 104″
Double	81″ x 104″
Queen	90″ x 110″
King	108″ x 110″

These measurements are useful if you're doing sheets on walls or ceilings.

SQUARE FOOTAGE OF FLAT SHEETS:
Twin	about 52 square feet
Double	about 58 square feet
Queen	about 69 square feet
King	about 83 square feet

BEDSPREAD SIZES:
Twin	76″-81″ x 105″-110″
Double	88″-96″ x 105″-110″
Queen	100″-102″ x 116″-120″
King	116″-120″ x 120″

Note 1: Sizes are approximate. Quilting may take up some of the width and length.
Note 2: Double beds are also known as full size.
Note 3: King size may also refer to Dual King which is two twin beds pushed together.
Note 4: The drop (height from top of bed clothes to the bottom of the spread) is usually 20″-21″.

MATTRESS SIZES:
Youth	33″ x 66″
Day	30″ x 75″
Twin	39″ x 75″
¾	48″ x 75″
Double	54″ x 75″
Queen	60″ x 80″
King	76″ x 80″
Bed Height	About 19½″-20″

WHEN A TAPEMEASURE IS A WOMAN'S BEST FRIEND

Always when you're into a sheeting project of any kind bring your tape measure when you go shopping, and if you're into big work, buy a really good 12 foot roll up metal tape or the carpenters folding kind.

A professional stapler is also a necessity if you are doing wall work with sheets. Buy a good one, but try it out yourself before you buy. A stapler should be heavy enough to do the job—but it should also be light enough to work with one hand. Make sure you do this before you invest.

If you're planning to do a room with sheeting, good planning is necessary. Make a floor plan of the room, laying out the height and width of each wall, carefully measuring where the windows and doors are. If you make a chart (preferably on graph paper) of each side of the room, and then consult the sheet size chart above, you'll know instantly how many sheets you need for the job.

The best economics is to use as much of the wide width of sheets as possible, placing them so that the patterns work to your best advantage. Not all sheets of the same pattern are identically printed so it's a good idea to spread out each sheet and check that the patterns match. Precise, linear patterns, like checks and stripes, can be difficult to match in large areas. Overall, random patterns are often easier.

When you do a whole room in sheeting—walls, bed, curtains, pillows, etc., buy all the sheets you will need at the same time. Patterns can be discontinued or dye-lots changed, and if you underestimate, you may be in trouble. One Mademoiselle editor who claims to have sheeted everything but her dog (and he sleeps on a sheeted pad!) says the best way to insure against this is to overbuy. She buys two extra sheets of her bed size and doesn't use them, puts them away wrapped for the inevitable day when wine spills on the round table cloth or when a curtain gets torn.

The borders of some sheets are often the most attractive part of the design. Use them to best advantage—don't waste them. They can be cut off and joined together to make more elaborate pillows (see page 88).

• Always rip hems from sheets—unless you can use existing hems in your project. Press opened-out hems with a steam iron.

• Don't wash sheets before using them—unless your project is one that will need to be washed often and you are afraid of shrinkage or fading.

1 PICNIC PAD

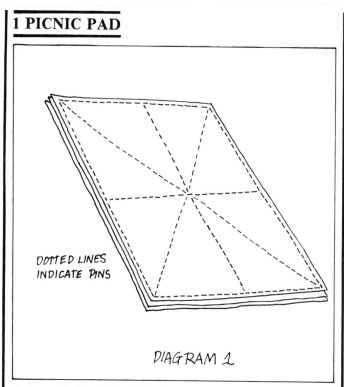

DOTTED LINES
INDICATE PINS

DIAGRAM 1

You'll need: Double bed size flat mattress pad. 2 twin-size sheets without borders.

1. Remove elastic bands from bed pad and wash it. This will eliminate future shrinkage.

2. Cut sheet to size of bed pad, allowing 1 inch all around.

3. Place sheet on floor, wrong side up; center pad on sheet; place second sheet on top, right side up.

4. Starting in center, pin diagonally out to corners, then straight out to each side (Diagram 1). Baste all pin lines and baste around outside edge.

5. Mark and stitch parallel quilt lines diagonally over entire surface of pad. Lines should be about 3 inches apart. Bind edges of pad with bias tape. Instead of tape you might use a self binding if you have enought sheeting left. Just cut 1½ inch wide bias strips and join together.

Mademoiselle editors' tip

This basic idea can be more than a picnic pad. Using a mattress pad as a base you can get flat-quilting of any sheet pattern you want. Nice for upholstering a chair seat, for a child's crib quilt, for making a dog mat.

2 HOW TO MAKE 11 GREAT PILLOWS

GENERAL DIRECTIONS

• Stuffing for pillows can be foam, foam chips, kapok, cotton batting or polyester wadding. The most luxurious is down or down and feathers. If you are lucky enough to have an old down or feather pillow, use it for stuffing. If you do this, don't try and transfer the feathers themselves. Just shake the feathers down in the pillow till you get it plump and stitch down the original covering to make it a square shape.

• A really long wearing pillow is one that has a muslin inner cover which is made to the basic shape of the pillow—not including welting, flanges or the like. If you are making a quickie and it's a simple knife edge or box pillow, just omit the inner muslin.

• Although purists insist that pillows be equipped with zippers for quick on-and-off covers, they have been omitted from these pillows to make them easier to sew. They are slipstitched together on the open side and can be easily ripped for removal of cover. If you insist, insert a zipper on the open side.

• If you're using a ready-made foam pillow form, make your muslin and cover ½ inch smaller on each measurement than size of pillow to insure a close fit.

• If you are filling a pillow with feathers or foam chips, do it in the bathtub for easy cleanup. With the door shut!

• Making Welting: Some pillows look more professional with a welted edge. Either use commercial welting or make your own. To make welting: measure length of welting needed; cut cord to this measurement plus 3 inches. Cut bias strips of fabric 2 inches wide. Piece as necessary, making seams on the diagonal. Place cord along center of fabric strip on wrong side. Enclose it in the strip (Diagram 1). Stitch close to cord, using a zipper foot on machine.

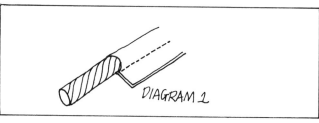

DIAGRAM 1

• When stuffing pillows, get stuffing well into corners. Use the eraser end of a pencil for the very corner, then try a soup spoon for the rest of the corner area.

2A KNIFE EDGE PILLOW

You'll need: Muslin. Stuffing. Sheeting.

1. Cut 2 pieces muslin the size of pillow desired plus ½ inch on all edges.

2. Baste pieces together. Stitch around edges with ½ inch seams, leaving 4 inches open on center of 1 side. Trim seams, clip corners. Turn.

3. Stuff firmly.

4. Turn in edges. Slipstitch opening closed.

5. Make outer covering exactly like muslin except leave a 6 inch opening on center of 1 side. Press.

6. Insert muslin pillow form. Turn in edges. Slipstitch opening closed.

2B KNIFE EDGE PILLOW WITH WELTING

DIAGRAM 1

You'll need: Same as plain knife edge pillow. Commercial welting or cord and extra fabric.

1. Follow 1, 2, 3, 4 for 2A Knife Edge Pillow.
2. Cut outer cover exactly like muslin.
3. Make welting as in General Directions.
4. Baste welting to 1 piece of outer cover on right side with raw edges on edge of cover (Diagram 1). Cut away extra cord at ends of welting. Turn in ends of welting fabric. Sew together by hand.
5. Stitch around welting with a zipper foot on machine.
6. Baste other piece of outer cover to first piece, right sides together, with welting sandwiched between. Stitch around covers, using a zipper foot on machine.
7. Trim seams, clip corners of fabric. Snip into welting at corners.
8. Turn cover. Press. Insert muslin pillow form. Turn in edges of opening. Slipstitch opening closed.

2C BOX PILLOW

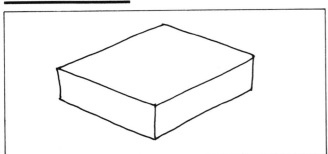

You'll need: Muslin. Stuffing. Sheeting.

1. Cut 2 pieces muslin the size of pillow desired plus ½ inch on all sides. Plan a boxing strip as wide as depth of pillow desired, long enough to go completely around pillow. Add ½ inch on all sides and cut piece. Boxing strip may be pieced if necessary.
2. Stitch short ends of boxing strip together with ½ inch seam.
3. Pin and baste boxing strip around edge of pillow piece. Stitch. Repeat with other pillow piece, leaving 4 inches at center of 1 side open. Trim seams, clip corners. Turn right side out.
4. Stuff pillow.
5. Turn in edges of opening; slipstitch opening closed.
6. Make pillow cover like muslin pillow. When stitching boxing strip to front and back pieces, be sure seam of boxing strip is in the center of 1 side—not in a corner. Also leave a slightly larger opening on last side. Trim seams, clip corners. Turn right side out. Press.
7. Insert pillow in cover. Turn in edges of opening; slipstitch opening closed.

2D BOX PILLOW WITH WELTING

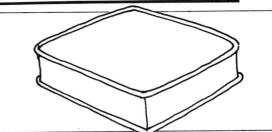

You'll need: Same as plain Box Pillow. Commercial welting or cord and extra fabric.

1. Follow 1, 2, 3, 4, 5 for 2C Box Pillow.
2. Cut pillow cover like muslin pillow.
3. Make welting as in General Directions.
4. Follow steps 4 and 5 under 2B Knife Edge Pillow with Welting for both front and back of pillow cover.
5. Stitch boxing strip to front and back pieces as in step 6 of 2C Box Pillow. Be sure to snip into welting at corners.
6. Finish as in Step 7 of 2C Box Pillow.

2E PILLOW WITH WIDE FLANGE

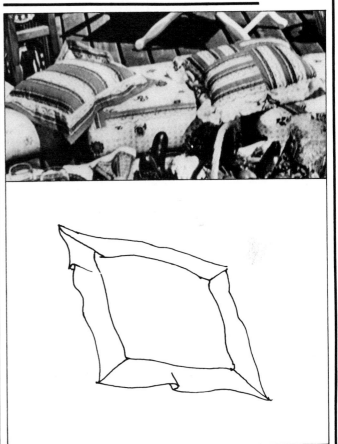

You'll need: Muslin. Stuffing. Sheeting.

1. Make muslin pillow form following Steps 1, 2, 3, 4 for 2A Knife Edge Pillow.
2. Plan fabric cover, adding 3½ inches on all sides of basic pillow requirements. Cut front and back to these measurements.
3. Follow Step 2 of 2A Knife Edge Pillow, leaving 6 inches open.
4. Working on right side of pillow cover, mark a chalk line 3½ inches in from edge on all sides. Stitch around, leaving 6 inches open in the center of the same side which you left open on the outer edge.
5. Insert muslin pillow form. Pin and baste open section of inner stitching line. Machine stitch.
6. Turn in opening on outer edge. Slipstitch opening closed.

2F ALL AROUND RUFFLED PILLOW

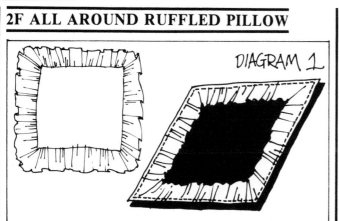

DIAGRAM 1

You'll need: Muslin. Stuffing. Sheeting. Ruffled trimming or extra fabric.

1. Make muslin pillow form following Steps 1, 2, 3, 4 for 2A Knife Edge Pillow.

2. Cut 2 pieces outer covering following Step 1 for 2A Knife Edge Pillow.

3. Use ready-made ruffling or make fabric strips 2¼ inches wide, piecing as necessary until they are 2½ times the perimeter of pillow. Make ¼ inch finished hem on outer edge. Shirr ⅜ inch from inner edge.

4. Measure ruffling around edge of front cover piece and seam short ends together.

5. Baste ruffling on front piece, raw edges and right sides together (Diagram 1). Stitch ½ inch from edge.

6. Place pillow front and back pieces right sides together with ruffling sandwiched between. Baste. Stitch around edges with ½ inch seams, leaving 6 inches open on center of 1 side. Trim seams, clip corners. Turn. Press.

7. Insert pillow form. Turn in open edges. Slipstitch opening closed.

2G PILLOW WITH END RUFFLES

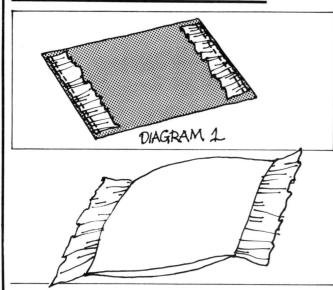

DIAGRAM 1

You'll need: Muslin. Stuffing. Sheeting. Ruffled trimming or extra fabric. It could be a left over sheet border.

1. Make muslin pillow form following Steps 1, 2, 3, 4 for 2A Knife Edge Pillow.

2. Cut front and back of fabric cover to same measurements as muslin form.

3. Cut 2 pieces ruffled trimming same length as sides of pillow. Or make 2 fabric strips 2¼ inches wide and 2½ times the length of sides of pillow. Make ¼ inch finished hem on outer edge. Shirr ⅜ inch from inner edge. Make narrow finished hems on readymade

or handmade ruffling so it is 1 inch shorter than edge to which it will be attached.

4. Baste ruffling to pillow front, right sides and raw edges together (Diagram 1). Short sides of ruffling should be ½ inch from edge of pillow front. Stitch ½ inch from edge.

5. Place pillow front and back pieces right sides together with ruffles sandwiched between. Baste. Being careful not to catch short ends of ruffles, stitch around edges with ½ inch seams, leaving 6 inches open on center of 1 side without ruffle. Trim seams, clip corners. Turn. Press.

6. Insert pillow form. Turn in open edges. Slipstitch opening closed.

2H QUILTED BED PILLOW COVER

You'll need: Bed pillow. Pieces from a quilted bedspread. Zipper.

1. Measure bed pillow. Cut 2 pieces quilted fabric to these measurements plus ¾ inch all around.

2. Right sides together, stitch front and back together with ½ inch seams around outer edges, leaving an opening the length of zipper in center of 1 side. Trim seams, clip corners. Turn.

3. Insert zipper. Press.

4. Insert pillow.

Note: If you want matching welting on this pillow, just rip the quilting stitching and remove the padding from bedspread pieces. Make welting as described in General Directions and insert welting as in Steps 4, 5, 6, 7 of 2B Knife Edge Pillow With Welting.

2 I PILLOWS USING SHEET BORDERS

If you have been working with sheets, you may have a collection of borders asking to be used. One way is to put them together, patchwork fashion, then handle the joined pieces as a plain piece of fabric. Or use them to trim simple knife-edge pillows as in 2I.

You'll need: The usual materials for a knife-edge pillow. Sheet borders.

Pillow A—With borders across the corners:
   1. When you have cut the usual pillow top, cut borders to fit across each corner, allowing for seams.
   2. Place borders on pillow top. Turn in one quarter inch on inner edges of borders. Baste. Stitch.
   3. Finish as for 2A Knife Edge Pillow, catching outer edges of borders in seams.

Pillow B—With plain borders:
   1. When you have cut the usual pillow top, cut long borders to fit each side, allowing for seams on long edges.
   2. Place top and bottom borders on pillow top. Turn in

one quarter inch on inner edges. Baste. Stitch.

   3. Place other two borders along edges. Turn in one quarter inch on inner edges. Baste. Stitch.

   4. Finish as for 2A Knife Edge Pillow, catching outer edges of borders in seams.

Pillow C—With center stripes:

   1. When you have cut the usual pillow top, cut border strip to extend down length of pillow, allowing one quarter inch for seam down each long edge.

   2. Turn under one quarter inch on each long edge. Baste border in place down center of pillow top. Stitch down each side.

   3. Finish as for 2A Knife Edge Pillow, catching ends of strip in seams.

2J BOLSTER PILLOW

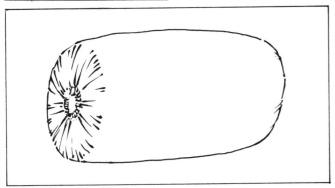

You'll need: Foam bolster pillow form (they come 9 inches in diameter x 36 or 54 inches long). Sheeting. 1 yard cord.

   1. Measure around bolster. Cut piece of sheeting to the width of this measurement plus 1 inch. The length should be 46½ inches for a 36 inch bolster, 64½ for a 54 inch bolster.

   2. Right sides together, join the long edges with a generous ½ inch seam. Press seam open.

   3. Turn ¼ inch on each end to wrong side, then turn ½ inch to wrong side for casing. Press. Stitch. Turn cover right side out.

   4. Make a small opening in each casing and whip edges neatly.

   5. Cut cord in half. Attach a safety pin to end of cord and run a piece through each casing.

   6. Slip cover on bolster and draw up cords as tightly as possible. Tie.

   7. If there is a small opening at each end of bolster, it can be concealed with a scrap of sheeting tacked inside the opening.

2K THE FRENCH FOLD PILLOW CASE

You'll need: Pillow form. Sheeting.

   1. Cut your pillow top to size with necessary seam allowances. Cut pillow back in 2 pieces. Each should be the same width as pillow front. One is 1/3 the length of the front plus 3 inches; the other is 2/3 the length of the front plus 3 inches.

   2. Turn ½ inch finished hems on the 2 back pieces as in Diagram 1.

   3. Right sides together, assemble the front and 2 back pieces as in diagram. Baste. Stitch outer edges with ½ inch seams. Trim seams, clip corners.

   4. Turn cover right side out, press and slip over pillow form.

Mademoiselle editors' tip

If there is one quick easy way of covering a pillow, this is it. The pillow slips between the back folds and you can have complete coverage. The French use this method for covering big square bedpillows, but it works just as well on oblongs. The French fold is the one to use for pillows whose covers have to be washed often.

3 SHEET "WALLPAPER"

GENERAL DIRECTIONS

Sheets are easy to use for walls because they come in wide widths. Less seaming—and matching—for you to do.

   • When buying sheets, open up the packages to make sure that the pattern is similarly placed on all sheets so that your patterns can be properly matched later.

   • If you have average 8 foot ceilings, just cut the hems off sheets. If your ceilings are higher, rip hems and press out creases. If your ceilings are extremely high, buy longer sheets.

   • Press all sheets thoroughly. You can't get out wrinkles once the sheets are in place.

   • Do not use white background sheets on colored walls. Check your sheets on the wall to see if the color shows through.

   • Sheets can be glued to walls with special paste for fabrics but stapling is much easier.

3A SHEET "WALLPAPER": FLAT

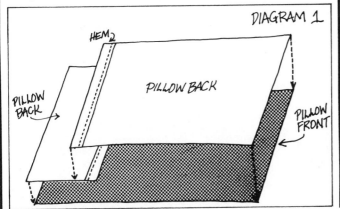

DIAGRAM 1

HEM

PILLOW BACK

PILLOW BACK

PILLOW FRONT

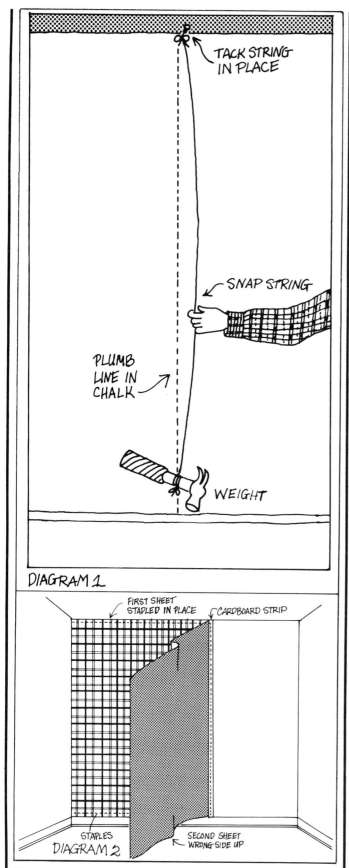

DIAGRAM 1

FIRST SHEET STAPLED IN PLACE — CARDBOARD STRIP

STAPLES

DIAGRAM 2 SECOND SHEET WRONG SIDE UP

You'll need: Sheets. Staple gun. Masking tape. ½ inch wide strips of lightweight cardboard. Trimming tape. White glue.

1. Measure square footage of wall. If the room is 12 feet long and you have 8 foot ceilings, the square footage is 8 x 12 = 96 square feet. Since there is about 52 square feet in a flat twin size sheet, 2 sheets should be enough. But don't be fooled. Twin sheets may not be quite 72 inches wide—and you need a little extra for fold-backs. Better use 1 twin and 1 double.

Note: All directions that follow assume that you are working from the left side of wall to the right.

2. Walls may not be absolutely straight. To get a straight line to work from, make a plumb line. Run colored chalk down a long string. Put a thumbtack through 1 end of string, tie a weight (any heavy object) at the other end. Insert tack at ceiling 1 sheet width from left corner of room (see Diagram 1). Snap the string and the chalk will transfer to the wall.

3. Cut off sheet hems (or rip them open if needed). Press.

4. If your room has ceiling moldings or baseboards, remove them. Or you can leave them in place and work just within them.

5. Run a strip of masking tape across top of room, also across the floor line and straight down in line with plumb line. These will prevent the staples from cracking the plaster.

6. Staple sheet across just below ceiling, first stapling about 6 inches apart to anchor sheet in place, then go back and staple about 1 inch apart. (Use this method when stapling all other edges.) Now draw sheet down firmly and staple at bottom.

7. Using a metal ruler as a guide, cut off excess fabric at both sides and bottom with a craft knife. Staple sheet at edge near plumb line.

8. Now place next sheet over first one, right sides together. Lay cardboard strip over edge near plumb line and staple through cardboard and both sheets (Diagram 2). This method hides the staples. You may need someone to help you with this step, however.

9. Turn top sheet right side out and staple to wall at ceiling. Draw taut to bottom and staple.

10. At right-hand corner of wall cut off excess as before.

11. Free edges of sheets at corners of room can be carefully glued in place (staples would show) or just staple and cover later with trimming.

12. If you have removed them, replace ceiling molding and baseboards. Or finish ceiling and floor edges with trimming cut to length and glued in place. If you have stapled the corner sides, these can also be finished with trimming glued in place.

HANDLING A WINDOW OR DOOR

1. Work sheet right up to window or door frame. Staple down side edge and cut off extra sheet.

2. Cut a piece to fit over window (or door) and another piece for under window, adding 2 inches on width of each piece. Watch the matching on this. The better the match, the more professional the finished job will look.

3. Attach top piece with a cardboard strip on the left. Then staple at top and bottom. Staple down right side.

4. Repeat Step 3 for under-window piece.

5. Now using cardboard strip, apply next section of sheet down right side of window (or door), working from the ceiling down and overlapping the over-window (door) and under-window pieces.

6. Cover staples around frame with trimming glued in place.

GOING AROUND A CORNER

1. When you staple down a corner, put staples as close to corner as possible.

2. Let fabric continue around corner and cut off 4 inches beyond corner. Staple all down loose edge.

3. Begin again with new plumb line on this wall.

4. Attach next sheet at top, bottom and right edges. Then return to corner and treat as for first corner, overlapping the extra fabric that extended around from adjoining wall.

4 SHEET "WALLPAPER": GATHERED

If you want a gathered fabric effect on your walls, sheets are a good way to do it. There are basically two ways; hanging the gathered sheeting from the top, leaving the bottom free, or shirring the sheets on curtain rods at the top and bottom of the walls. The first method is fuller. The second method keeps the gathers flat against the walls. If you are covering a wall of ugly doors, use the first method. If you are working in a small room or a hallway where space is important, it's better to use the second one.

You'll need: Sheets. Shirring tape. Masking tape. Tacks or staples.

1. Measure the width of wall to be covered. You will need 2-3 times that width in sheets. If wall is 10 feet wide, you'll need 20-30 feet width of sheets, or 4-5 twin flat sheets, or 3 king size sheets. And you will also need 20-30 feet of shirring tape.

2. Rip hems from sheets if you need the length. Or cut them off. **Note:** Occasionally the wide top hem can be used as the bottom hem of your curtains. Plan them accordingly.

3. Place 2 sheets right sides together and stitch long edges with 1 inch seam. Join other sheets in same manner until you have 1 giant piece. Snip into seams at 4 inch intervals to prevent seams from puckering when hung on walls. Press seams open.

4. Turn 1 inch to wrong side on top edge. Press.

5. Pin shirring tape over the 1 inch turnback on wrong side of sheets all along top edge. Stitch at top and bottom edges of tape, being careful not to catch the cords in stitching.

6. Measure sheets for length. Mark an ample hem of 5-6 inches. Turn under ½ inch, then turn hem. Press. Stitch.

7. Press the sheets.

8. Pull up shirring cords so sheets are width of wall. Do not cut off cords. Just wind up and fasten each with a rubber band.

9. Run a strip of masking tape all along top edge of wall.

10. Tack or staple sheets to wall, hiding the tacks or staples in the shirring.

HANDLING WINDOWS AND DOORS

If you have doors or windows to consider, make large shirred section of sheet which just comes to the door (or window). Make a short shirred section which will hang over door (or window). Then start another large shirred section which will begin on other side of door (or window).

The section which hangs below the window should be shirred only slightly to conform with the other lower sections.

Mademoiselle editors' tip

On curtain rods. There is nothing more frustrating than getting all set to hang your shirred wall of sheets and find that you've bought the wrong curtain rods. Explain to the salesperson when you buy your rods *exactly* what you plan to do. (This is where a drawing helps.) Make sure you buy the flattest possible rod, that you have enough extenders to bridge the long walls, and that you have sufficient plugs and/or Mollys to insert the screws firmly. Shirred walls of sheets must have even tension. Attach the top curtain rod first, put the curtain on, and leave it to hang out overnight. Then, the next day, insert the bottom rod in the lower hem and gently pull it down till you get the right tension. Then attach the lower rod. Remember that you will, with certain kinds of rods, have to attach the lower ones *in reverse*, to keep the curtain rod in the hook and maintain tension.

5 SHEET "WALLPAPER": SHIRRED

You'll need: Sheets. Curtain rods and hardware (for sizes see Step 3 below).

1. See Step 1 at left for width of sheets needed.

2. See Step 2 at left.

3. 72 and 81 inch wide sheets will take a curtain rod about 3-4 feet wide; 90 and 108 inch wide sheets will take a curtain rod about 4-5 feet wide.

4. Attach curtain rods 1½ inches below ceiling as close together as possible. Also attach rods at bottom of wall 2 inches above the floor.

5. Measure space between top and bottom rods, add 5 inches and cut sheets to this length.

6. At top and bottom of sheets turn ¼ inch to wrong side, press. Turn 2¼ inches to wrong side, press. 1 inch from edge stitch across, forming heading. 2⅛ inches from edge stitch across, forming casing.

7. Press thoroughly, then insert curtain rods in casings. Hang curtain.

8. When all curtains are in place, pin edges of curtains together if they show any wall space between them.

HANDLING WINDOWS AND DOORS

Plan curtain rods so they stop on each side of door or window. Hang a rod just below ceiling over door (or window) and another one directly over door (or window). Make a small section of sheet that will fit between these 2 rods.

For a window also attach a rod directly under the window and another one 2 inches above the floor. Make a small section of sheet that will fit just between these 2 rods.

Note: You can also use this curtain rod method for hanging curtains that are loose at the bottom. Omit bottom rods and hem bottom edge of curtains.

6 SHEETS AS ARCHITECTURE: WALL PANELS

This is a technique which should not be attempted unless you have had some woodworking experience.

You'll need: Pieces of sheet or fabric. Masking tape. Staple gun. Molding. Miter box. Paint. Brads.

1. Plan your panel carefully and make a paper pattern of the shape. Tape pattern up on wall to check the effect.

2. Measure the perimeter of paper pattern to get length of molding needed. Add on at least a foot for waste. Take measurements and pattern to lumberyard and let the lumberman show you a variety of moldings to select from. Some lumberyards will even cut the miters for you.

3. If the lumberyard did not cut the miters, saw the molding to the proper lengths and cut miters. Set aside.

4. Cut sheet following paper pattern. If you are using more than 1 panel, be sure that the design of sheets line up on all panels. If the design of your sheet has a large motif, be sure it's centered; in other words, don't have a large bunch of flowers off to 1 side.

5. Pencil outline of panel on wall. Run masking tape all around panel just within the outline.

6. Staple 1 side of fabric piece over masking tape, placing staples 6 inches apart. Then go back and staple 1 inch apart. Draw opposite side firmly across and staple in place. Staple third side, then fourth, keeping fabric taut. If your panel is a hexagon or has diagonal corners, also staple those sides.

7. Paint moldings. When dry, sand lightly and give a second coat of paint.

8. Nail 1 strip of molding in place, being careful not to scar molding. Carefully fit joint of next strip and nail. Continue around until molding is all in place.

9. Touch up nail heads with dabs of paint.

7 SHEETS AS ARCHITECTURE: WALL & WAINSCOT

If your room already has a chair rail, just apply sheets to the walls as described in direction 3A Sheet Wallpaper, p. 89. Put on the section above the chair rail first and complete with wainscoting below the chair rail. If you are planning to add a chair rail:

You'll need: All the materials under direction 3. Sufficient molding to extend around the room. Paint or stain and varnish or wax. Brads.

1. If you are planning 1 pattern on the walls, put up sheets from ceiling to floor as described in direction 3A, p. 89.

2. Plan molding and cut miters for all corners. If you are not a skilled carpenter, just use butt joints in corners.

3. Sand molding. Paint or stain it. Give painted molding a light sanding and a second coat of paint. Give stained molding a going over with fine steel wool, then varnish or wax it.

4. Mark a guide line all around room for chair rail.

5. Nail up molding, following guide line. Be careful not to scar molding.

6. Touch up nail heads with dabs of paint.

* * * * * * *

Note: If you want 2 coordinated sheet patterns on the wall as in our picture, mark a line for chair rail all around the room. Put 1 pattern above the line, another pattern below the line. Then the chair rail will hide the raw edges of the upper and lower sheets.

8 SHEETS AS ARCHITECTURE: WINDOW FRAME

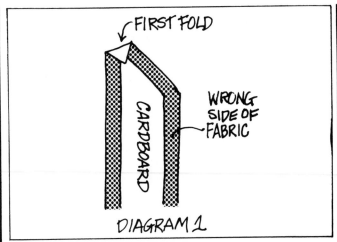

A METHOD THAT IS EASY TO REMOVE:

This method takes about as much time as the above one—but has one advantage. You can remove the whole frame at the end of your lease and no scarred walls. Fiberboard can also be used instead of cardboard, but you'll have to nail it up.

You'll need: Sheets as above. Large pieces of cardboard. White glue. Brush. Heavy-duty double-faced tape.

1. Follow Step 1 for Simple Method.

2. Following pattern, cut sheet for most attractive use of fabric, adding 1½ inches on all edges.

3. Cut cardboard piece for each side of frame, following pattern.

4. Place fabric for 1 side of frame wrong side up. Center its matching cardboard piece on it, draw the extra fabric over cardboard and glue in place. Trim away some of the excess fabric when working at the point of miter and fold down miter corner as in Diagram 1. Repeat on all sides of frame.

5. Mark position of frame around window and use this as a guide for putting strips of double-faced tape around entire outer edge of frame. Also put strips around inner edge of frame and where miters or other joints will come.

6. Stick each section of frame in place.

8A SHEETS AS ARCHITECTURE: CHANGING A WINDOW SHAPE

SIMPLE METHOD

You'll need: Sheets with borders, stripes or the like. Fabric wall paste. Brush.

1. Measure the window. Decide on size of border and lay out the pattern on paper. Plan corners for miters or plain butt corners.

2. Cut sheet for most attractive use of fabric.

3. Mark outline of border on wall around window. Carefully apply paste within outline on top border area and attach fabric. Continue with sides, then bottom borders. **Note:** If your window has prominent moldings and a sill which might interfere with this window treatment, you might make them a feature of the design. First paint them a color to match one of the colors in your fabric, then add the border (see the niche bed picture on page 83 where paint has been used to pick up the color of the curtains).

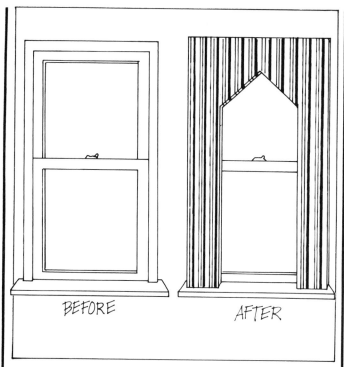

BEFORE   AFTER

You'll need: ½ inch plywood. ¾ x 4 inch lumber. Nails. An old blanket. Sheet. Staples and staple gun. 2 angle irons and screws.

1. Plan your window treatment and make a paper pattern to exact size. **Note:** 4 inch boards are called for to clear the window sill. You may need slightly wider boards. If you don't need the full 4 inch depth, by all means make your frame shallower.

2. Cut plywood to shape of paper pattern. Cut top board to fit width of plywood frame. Cut 2 side boards to fit under top board and extend to bottom of frame (Diagram 1).

3. Nail together the 4 pieces of frame.

4. Cut blanket large enough to fit over plywood and side and top boards. Leave center section intact. Center frame on blanket and staple blanket to frame, cutting away extra thickness at corners. Now cut out center section, leaving 2 inches all around opening to extend to back of frame. Slash around curves or at corners. Pull blanket to back and staple in place.

5. Cut sheet large enough to fit over plywood and side and top boards and extend 2 inches over back of frame. Leave center section intact. Center frame on wrong side of fabric. Draw excess fabric to back and staple in place, folding in corners neatly. Now cut out center section, leaving 2 inches to extend to back of frame. Slash around curves or at corners. Pull fabric to back of frame and staple in place.

6. Screw angle irons onto top board (Diagram 1) and screw the frame in place.

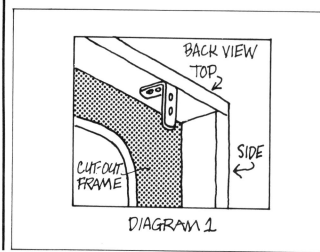

BACK VIEW
TOP

SIDE

CUT-OUT
FRAME

DIAGRAM 1

9 SHEETING A CEILING

It's better not to try applying sheets to a large ceiling—not any larger than could be covered with one queen or king size sheet. You'll need: Sheet. Staple gun. Masking tape. Trimming. White glue.

1. Rip open hems of sheet if you need the fabric. Or cut them off. Press.

2. Run masking tape all around outer edge of ceiling to prevent the staples from cracking the plaster.

3. Attach 1 edge of sheet to 1 side of ceiling, stapling 6 inches apart. Then go back and staple 1 inch apart.

4. Have 2 people pull sheet tightly across ceiling and hold it while you staple the opposite side as in Step 3.

5. Now staple the third side.

6. Again have 2 people pull the sheet while you staple the fourth side.

7. With a sharp craft knife cut off the excess sheet at the sides of the ceiling.

8. With glue attach trimming to cover raw edges of sheet. If the staples will not show, trimming may be stapled in place.

Note: If the sheet sags slightly, you can scatter staples here and there so they are lost in the pattern. This step may not be necessary until the sheet has been in place for a while.

10 BED SKIRTS & DUST RUFFLES

10A TAILORED BED SKIRT

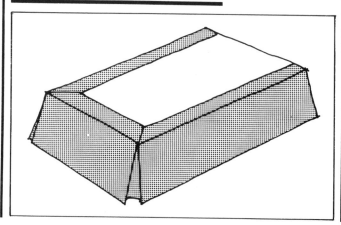

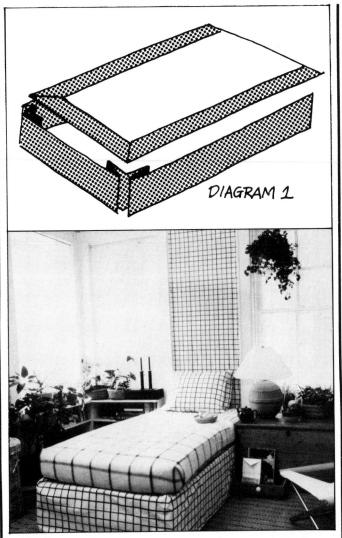

DIAGRAM 1

You'll need: Patterned or plain sheet. For twin bed you need a twin flat sheet. For double, queen and king size bed you need a double flat sheet. Muslin or an old sheet.

1. Measure width and length of your box spring and cut a muslin top to these measurements plus ½ inch on each long side, 1 inch on each short side.

2. Cut 2 pieces of patterned fabric 3¼ inches wide and the same length as the long edges of muslin piece. Cut one 3¼ inch wide strip the same length as width of muslin.

3. Right sides up, lay the long patterned strips *over* each long edge of the muslin; pin. Lay shorter strip *over* the foot end of muslin piece; pin. Turn in ¼ inch on inner edge of all strips; pin. At foot end, miter the 2 corners of strips (see Diagram 1). Stitch strips to muslin on inner and outer edges. These strips keep the muslin from showing around the edges of the bed.

4. For skirt, cut a long piece whose width is the distance from floor to top of box spring plus 3¼ inches. Make it twice the length of box spring plus the width of box spring plus 16 inches for the 2 pleats at each front corner (32 inches all together), plus 3 inches for hems—for a double bed, 19 feet, 11 inches. Since you will have to piece this long ruffle, plan seams to be hidden in the corner pleats. Add ½ inch on each section for seams. Join into 1 long strip with French seams.

5. Pin center of skirt to center of foot end of muslin piece. Right sides together, pin skirt all across foot end along edge. Fold in 4 inch deep pleats in corners (Diagram 1). Continue pinning along sides to head end of piece. Baste. Stitch with ½ inch seams.

6. Make 3 inch finished hem on lower edge of skirt, making sure that skirt clears the floor and rugs.

7. Turn under a 1 inch finished hem across both skirts and muslin at head end. Stitch.

8. Press and place skirt between box spring and mattress.

10B GATHERED DUST RUFFLE

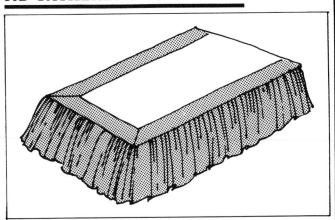

You'll need: Patterned or plain sheet. (For twin bed you need a queen flat sheet. For double or queen size bed you need a king size flat sheet.) Muslin or an old sheet.

1. Follow steps 1, 2, 3 for 10A Tailored Bed Skirt.

2. For ruffle cut a long piece the distance from floor to top of box spring plus 3¼ inches. Make it twice the length of box spring plus the width of box spring. Double this measurement and add 3 inches. That's the length of your ruffle (for double bed, 34 feet 3 inches). Since you will have to piece this strip, add ½ inch on all joining edges. Join into 1 long strip with French seams.

3. Using ruffler on your machine or 2 rows of long stitches on machine, shirr 1 edge of strip.

4. Mark center of strip and draw up a shirring to fit around muslin top. Pin center of strip to center of foot end of muslin piece. Right sides together, pin ruffle all across foot end of muslin piece. Continue pinning along sides to head end, adjusting ruffling as you pin. Baste. Stitch with ½ inch seam.

5. Make 3 inch finished hem on lower edge of ruffle, making sure that ruffle clears the floor and rugs.

6. Turn under a 1 inch finished hem across ruffles and muslin piece at head of bed. Stitch.

7. Press and place dust ruffle between box spring and mattress.

10C KNIFE PLEATED BED SKIRT

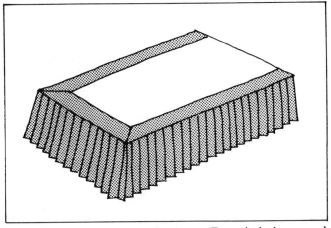

You'll need: Patterned or plain sheets. (For twin bed you need 1 twin and 1 double flat sheet. For double bed you need 1 twin and 1 double flat sheet. For queen size bed you need 1 twin and 1 queen flat sheet. For king size bed you need 1 twin and 1 queen flat sheet.) Muslin or an old sheet.

1. Follow steps 1, 2, 3 for 10A Tailored Bed Skirt.

2. For skirt cut a long piece whose width is the distance from floor to top of box spring plus 3¼ inches. Plan the length by figuring how many pleats you want around the skirt. Each 2 inch

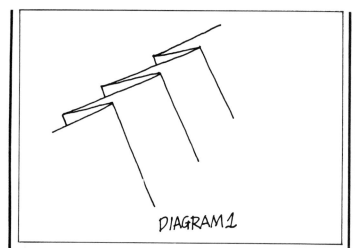

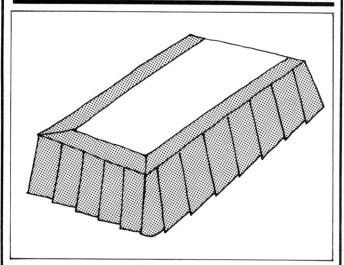

DIAGRAM 1

wide pleat takes 6 inches of fabric—100 pleats require 100 x 6 = 600 inches or 50 feet. Add 3 inches for hems. Since you will have to piece this skirt, plan seams to be hidden in a pleat. Add ½ inch on each section for joining seams. Join into 1 long strip with ½ inch seams.

3. Make 3 inch finished hem on long edge of skirt. Press.

4. Make pleats all along raw edge of skirt, using your planned measurements and following Diagram 1. You may find it helpful to pad your worktable so that you can iron pleats as you measure and pin them. Baste and stitch securely all across top edge.

5. Mark center of skirt and pin to center of foot end of muslin piece. Right sides together, pin skirt all across foot end along edge. Be sure that a pleat falls at each corner. Continue pinning along sides to head end. Check on bed to see if skirt clears the floor. If not, adjust. Baste. Stitch with ½ inch seam.

6. Turn under 1 inch finished hem across skirts and muslin piece at head of bed. Stitch.

7. Place ruffle between box spring and mattress.

10D SIDE PLEATED BED SKIRT

You'll need: Patterned or plain sheets. (4 inch deep pleats about 7½ inches apart. For all size beds you need a king size flat sheet.) Muslin or old sheet.

1. Follow steps 1, 2, 3 for 10A Plain Bed Skirt.

2. For skirt, cut a long piece whose width is the distance from floor to top of box spring plus 3¼ inches. Make it twice the length of box spring plus the width of box spring plus 8 inches for each pleat desired plus 16 inches for each front corner pleat (32 inches for the 2 front corners) plus 3 inches. Our pleats were about 7½ inches apart. You may have to adjust spacing depending on size of your bed. Since you will have to piece long skirt, plan seams to be hidden in pleats. Add ½ inch on each section for joining seams.

3. Mark top muslin piece with pins at regular intervals where pleats will occur on skirt.

4. Mark center of skirt edge. Pin center of skirt to center of foot end of muslin piece. Right sides together, pin skirt all across foot end of muslin piece, making 4 inch deep pleats at each pin mark. At corners, make pleats as in Diagram 1 for 10A Tailored Bed Skirt. Continue pinning along sides to head end of piece, making pleats where indicated by pins. Baste. Stitch with ½ inch seam.

5. Make 3 inch finished hem on lower edge of skirt, making sure the skirt clears the floor and rugs.

6. Turn under a 1 inch finished hem across skirts and muslin at head of bed. Stitch.

7. Place bed skirt between box spring and mattress.

11 MAKING A NICHED BED

The ensemble shown was used on a 39 x 80 inch (long twin) bed set across the end of a small room just 7 feet wide. That left 2 inches of clearance at each end of bed. For entire bed ensemble 2 king size throw-type quilted bedspreads were used. You could also do the same niched bed idea using sheets. It's suggested that you work out your patterns in advance and lay them out. You may be able to use 2 smaller-size spreads (or sheets). Other materials will be included in the directions that follow.

11A FAKE BED SKIRT

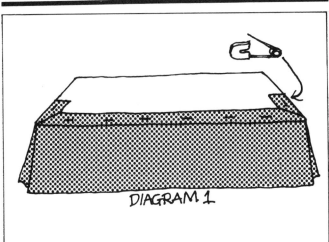

DIAGRAM 1

This fake bed skirt can be used whenever you niche a bed. Why make a full bed skirt when only the front shows!
You'll also need: 2½ yards wide bias tape. Large safety pins.
1. Measure height of bed from floor. Add 4 inches. From side edge of bedspread cut a skirt strip whose width is the measurement you just worked out. Length should be length of bed plus 11 inches. Cut strips so that both ends are free of stitched borders, etc., at ends of bedspread and outside edge of bedspread is lower edge of skirt.
2. Make 1 inch finished hems at both narrow ends of strip.
3. On raw top edge of strip apply bias tape.
4. Pin taped edge of skirt to box spring (at 6 inch intervals) so that skirt just clears the floor.

11B BEDSPREAD

1. Plan size of spread. Length should be length of mattress plus 6 inches to tuck down at foot and at head (ours was 92). Width should be width of mattress plus 6 inches to tuck down at back and enough to hang down to cover mattress at front (ours was 33 + 6 + 12 = 51 inches). All measurements include 2 inch hem allowances.
2. Cut a piece to your measurements from the best section of spread, skipping seams if possible. If you have to include the seams on the original spread, be sure they will be evenly spaced on your spread.
3. Turn under and press ½ inch on all edges. Turn under and press 1½ inch hem on all edges. Stitch.

11C VALANCE FOR NICHED BED

You'll also need: Strip of ½ inch plywood 10-12 inches wide by the length of the area into which it will fit (ours was 12 x 84 inches). Strip of sateen or other plain cotton to match the bedspread as wide as valance board plus 2 inches. Its length should be length of board plus 2 inches (bedspread fabric can be used in place of sateen). Staple gun and staples. 4 angle irons and screws.
1. Sandpaper valance board well.
2. Cut bedspread same size as valance board plus 2 inches on all sides. If there are seams on bedspread be sure they are evenly placed on valance. However, it is better to use area of bedspread that has no seams.
3. Center valance board on wrong side of bedspread fabric. Draw edges over board and staple in place, folding corners in neatly.
4. Turn in 1¼ inches on each edge of sateen lining, press. Center

on back of valance. Staple along edges. If staples show, you may want to slipstitch lining in place with a curved needle. **Note:** If you have enough bedspread material, you can line the valance with bedspread fabric.
5. Screw angle irons, evenly spaced, to back of valance near top edge. Screw angle irons to ceiling.

11D BED CURTAINS

You'll also need: Sateen lining to match bedspread (or use extra bedspread fabric). Curtain rings. Curtain rods. The curtain rods must attach from the ceiling.
1. Measure from floor to ceiling. Add 4 inches. This is length of curtain. Width should be from 12-18 inches. Double this measurement for fullness and add 1½ inches. Cut 2 curtains. Also cut 2 linings of sateen or bedspread fabric.
2. Place curtain and lining right sides together. Stitch long sides and across top with ¾ inch seams. Trim seams, clip corners. Turn right side out. Press. Repeat for second curtain.
3. Sew curtain rings across top edges.
4. Attach curtain rods to ceiling behind valance.
5. Hang curtains.
6. Measure bottom edge of curtains for hems, making sure they clear the floor. Cut off excess fabric if necessary, leaving 4½ inches for hems. Make a 4 inch finished hem on curtains and linings, leaving an opening between the 2 hems at the bottom.

CURTAIN TIE BACK

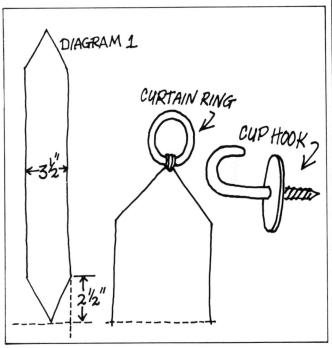

DIAGRAM 1
CURTAIN RING
CUP HOOK
3½"
2½"

You'll also need: Small amount buckram. Scraps of sateen lining to match bedspread fabric. 4 curtain rings. 2 cup hooks.
1. Loop a tape measure around curtain as if it were a tie back. With this measurement draw a tie back pattern, making it 3½ inches wide (Diagram 1). Point ends as in diagram.
2. Cut buckram following pattern. Cut front and lining, adding ½ inch to all edges.
3. Center buckram on wrong side of front piece. Baste.
4. Right sides together, join lining to front with ½ inch seams, leaving center of 1 long side open. Trim seams, clip corners. Turn right side out.
5. Slipstitch opening closed.
6. Sew a curtain ring to each point of tie back.
7. Make second tie back in same manner.
8. Attach cup hooks to wall at right height to catch tie backs.

You'll need: Sheeting—matching print in 2 colors. Borders from sheets or 2 inch wide braid. Polyester wadding.

1. Measure your table top. Cut 2 pieces of sheeting (1 of each color) to these exact measurements. Cut wadding to these same measurements. Cut 2 center panels (1 of each color sheeting) about 1/3 the size of table top.

2. Center a panel (of opposite color) on each large piece of sheeting. Baste. Edge panels with sheet borders, turning in raw edges of borders. Miter borders in each corner. Baste and stitch along inner and outer edges of borders and along miters. Use braid if you don't have extra sheet borders. **Note:** If you are using commercial braid rather than borders, do not turn in long edges.

3. Place the 2 pieces right sides together. Lay wadding on top. Baste and stitch with 1 inch seam all around edges, leaving 12 inches open at center of 1 side. Trim seams, clip corners. Turn right side out.

4. Turn in open edges and slipstitch opening closed.

5. Baste all around outer edges. Baste from center out to each side and from center out to corners.

6. Mark runner with chalk for quilting. You can plan diagonal lines in each direction—forming diamonds. Or use simple horizontal and vertical lines. In any case make lines about 6 inches apart.

7. Roll up runner to make it easier to handle and stitch all quilting lines.

8. Tie all thread ends carefully.

You'll need: An old fabric-covered lampshade. Sheeting. Borders from sheeting or 1½ inch wide braid. Heavy weight buckram.

1. Measure height and circumference of lampshade. Add 1 inch to each measurement. Cut a piece of sheeting to these measurements.

2. Make ¼ inch finished hems on both edges of piece. Join ends of strip with ½ inch seam, forming a ring.

3. Slip ring of fabric over lampshade, wrong side out. Pin around bottom. Pin evenly spaced darts until sheeting fits lampshade perfectly (Diagram 1). Take off sheeting cover and stitch darts in place. Cut away extra fabric from darts and press darts open.

4. Slip the cover over lampshade and tack in place around top and bottom.

5. For trim cut sheeting borders about 2 inches wide and the length should be the circumference of the top (and bottom) of the shade plus 1 inch. Cut a similar lining piece of matching border or plain sheeting.

6. Turn under and press ¼ inch on all long edges. Cut a strip of buckram to this width but 1 inch shorter than length. Right sides out, place the sheeting and lining pieces together with the buckram sandwiched between, but coming ½ inch from the ends. Stitch along long edges.

7. Turn in ½ inch at each end. Butt ends of strip together and whip ends together, forming a ring.

8. Slipstitch ring to top (or bottom) of shade.

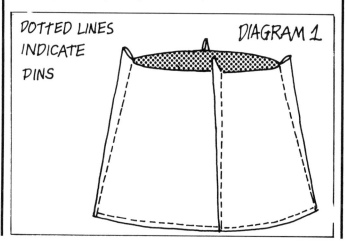

DOTTED LINES INDICATE PINS   DIAGRAM 1

14 CHAIR BACKS, SEAT CUSHIONS

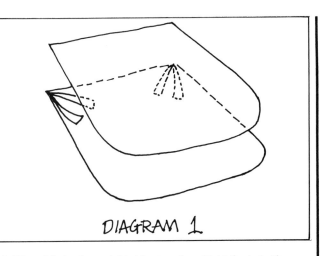

DIAGRAM 1

3. Place fabric pieces right sides together. Fold ties in half crosswise and slip between fabric pieces with a fold in each back corner (Diagram 1). Place double thickness of wadding on top. Stitch outer edges with ½ inch seams, leaving center of 1 side open. Trim seams, clip corners. Turn right side out.

4. Turn in raw edges. Slipstitch opening closed.

5. Place pad on chair and tie ties in corners around uprights.
Note: If you want welting, follow directions for 2B Knife Edge Pillow With Welting.

15 SHEET SHOWER CURTAINS

You'll need: A double bed sheet. Borders from a sheet or braid. Grommets and grommet setter. Shower curtain liner. Shower curtain hooks. Small amount buckram. 4 curtain rings. 2 cup hooks.

1. Measure height of shower curtain rod from floor. Rip hems from sheet and cut sheet in half lengthwise. Cut each panel to the height you measured plus 6 inches.

2. On each panel fold 2 inches under at top. Press. Make a 4 inch finished hem at bottom.

3. Trim inner vertical edges of each panel with a sheeting border sewn in place. Or use braid as trim.

4. Mark top edges for grommets on 2 inch foldback. Start 1 inch in from each side and space them evenly about 6 inches apart. Put a 2 inch square of scrap fabric inside foldback at top edge to strengthen each grommet. Set grommets.

5. Split curtain liner to go behind each panel. Hang shower curtain with lining hanging on same hooks.

6. For tie backs follow directions on page 97.
Note: It's wise to remove the tie backs completely when using the shower.

CHAIR BACK:
Note: This type of chair back is suitable only on ladder back chairs.
You'll need: Sheeting (we used parts of 3 different color sheets). Old sheet. Polyester batting.

1. Measure from top rung of chair back to lower rung. Be sure to include ½ the thickness of top and bottom rungs. Measure width of rungs. Cut sheeting the width of rungs plus 2 inches. The length should be twice the height measurement plus 2 inches. Cut old sheeting and batting to these measurements. Also cut 4 ties 1¼ x 8 inches.

2. Place batting on old sheet piece. Baste around edges and from center out to corners. Right sides together, place old and new sheeting pieces together with batting on top of pile. Stitch around edges with 1 inch seams, leaving center of 1 end open. Trim seams. Clip corners. Turn right side out.

3. Turn in edges of opening and slipstitch close.

4. With pencil, lightly mark quilting lines on chair back. Stitch. Tie thread ends securely.

5. Turn under ½ inch all around tie pieces. Press. Wrong sides together, fold ties in half lengthwise. Press. Stitch. Sew a tie just inside each corner of chair back.

6. Place chair back on chair and tie ties around uprights.

SEAT CUSHIONS
You'll need: Sheeting. Polyester wadding.

1. Make a paper pattern following outline of chair seat. Fold pattern in half to see if both halves are identical. Cut 2 pieces of fabric and 2 thicknesses of wadding following pattern plus ½ inch all around. Cut 2 ties 1¼ x 16 inches.

2. Turn under ¼ inch all around tie pieces. Press. Wrong side together, fold ties in half lengthwise. Press. Stitch.

16 VALANCES

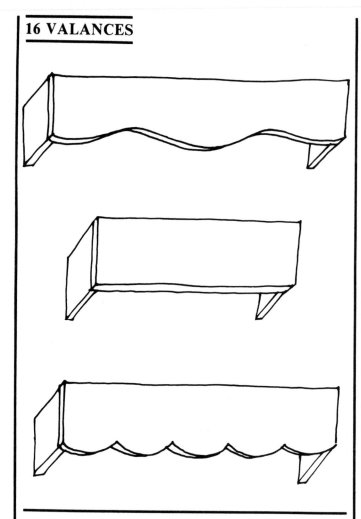

Although making and hanging a valance may be a bit of trouble, the great look it gives a window makes it all worthwhile. First of all, it hides moldings or a plain window frame. It keeps a rolled-up window shade out of sight and finishes off a window treatment the way curtains alone can never do.

In fact, if you like an uncluttered window, (and many decorators today do), just placing valances over the windows is a great way to achieve that look.

You can also conceal lighting under a valance. Long, narrow lighting fixtures should be used, and it's important to attach the fixture before you do the valance. That way you'll be sure to make the valance deep enough and wide enough to control the light.

16A WINDOW VALANCE

You'll need: ½ inch plywood. Small amount ¾ inch pine. Wood screws. Polyester wadding. Staples and staple gun. Sheeting. Hardware for hanging valance.

1. Put up all hardware for hanging draperies and/or curtains. Measure depth they protrude from wall to determine how deep your return boards (see Diagram 1) should be. Make a full size paper pattern of valance design. If you have made a curved or elaborate design, fold pattern in half crosswise to check if both ends are identical. Trace design on plywood and cut out. Cut out 2 returns for valance from pine. If valance is particularly wide put an extra support in center. Screw returns and support in place.

2. Sandpaper valance thoroughly.

3. Following your pattern, cut wadding for front surface of valance and long enough to cover each return. Staple in place.

4. Following pattern, cut sheeting but make sides long enough to cover each return and add 1½ inches all around.

5. Center valance, wadding side down, on wrong side of sheeting. Draw fabric firmly to back over valance board and returns and staple in place. If you have a curved or angled front board, slash the fold-over allowance around curves or at corners to help make a neat job.

6. With a curved needle sew on any trim desired.

7. Screw on hardware to hang valance. Diagram 1 shows an angle iron in place for hanging. Attach valance to wall.

16B SHOWER VALANCE

This valance could be used above the shower curtains in Direction 15.

You'll need: Strip of ½ inch plywood as wide as valance desired by length of area into which it will fit. Sheeting. Polyester wadding. Strip of vinyl fabric ¼ inch smaller all around than valance board. Staple gun and staples. 4 angle irons and screws.

1. Sandpaper valance board thoroughly.

2. Cut sheeting same size as valance board plus 2 inches on all sides.

3. Cut wadding to size of valance. Staple to front of board.

4. Center valance, wadding side down, on wrong side of sheeting. Draw edges over board and staple in place, folding corners in neatly.

5. Center vinyl piece on back of valance. Staple along edges.

6. Screw angle irons evenly spaced to back of valance at top edge. **Important:** Let angle irons protrude so that when they are screwed to ceiling there will be a space between valance and ceiling. This will allow the steam to escape when shower is in use.

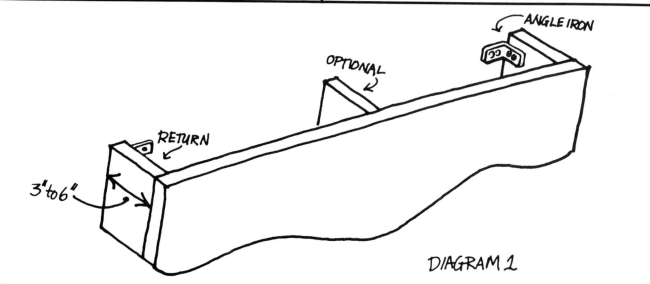

DIAGRAM 1

21

3 A

15

22

25

23

24

SHEETS
ALL OVER

10 B

14

6➤

Mademoiselle editors' tip
Making a sheet an architectural element on a wall or around a window works best if you use a bold and simple graphic—like a stripe or supersize plaid.

SHEETS ALL OVER

15

21

22

3ᴬ

25

23

24

SHEETS ALL OVER

10ᴮ

14

6➤

Mademoiselle editors' tip
Making a sheet an architectural element on a wall or around a window works best if you use a bold and simple graphic—like a stripe or supersize plaid.

SHEETS ALL OVER

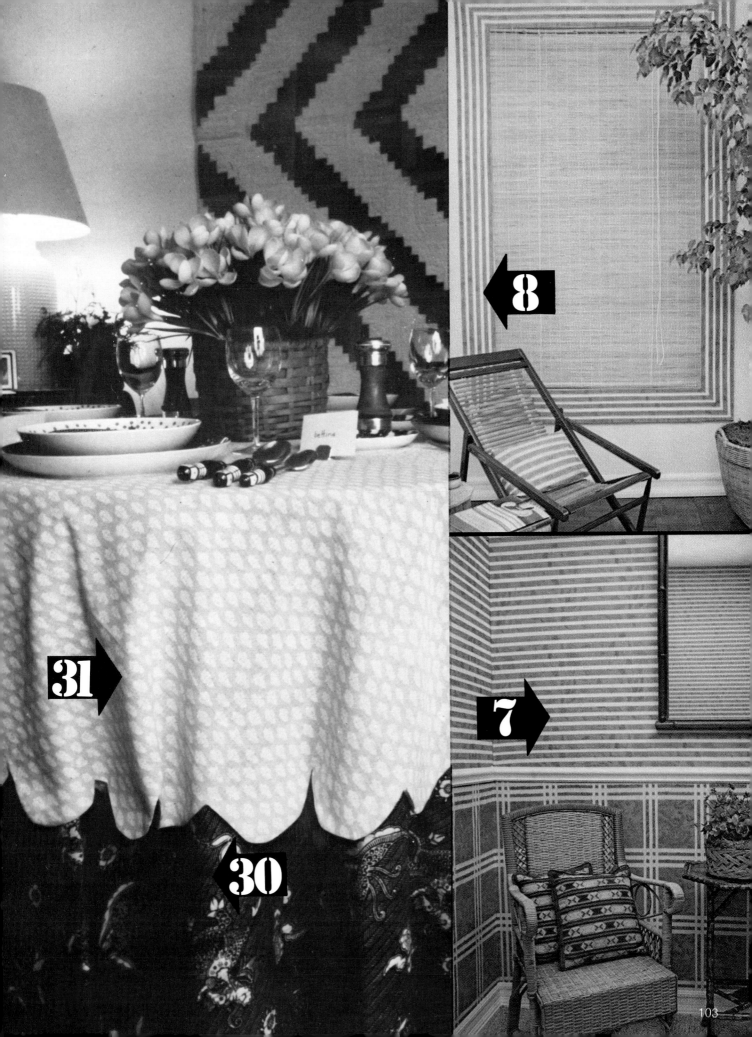

4

25

26

29

27

2A

2B

28

SHEETS ALL OVER

35

36

3A

10D

3a Sheet "wallpaper": flat
See page 89

10d Side-pleated bedskirt
See page 96

35 Chest flowered with sheets
See page 113

36 Slipcovered shelves
See page 114

SHEETS ALL OVER

17 LOFT BED COVER

You'll need: Bedspread (twin size will fit up to a double loft bed). 1¼ yards ¾ inch wide elastic.

1. Measure length, width and height of mattress. Cut bedspread to length of mattress plus twice the height plus 4 inches. Width should be width of mattress plus twice the height plus 4 inches. **Note:** If bedspread has seams, place them evenly on new bedspread piece.

2. Make 1 inch finished hems all around piece.

3. Make up bed with sheets and blankets as it will be when used. Center bedspread on top of bedclothes and make neat turned-in corners. Pin. Take bedspread off and sew corners in place.

4. Cut elastic in fourths. On wrong side pin a piece across each corner. Turn in raw ends and stitch in place.

18 QUILTED FABRIC RUG

You'll need: Sheeting (ours had a braided design which we cut out of the center). Canvas or duck. An old blanket. Container of anti-skid rug backing.

1. Plan shape and size of rug (ours was oval). Cut sheeting to size plus 1 inch on all edges. Cut canvas backing same size. Cut blanket same size without 1 inch seam allowances.

2. Center blanket piece on wrong side of canvas piece. Baste.

3. Right sides together, place sheeting and canvas pieces together. Baste around edges. Stitch with 1 inch seams, leaving 15 inches open on center of 1 side. Trim seams, clip corners or notch curved edges. Turn right side out.

4. Turn in edges of opening. Slipstitch opening closed.

5. Baste around edges. Then baste from center to center of each side. Baste from center diagonally out to each corner.

6. Mark rug with chalk for quilting—can be squares, diamonds, concentric circles or can outline parts of the design. Stitch, making sure to tie all loose thread ends carefully.

7. Paint around edges of back of rug with anti-skid backing following directions on the container.

19 COVERLET FOR A PLATFORM BED

DIAGRAM 1

You'll need: 2 flat sheets (twin size for twin bed, double size for double bed, etc.). 2 polyester quilt batts.

1. Plan size of comforter. Most comforters are 20-27 inches wider than the bed and 86-92 inches long. Rip hems from sheets. Press. Cut sheets to size plus 1 inch all around. Cut batts to size *without* the extra seam allowances.

2. Center the 2 batts—1 on top of the other—on the wrong side of 1 sheet piece. Baste.

3. Place the 2 sheets right sides together, the batts on top. Baste. Stitch around edges with 1 inch seams, leaving 15 inches open on center of 1 side. Trim seams, clip corners. Turn right side out.

4. Turn in edges of opening. Slipstitch opening closed.

5. Baste around edges. Baste from center diagonally out to corners.

6. Mark quilting lines on comforter lightly with pencil. (Ours was quilted in large blocks and with double rows of stitching. There was also stitching around the edges.) Roll up the comforter and run through the machine as in Diagram 1. Stitch. Tie all thread ends securely.

20 SLIPCOVERING A COMFORTER

DIAGRAM 1

This forms an easy-care set of bottom fitted sheet and slipcovered comforter which acts both as comforter and top sheet. The set is completed with matching pillow cases.

You'll need: 2 flat sheets (size depends on size of comforter).

1. Rip out hems from sheets. Press. Cut sheets to size of comforter plus 1 inch all around. Cut 6 ties each 2¼ x 9 inches.

2. Baste sheets right sides together. Stitch around with 1 inch seams, leaving 1 end open. Trim seams, clip corners. Turn right side out.

3. Turn in a ½ inch finished hem on each raw edge of opening. Stitch.

4. Turn under raw ends of ties; press. Fold ties in thirds lengthwise, right side out. Turn under ¼ inch on long raw edge; press. Stitch.

5. Place 3 ties, evenly spaced along each edge of opening (Diagram 1). Stitch.

6. Insert comforter in slipcover and tie each pair of ties.

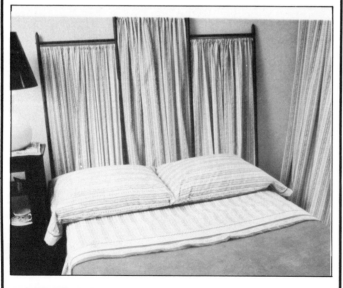

21 SCREEN HEADBOARD

You'll need: Sheeting.

1. Measure each panel of screen—height and width inside the frame. Cut sheeting for each panel—height plus 5 inches; width is double the measurement plus 2½ inches.

2. On all panels make side hems by first turning under ¼ inch, then turning under 1 inch. Press. Stitch.

3. Turn under ¼ inch at top and bottom. Press. Then turn under 2 inches. Press. Stitch along open edge, then stitch 1 inch from edge to form casing.

4. Slip rods inside casings. Attach rods to screen.

22 BLANKET BINDING

You'll need: Blanket. Sheeting.

1. Wash blanket and sheet to take care of any shrinkage.

2. Cut sheeting into two 6½ inch wide strips on the true bias (Diagram 1). Strips should be long enough to fit across ends of blanket plus ½ inch.

3. Turn under ¼ inch on all edges of strips. Press. Fold strips in half lengthwise, right side out. Press. Insert top and bottom edges of blanket inside fold of strips. Pin and baste. Stitch; also stitch across ends of strips as well. **Note:** For a really elegant job, slip-stitch strips in place by hand, sewing ends of strips as well.

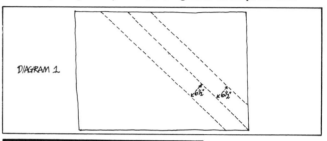

DIAGRAM 1

23 PADDED HEADBOARD

You'll need: ½ inch plywood. Sheeting. Also used sheet. Polyester batting. Staple gun and staples. Hanging plates and screws.

1. Plan size of headboard and cut plywood to size or have it cut at lumberyard.

2. Cut sheeting, old sheet and batting to size of plywood plus 2½ inches all around.

3. Place sheet piece and old sheet wrong sides together with batting sandwiched between. Baste around edges, then from center out to center of each side, then from center diagonally out to each corner.

4. With pencil lightly mark sheet for quilting lines. (Ours were widely spaced diagonals.) Stitch.

5. Center plywood on back of quilted piece. Draw excess fabric to back of plywood. Working from center out, staple 1 side to plywood. Always working from center out, staple opposite side. Repeat with other 2 sides, neatly folding in corners. Cut off any excess.

6. Screw on hanging plates to back of headboard and hang on wall on large screws.

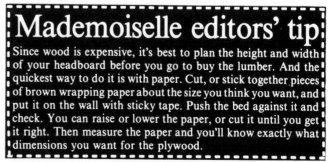

Mademoiselle editors' tip

Since wood is expensive, it's best to plan the height and width of your headboard before you go to buy the lumber. And the quickest way to do it is with paper. Cut, or stick together pieces of brown wrapping paper about the size you think you want, and put it on the wall with sticky tape. Push the bed against it and check. You can raise or lower the paper, or cut it until you get it right. Then measure the paper and you'll know exactly what dimensions you want for the plywood.

24 DORMER DRESSING TABLE

We made a dressing table, but the principle of a covered, skirted board fitted in a dormer space could also be a little bedroom desk. You'll need: ¾ inch plywood. Sheeting. Staple gun and staples. Nylon tape fastener. 4 angle irons. Screws. Glass.

1. Measure space inside dormer and plan table just to fit. Cut plywood to size. Sandpaper thoroughly.

2. Cut sheeting to size of plywood tabletop plus 2 inches all around. Center plywood on wrong side of sheeting piece. Draw extra fabric over plywood and staple in place.

3. Staple half the strip of nylon tape fastener all along the front edge of tabletop.

4. On each side of tabletop screw on angle irons underneath near each corner. Attach angle irons to side walls of dormer.

5. Have glass cut to size of tabletop and lay in place.

6. For skirts measure area between side walls of dormer. Cut 2 pieces of sheeting to this width plus 2½ inches. Make length of pieces the height of tabletop from floor plus 3¼ inches. Cut 2 pieces for ruching, each 3½ inches wide by 2½ times the width between side walls of dormer.

7. Make ¼ inch finished hems all around each ruching piece. Run 2 rows of machine or hand shirring down center of length of each piece.

8. Make 1 inch finished hem on side edges of each skirt. Make 2 inch finished hem on lower edges. Turn under 1 inch at top edge and press. Run 2 rows of shirring across doubled top edges. Draw up shirring so that the 2 skirts fit the tabletop. Tie thread ends securely.

9. Draw up the shirring on ruching so that each piece fits across a skirt piece. Pin and baste to the shirring line of each skirt. Stitch in place.

10. Cut remaining half of the nylon fastener tape in 2 equal pieces. Stitch a piece to back of each skirt along shirring line. Stick skirts in place.

Note: The sheeting along the center of the window was put on just for the picture. You may want to do it for a special occasion by sticking it in place with double-faced tape.

25 SHEET-CURTAINS

Curtains, because they need so much fullness, are perfect to make from sheets since sheet widths give you lots of fabric. Be generous. Make curtains with double the width of fabric. Since sheet-curtains are unlined, they will be translucent rather than completely opaque. And the hems, being double, will be silhouetted, so measure carefully to be sure of having even hems. If you want a more expensive effect, and have the fabric, double the width of the hem. Your curtains will hang better. Lower hems of curtains can be machine stitched but they look much more elegant if they are hemmed by hand.

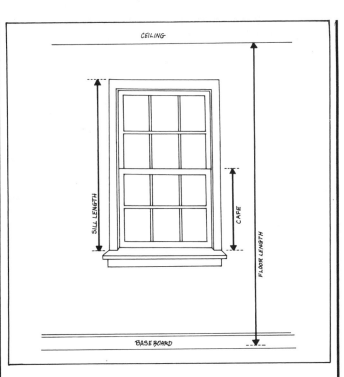

CAFE CURTAINS:

Cafe curtains generally cover the lower half of the window. You can also have double cafes which consist of a pair of curtains on the lower half of the window and a pair on the upper half. Just be sure the pair on the upper half covers the lower pair by a couple of inches.

There are also triple cafes. Divide the height of the window in threes and install 3 curtain rods. Again be sure each upper pair of curtains covers the pair just below it by a couple of inches.
You'll need: Sheeting.

1. Measure the width desired. Cafes can go inside the frame, on the frame or on the wall outside the frame. Measure length desired. Add 2½ inches to width, 5½ inches to length. Cut out curtains. **Note:** If the sheet is patterned, be sure that the design is identically placed on both curtains. If you are making more than 1 pair, be sure that all curtains have the designs lined up identically. This may require extra fabric.

2. Turn under ¼ inch at side edges. Press. Turn under 1 inch. Press. Stitch.

3. Turn under ¼ inch at top edge. Press. Turn under 2 inches. Press. Stitch along open edge. Then stitch 1 inch from edge, forming a 1 inch heading and a 1 inch casing.

4. Turn under ¼ inch at lower edge. Press. Turn under 3 inches. Press. Stitch.

5. Insert curtain rod and hang curtains.
See page 115 for directions on cafe curtains made from pillowslips.

SILL LENGTH CURTAINS

These curtains are made just like cafe curtains. Since they will block out more light than cafes, you may want to hang them farther out on the wall with more open space between them. Or try using tiebacks.

FLOOR LENGTH CURTAINS

Floor length curtains can start at the top of the window frame or can hang all the way from the ceiling. Just make sure they come 1 inch above the floor or rug. These curtains can be made just like cafes.

SHIRRED TOPS

For a really elegant look in curtains make shirred tops. There is commercial shirring tape available. Choose 2 or 4 cord tape.

1. Turn down ½ inch at top of curtain. Place tape on back of curtain, overlapping turn-down by ¼ inch. Knot cords to prevent them from pulling out. Stitch tape at top and bottom.

2. Unknot cords and pull up cords to desired width of heading. Reknot cords but do not cut off. Just wind them up and fasten with rubber bands.

3. Slip drapery pins in shirring tape on back to hang curtains.

26 RADIATOR/AIRCONDITIONER DISGUISE

This is a disguise that came about because our photographer kept saying "Can't you do anything about hiding that ugly radiator/airconditioner? It shows up in every picture!" Our decorating editor went to work and devised this quick cover-up. It worked out just fine for the picture, but everyone had doubts about its permanency. Six months later, the woman whose apartment we photographed came in to report that her "party cover" was considered one of the best features in her all-sheeted room. What she did was put it on for special occasions. Left it off for practical day-to-day life. So if you have a disguisable radiator/airconditioner, herewith the directions for a "temporary" cover.

You'll need: Sheeting. Double-edged masking tape.

1. Measure width, height from floor and depth of unit (Diagram 1). Cut sheeting to twice the width plus 2½ inches. Length should be height plus the depth plus 3¼ inches.

2. On side edges turn under ¼ inch. Press. Turn under 1 inch. Press. Stitch.

3. On lower edge turn under ¼ inch. Press. Turn under 2 inches. Press. Hem.

4. Turn under 1 inch on top edge. Press. Run 2 rows of shirring ½ inch from edge. Draw up to fit area to be covered. Knot thread ends securely.

5. Apply double-faced masking tape across back edge of air conditioner or radiator cover. Press shirred fabric onto tape firmly.

6. To remove, just pull it off. Each time, reapply masking tape.

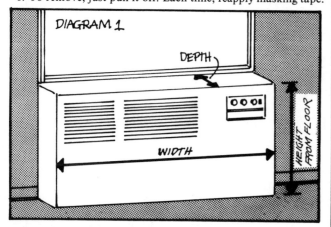

DIAGRAM 1
DEPTH
WIDTH
HEIGHT FROM FLOOR

27 DIRECTOR'S CHAIR COVER

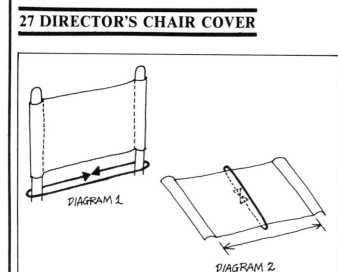

DIAGRAM 1

DIAGRAM 2

You'll need: Sheeting or toweling.
Chair Back:

1. Remove old chair back and use it as a base for new one. Cut sheeting long enough to go around back (see Diagram 1) plus 2 inches. Make height as in diagram plus 2½ inches.

2. Join edges of length of strip, right side together, and stitch with 1 inch seam. Press seam open. You have formed a tube.

3. Make 1 inch finished hems on raw edges of tube. Turn right side out.

4. Slip tube over old chair back with seam in center back. Stitch down each side about 2½ inches from sides, forming openings for chair posts.

5. If the old chair back shows out at top edge, whip together the front and back of new chair back along top edge.

Chair Seat:

1. Remove old chair seat and use it as a base for new one. Cut sheeting long enough to go around seat (see Diagram 2) plus 2 inches. Make width as in diagram plus 2½ inches.

2. Repeat 2 above.

3. Repeat 3 above.

4. Slip tube over old chair seat with seam in center back, open edges at sides. Whip side edges in place just inside area for side rods.

5. Slip on chair.

28 SLIPCOVERING CUSHIONED FURNITURE

You'll need: Sheeting. Commercial welting or cord and extra fabric. Zipper long enough for 1 side of cushion less 2 inches.

1. Cut top and bottom of cover to size of cushion plus 1 inch all around. Cut boxing pieces to depth of cushion plus 2 inches. Cut 1 for each side, each piece 2 inches longer than side.

2. If you are making welting, follow General Directions for Pillows (page 86).

3. Slit the boxing piece (which will have the zipper) down the center lengthwise. Turn in the slit edges ¼ inch and baste. Center zipper between these edges and stitch in place. Hand sew the openings at ends of zipper.

4. Join all boxing pieces with 1 inch seams into a circle.

Complete as for Box Pillow With Welting (page 87), only placing seams on boxing strip in corners.

29 SQUARE RUFFLED TABLECLOTH

You'll need: Sheeting.

1. Measure tabletop (Diagram 1). Cut sheeting to size of top plus ¾ inch all around. Measure depth of skirt desired (C on Diagram). Cut a strip to this measurement plus 3¼ inches. Length of strip = 2 x A on Diagram + 2 x B on Diagram + 5½ inches. For example, let's say A and B are both 40 inches. 2 x 40 + 2 x 40 + 5½ = 165½ inches. You will have to use 2 equal pieces joined together.

2. Right sides together, join ends of strip with ¾ inch seam. Press seam open.

3. Turn under ¼ inch on lower edge of skirt. Press. Turn under 2½ inches. Press. Hem.

4. Pin skirt to top, placing the 2 seams in corners and easing in the fullness at each corner. There should be about 1 inch ease at corners. Join with ¾ inch seam.

Ruffle:

1. Make tablecloth as above, cutting skirt to width desired plus 1½ inches for top and bottom seams. Omit hem on skirt.

2. Cut ruffle 2½ times the length of skirt strip and width desired plus 2 inches. You will have to piece this strip.

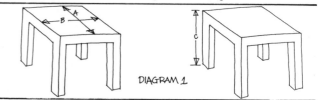

A
B
C
DIAGRAM 1

3. Right sides together, join ends of ruffle with ¾ inch seam. Press seam (and all piecing seams) open.

4. Turn under ¼ inch on lower edge of ruffle. Press. Turn under 1 inch. Press. Hem.

5. ¾ inch from raw edge of ruffle run 2 rows of shirring. Divide ruffle in quarters evenly and mark with pins. Draw up shirring.

6. Right sides and raw edges together, pin ruffle around skirt with pin marks at each corner. Adjust ruffle, pin and baste. Stitch ¾ inch from edge.

30 ROUND TABLECLOTH

You'll need: For a 30 inch diameter table a queen size sheet, for a 42 or 48 inch diameter table a king size sheet. String. Thumbtack. Bias tape. Pencil.

1. Find radius of your table (half the diameter). Add it to the height. If the table is 30 inches in diameter, the radius is 15 inches. Add it to the height (29 inches) = 44 inches—the finished radius of cloth. Add 1 inch for hem—cutting radius will be 45 inches.

2. Cut sheet into a square twice the size of your radius. Fold in half horizontally and vertically (Diagram 1).

3. Cut a piece of string 2 inches longer than your radius. Tie 1 end around pencil. Put a thumbtack through opposite end of string. Make sure there is exactly the length of radius between thumbtack and pencil.

4. Place thumbtack at point A (Diagram 2) on folded sheet. Draw an arc from 1 edge to the other.

5. Cut sheet through all thicknesses, following drawn arc.

6. Open out cloth and press under a 1 inch hem all around. Clip hem at close intervals all around.

7. Face hem with bias tape and stitch twice.

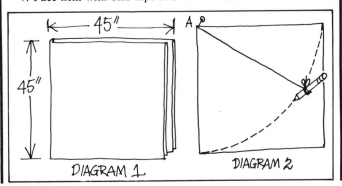

31 SCALLOPED TABLECLOTH COVER

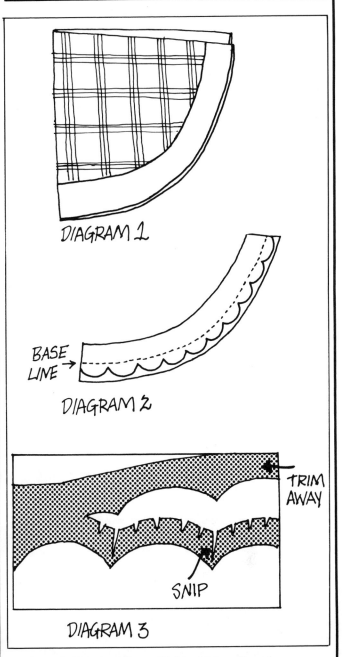

You'll need: Sheeting. Piece of lightweight cardboard.

1. Make a round tablecloth of size desired, following directions above. Allow 1 inch beyond edge of scallops.

2. Fold cloth in quarters and make a cardboard template (Diagram 1) of edge of ¼ of cloth. Draw a base line on template to indicate top point of scallops (about 2 inches from edge) (Diagram 2). Decide on depth and width of scallop. See if the width will work out evenly across the full width of template. If not, adjust the width of scallop slightly. Draw scallops on template with compass or cup or small ashtray or coaster. Use base line as a guide.

3. Use template as a guide to cutting out ring of sheeting for facing edge of cloth. Piece as necessary, forming a ring. Right sides together, place facing around edge of cloth. Baste.

4. Cut out scallops on template. With pencil lightly mark scallops on facing, joining scallops carefully at edge of template. Stitch scallops, pivoting the machine needle carefully where scallops meet.

5. Trim extra fabric around scallops. Snip and notch as in Diagram 3. Turn scallops right side out. Baste along edges of scallops. Press.

6. If you want, tack inner edge of facing in place.

SKIRTING A SINK

Bathroom sinks usually come two ways—the kind where the basin ends and the plumbing shows below, or the more modern vanity, where the lower portion is enclosed in a cupboard or shelf arrangement.

By running a skirt around the basin part in the first case, you hide the ugly plumbing and gain storage space; in the second case, the skirt adds a decorative element often lacking in most under-sink cupboard arrangements.

If you are skirting an ordinary sink, no matter what the shape, you should make a continuous skirt (direction 32). If you are skirting a vanity, you'll need the front split skirt for cupboard access (direction 33).

32 BATHROOM SINK SKIRT

You'll need: Sheeting. Nylon tape fastener. Household cement.

1. Measure around sink (Diagram 1). Cut skirt strip twice that length plus 2½ inches. Height is height from floor as in diagram plus 3½ inches.

2. On side edges turn under ¼ inch. Press. Turn under 1 inch. Press. Stitch.

3. On lower edge turn under ¼ inch. Press. Turn under 2 inches. Press. Hem.

4. On top edge turn under 1½ inches. Press. 1 inch from edge make 2 rows of shirring. Draw up to fit around sink. Knot ends securely.

5. Cement half the strip of fastener tape around edge of sink. Stitch other half of strip to back of shirring with a row of stitching at top and bottom.

6. Join the halves of fastener tape to hang the skirt in place.

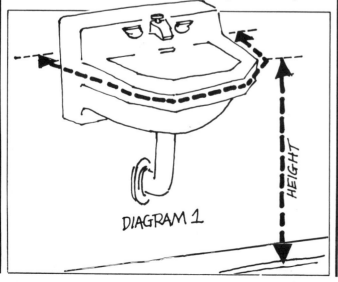

DIAGRAM 1

HEIGHT

33 VANITY SKIRT

Make same as for skirt for bathroom sink but cut 2 skirt pieces, each the measurement around vanity plus 2½ inches. Repeat Steps 2, 3 and 4 above. But when drawing up shirring make each skirt piece to fit half way around vanity. Then repeat Step 5, dividing half the tape into 2 equal pieces—1 for each skirt.

Hang skirt in place with pieces just meeting in the center so that you can get into vanity easily.

34 FABRICKED ROLLER BLIND

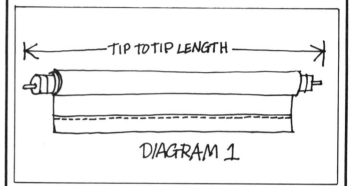

TIP TO TIP LENGTH

DIAGRAM 1

You'll need: Sheeting. Pressure sensitive window shade laminating kit. Transparent or masking tape. Iron. Several small heavy objects to act as weights. Triangle, T-square or the cardboard back from a notebook or writing tablet.
Note: Always measure with a steel or wood rule. Fabric tapes may stretch.

1. First attach brackets for hanging shade, following directions in kit to get exact size of roller. Measure between brackets. Measure roller for tip-to-tip measurements (Diagram 1). Subtract this last measurement from measurement between brackets. This gives you the amount to saw off roller.

Roll up the shade from the bottom until wood roller is exposed. At the pin end detach enough of shade cloth to expose roller. Saw off. Replace cap and pin on new end.

2. Trim away a strip of window shade down the full length equal in width to the amount sawed off the wood roller.

3. A shade should be 12 inches longer than the height of window frame opening. If you have to shorten the shade, cut it off at top edge. Use a triangle, square or piece of cardboard to get square corners. Reattach to roller.

4. Spread sheeting piece cut to approximate size of shade on table, wrong side up. *Lightly* draw a lengthwise line down center of fabric. Check that bottom edge is absolutely square and cut even. Cut a small V-notch in exact center of lower edge. Roll sheeting on a cardboard tube, right side in, from top to bottom.

5. Unroll shade, face side up, on table and lightly pencil on the clear plastic "skin" a center line from roller to hemline.

6. Reroll shade leaving about 18 inches of fabric exposed at bottom. Attach corners to table with tape. Lay plastic hem strip just below rolled part of shade to prevent it from rolling.

7. Lay tube with sheeting across exposed section of shade. Unroll 12 inches of sheeting and line up bottom edges with V-cut at center line of shade. Weight down.

8. Fold back sheeting about 6 inches. Starting at corner of shade, peel back and trim away a 3 inch section of clear plastic "skin" to expose the gummed surface. Return sheeting to position over the gummed area. Carefully smooth it down with an upward and outward movement from center of shade to sides.

9. Place the roll of sheeting over the laminated section and peel back another 12 inches of "skin." Continue laminating, always lining up center line of sheeting with center of shade. **Note:** If air bubbles should form, carefully peel back the sheeting and try again. Be careful not to stretch sheeting when doing this.

10. Go over laminated area with a *cold* iron to smooth it. Continue laminating until you reach the roller. Cut off any excess sheeting across top.

11. Place shade face down. Carefully trim away excess sheeting down both sides of shade.

12. Insert shade in plastic hem strips according to directions with kit.

13. Hang shade in brackets.

35 CHEST FLOWERED WITH FABRIC

GENERAL DIRECTIONS:

• Use old furniture or a new unpainted piece. Be sure that furniture has no raised surfaces such as carving or that legs are not fluted or banded. Simple shapes such as the little chest we used or straight legged tables are best.

• Unpainted wood must be primed with primer or shellac; otherwise the paste will not adhere well.

• Choose sheeting with a fairly small pattern. Drape the sheet over the chest or table first to make sure the pattern will be pleasing when repeated.

• If the furniture has a dark finish and your sheet has a light background, the color may show through. Better give it a coat of light paint first.

• Remove hardware, knobs, etc.

• Remove drawers from chest.

You'll need: Sheeting. Vinyl wallpaper paste. Mat knife or craft knife. Metal straight edge. 3 inch paint roller and small pan. Paste brush. Thumbtacks or push pins. 4 furniture glides.

1. Centering design, cut sheeting to fit top of furniture and adding enough all around to extend over thickness of top and fold 1 inch under top. Fasten in place with thumbtacks.

2. Mix paste according to package directions. Pour a small amount in roller pan. Roll half of fabric back (do not remove all tacks). With roller apply paste to half of top. Pat fabric in place; smooth from center out. Repeat for other half of top.

3. With brush apply paste to sides of top. Draw fabric over sides; smooth. Miter corners and with a straight edge and knife cut away excess at corners. Brush paste under top and draw edges underneath and stick down.

4. For rest of chest cut a piece of fabric, centering design. Width is height of chest from floor to just below top. Length is width of front and both sides plus 3 inches (Diagram 1).

5. Thumbtack fabric in place with 1½ inches extending to back on each side. Starting in center, paste sheeting in place, going right over drawer openings, legs and all. When paste is dry, carefully cut openings for drawers, saving the fabric. Slash fabric at legs (Diagram 2), fold back and paste down. Fold rest of fabric under chest and paste down.

6. Using the fabric from drawer areas, apply to drawer fronts. Trim.

7. Back may be covered in fabric if it will show.

8. Reapply hardware, knobs, etc.

9. Apply a furniture glide to each leg so that the fabric does not catch in rug and pull loose.

10. To keep piece clean finish it with several coats of non-yellowing polyurethane varnish. Test it on fabric first to see if fabric yellows. Or give piece a spray-on Scotchgard finish.

Note: If piece has curved legs, do not attempt to cover them. Just paint them (along with knobs) a coordinating color.

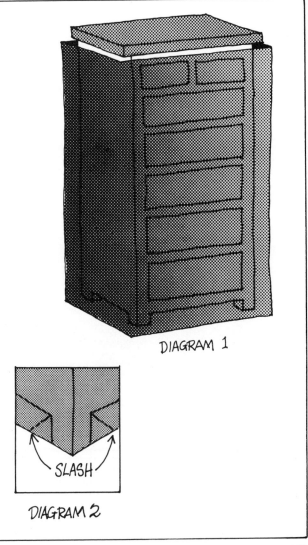

DIAGRAM 1

SLASH

DIAGRAM 2

36 SLIPCOVERED SHELVES

Covering shelves with sheeting gives a wonderful finish to a guest room closet, a linen closet or an armoire. If you plan to completely line a closet with sheeting, follow direction 3, Sheets as "Wallpaper" for the walls, and these directions for the shelves. Its easier to work in small tight spaces if you can remove the shelves before you work on the walls. Remember that since most closets and armoires contain things, a bad patch can usually be concealed by whatever is stored therein. It's the overall impression that counts!

STATIONARY SHELF:
You'll need: Sheeting. Staple gun and staples.

1. Cut sheeting to width of shelf plus 2 inches (Diagram 1). Length is twice the depth of shelf plus the thickness of shelf plus 2 inches.
2. Turn under 1 inch all around. Press.
3. Staple across back of shelf. Pull fabric firmly to underside of shelf and staple across. Put in a few staples at side edges to hold.

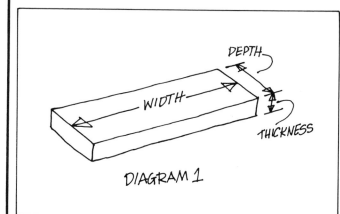

DIAGRAM 1

REMOVABLE SHELF:
You'll need: The same materials as above.

1. Remove shelf.
2. Repeat Step 1 above.
3. Wrap sheeting around shelf (Diagram 2). Staple 1 edge on back edge of shelf. Pull sheeting taut and staple other end over first end. Cut off excess.
4. Fold side edges of fabric over side edges of shelf and staple in place. Cut off excess.
5. Replace shelf.

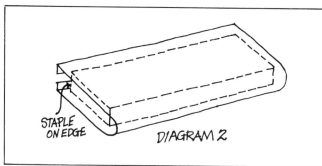

STAPLE ON EDGE   DIAGRAM 2

37 RE-COVERING A 3-PANEL SCREEN WITH SHEETS

You'll need: Sheeting. Ribbon or braid the width of screen frame and long enough to go around each panel. Staple gun and staples. **Note:** It is not necessary to remove old covering from screen.

1. Unscrew hinges from screen so that each panel is separate.
2. For each panel cut sheeting large enough to cover front and extend 1½ inches on back of panel on all sides.

3. Center a panel on wrong side of sheeting, draw extra fabric to back and staple. Starting in center, first staple 1 entire side, then opposite side, always working from center out. Then staple other 2 sides. Fold in corners neatly. Cover other 2 panels.
4. Starting at bottom, staple or tack ribbon (or braid) around outer edges of each panel (Diagram 1).
5. Reassemble screen by screwing in hinges where they were originally.

DIAGRAM 1

INSTANT DECORATING

You want a change, you want it fast...and you want it easy. You're a quick hand with a safety pin or a grommet setter and you're in no mood to do much sewing. You've got a dreary summer cottage or a dismal college room or maybe your living room looks as if it just died. For all those problems, these solutions....

38 SAFETY-PIN SLIPCOVERS

You'll need: Sheeting. Lots of big safety pins.
Note: This technique will work only on square or rectangular cushions and only on furniture made entirely of loose cushions.
1. Measure length of cushion plus depth on both sides. Measure width plus depth on both sides (Diagram 1). Add 20 inches to each measurement.
2. Cut sheet to measurements.
3. Place cushion right side up. Center fabric on it right side up.
4. Make hospital corners (as if you were making a bed) all around. Use large safety pins close together to hold fabric in place.
Note: You'll have to do a certain amount of smoothing after a party!

39 PILLOWSLIP CAFE CURTAINS

You'll need: Pair of pillowcases—standard size for windows up to 26 inches high, king size for windows up to 38 inches high. Each pair will fit windows 40 inches wide. For wider windows use more pillowcases.
1. Rip seams of pillowcase; press. Leave wide bottom hem to use as bottom of curtain.
2. Press under ¼ inch on all raw edges. Turn ⅝ hems on side edges; stitch.
3. Press top edge under 2 inches. Stitch hem close to inner edge. Stitch ⅝ inch from outer edge to form casing for curtain rod.

40 ONE HOUR CURTAINS

Both of these ideas work best if the length of the curtain needed is exactly the length of the sheet. This way you can use the hems as additional reinforcements. If your sheet has to be cut to fit the window, cut only one end, preserving, preferably, the widest hem.

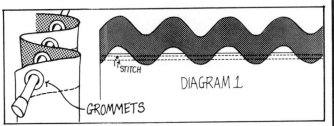

QUICK GROMMETTED WAY
1. Mark positions of grommets, measuring even intervals across top of sheet. Make them 4-6 inches apart with top edge of grommet ⅜ inch from edge of curtain.
2. Set grommets, following instructions with your set.
3. Thread curtain rod through grommets and attach.

QUICK RICKRACK WAY
1. Baste jumbo rickrack to top of curtain, allowing points to protrude beyond curtain as in Diagram 1. Turn in raw ends of rickrack.
2. Stitch rickrack twice as in diagram. Better by machine, but if none is handy, it can be done by hand.
3. Run rod through small spaces of rickrack or use shower curtain hooks in spaces.
Note: Notions stores carry cafe curtain heading, which can be used in the same way as the rickrack. It's a narrow tape which has small loops to hold the curtain rod.

41 ROD-LESS DRAPERY

This method makes a soft drape over a window, can be used alone or perhaps with other sheet-curtains. This kind of drapery is best made in a soft fabric, like Indian patterned bedspreads. It is important to first put up the coathooks, and then try bedspread before you cut it.
You'll need: Fabric long enough to go between coat hooks and extend length desired on each side plus 12 inches. 2 large ceramic coat hooks.
1. Attach coat hooks about 2 inches above each corner of window (Diagram 1).
2. Drape fabric to see if full width of fabric is not too wide for graceful draping. If it is, cut off necessary amount the full length of fabric.
3. Turn back 1 inch on long edges of fabric and hem. Make 5 inch finished hems on ends of fabric.
4. Drape fabric on coat hooks, anchoring folds with straight pins.

1 HOW TO MAKE A TOWEL REALLY YOURS

2 COZY UP A BASKET

DIAGRAM 1

MAKING THE BEST OF BITS

① Towel

You'll need: Bath-size towel. ⅛ yard, 45 inch wide washable cotton fabric. Package iron-on bonding fabric. Alphabet stencils, 2 to 3 inches high.

1. Cut fabric border 4½ inches wide and 1 inch longer than width of towel. Fold under long edges ¼ inch, short ends ½ inch; press. Pin border to towel and stitch in place.

2. Using stencils, trace initials *backwards* on wrong side of bonding fabric. Cut out letters.

3. Place letters on border and iron on letters following directions on package.

② Basket

You'll need: Basket. Piece of fabric (see below for size of fabric as it depends on size of basket). ¼ wide elastic long enough to fit around top of basket plus ½ inch.

1. Measure basket sides and bottom plus overhang desired on each side plus 2½ inches (Diagram 1). Use this measurement for diameter of circle you cut from fabric, piecing fabric if necessary.

2. Turn under ¼ inch on edge of circle, press. Turn under 1 inch hem; press. Stitch hem, leaving small opening. Stitch close to outer edge of circle. Then stitch ⅝ inch in from edge.

3. Put safety pin on end of elastic and thread through casing. Overlap ends ½ inch and stitch together. Stitch opening closed.

4. Slip lining in basket.

③ Makeup Bags

Size: 7½ inches wide. (For 6 inch bag see note below.) You'll need: 2 pieces fabric 8½ x 21 inches. 1 piece polyester batting 8½ x 15 inches. 7 inch zipper.

1. Press under top and bottom edges of front fabric piece ½ inch (Diagram 1). Measure down 5½ inches from top edge and mark with pin. From this point down, lightly pencil quilting design as in diagram.

2. Press under top and bottom edges of back piece. Lay front and back pieces wrong sides together. Sandwich batting between, positioning it ½ inch from bottom edge. Baste around edges of bag.

3. Set machine to 6-8 stitches per inches and quilt design through all thicknesses.

4. Center 1 side of zipper along bottom edge. With zipper foot stitch in place. Bring top down on wrong side, circle around and stitch top edge to zipper (Diagram 2).

5. Turn bag wrong side out as in Diagram 3. Stitch ½ inch side seams. Trim seams, clip corners. Turn and press.

Note: For 6 inch bag cut front and back 7 x 16 inches, batting 7 x 12 inches. Use a 5½ inch zipper. Make bag as above but reduce quilted area proportionately.

Two of these bags in different sizes make a marvelous gift. Pretty way to present them is to tie them together with matching cord.

SCRAPBOOK

There's almost no way you can do handwork and not end up with a lot of bits and pieces. You don't have to waste them, however; you can put your scraps to work. A handful of cotton can line a basket, make a bag. The yarn left over from your bargello pillow can be needled into a belt. Embroidery floss can floss up a sweater or an espadrille. And the ideas start right here....

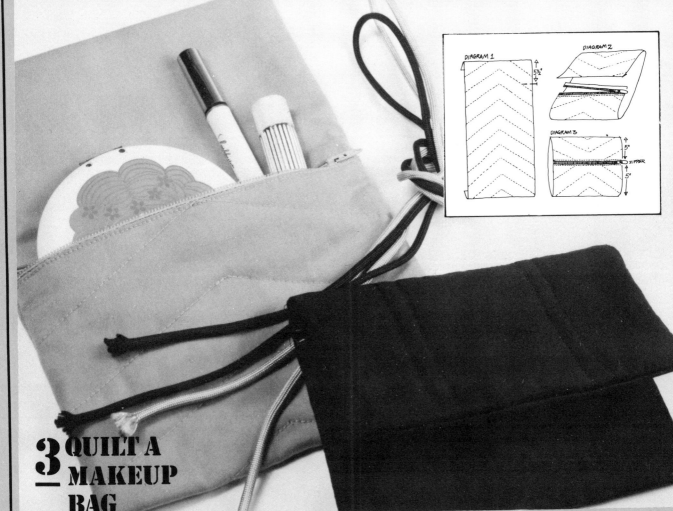

3 QUILT A MAKEUP BAG

THE BEST OF BITS

4 SLIPCOVER A BOX

DIAGRAM 1

A   B

DIAGRAM 2

DEPTH OF BOX + ½"

DIAGRAM 3

5 LINE A STRAW SATCHEL

DIAGRAM 1

HEIGHT

WIDTH

THICKNESS

④ Box

You'll need: Sturdy box with lid. Pieces of fabric. Cardboard. White glue. Glue brush.

Bottom of Box: 1. Measure width and depth of sides of box (A on Diagram 1), length and depth of sides (B on Diagram 1).

2. Cut a piece of fabric to above measurements plus 1 inch on each dimension. Slash in near 4 corners as in Diagram 2.

3. Mix 2 parts water with 1 part glue. Brush glue on bottom of box. Center box on wrong side of fabric. Smooth out bubbles and wrinkles.

4. Brush glue on front end of box and attach fabric as in Diagram 3. Draw excess fabric around sides and glue. Repeat with back end.

5. Glue sides in place.

6. Brush glue ½ inch *inside* top edge and draw extra fabric inside and stick down.

7. Cut a lining strip the depth of inside of box and long enough to go around all 4 sides plus ½ inch. Glue around inside of box, overlapping the end.

8. For base of box cut cardboard to fit loosely inside box. Cut fabric to the same measurements, adding ½ inch all around. Glue cardboard to center of wrong side of fabric. Glue excess fabric to back of cardboard. Glue fabric-covered cardboard inside box as a "floor."

Top of Box: 9. Repeat the same process to cover and line the lid.

⑤ Satchel

You'll need: Tote basket. Pieces of fabric. Thin polyester wadding. White glue.

1. Measure height and width of basket—and thickness if your basket has that (Diagram 1).

2. Cut wadding pieces for front and back of basket and 1 long gusset strip that will extend all the way around if basket has thickness.

3. With a few dabs of glue fasten wadding inside front and back of basket. Glue wadding gusset inside if needed.

4. From fabric cut front, back, (gusset, if necessary), adding ½ inch to all edges of each piece.

5. Right sides together stitch gusset around sides and bottom of front with ½ inch seam. Stitch gusset to back in similar manner. Do not turn. If lining has no gusset, just stitch front to back with right sides together and ½ inch seams around sides and bottom.

6. Turn ½ inch of upper edge to wrong side; press. Slip lining in basket and sew in place. Some baskets can be sewn right through the straw. On other baskets you have to work the stitches between the reed or other material.

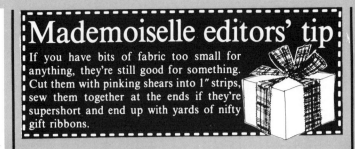

6 DO UP A TRAVEL BAG

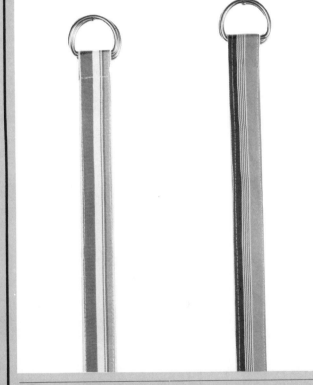

7 RUN UP – OR RIBBON UP – A BELT

⑥ Travel Bag

This is a drawstring travel bag that is exactly what's needed for a crowded suitcase. It's for all those little extras that get lost in the bottom. Make it in a bright print so that it'll surface at sight. We're giving you directions for just one size, but you can enlarge up or reduce down and make a whole set if you choose. They're great for everything from lingerie to lipsticks. A larger version of this—lined with clear plastic— carries a damp swimsuit. Great gifts!

Size: 9 x 13 inches. Just right for a traveler's suitcase. You'll need: 2 pieces fabric 10 x 14 inches. Rayon cord 22 inches long. Plastic (optional).

1. For pattern enlarge diagram (each small square = 1 inch square). Following pattern, cut front and back of bag from fabric.

2. Right sides together, stitch front and back together along sides and curved edge with ½ inch seam, leaving 1 inch unstitched at top of 1 side. Clip seam.

3. Turn ¼ inch of top edge to wrong side; press. Turn ¾ inch of top edge to wrong side; press. Stitch, forming casing.

4. Turn back seam allowance at casing opening. Handstitch in place. Turn bag right side out.

5. Tie cord to a large safety pin and pull through casing. Knot ends.

⑦ Belts

You'll need: Piece of fabric 2 inches wide x length of your waist plus 6 inches. Same length of 1 inch wide belting. 2 D rings or large notebook rings or a buckle.

1. Turn in ½ inch on all edges of fabric; press. Pin to back of belting. Cut off extra belting. Stitch around all edges.

2. Turn 1 inch of belt over straight edge of both D rings (or notebook rings) held together. Stitch across. Or fold 1 inch of belt over bar of buckle; stitch.

3. If you are using a buckle with a prong, punch holes as necessary.

Note 1: If you are using a clasp buckle, cut belt to waist measurement plus 2 inches. Fold 1 inch of belt over bar of buckle at each end.

Note 2: If you fall in love and buy an old-fashioned belt buckle, the method above works well. Belts can also be made of ribbon. Two lengths of grosgrain ribbon sewn together the long way and then attached to your old-fashioned buckle is the easiest way to do it.

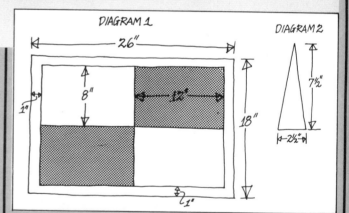

8 BACKGAMMON BOARD OUT OF BITS

(8) Backgammon Board

Size: 16 x 24 inches.

You'll need: 1 piece hardboard 16 x 24 inches. 1 piece plain cotton fabric 18 x 26 inches. 2 pieces light plain cotton fabric and 2 pieces contrasting plain cotton fabric, each 8 x 12 inches. About ¼ yard each of 2 different printed fabrics. ¾ yard of 1 inch wide trimming tape and ½ yard of 1¼ inch wide matching trimming tape. 1 piece polyester padding 16 x 24 inches. White glue.

1. Place plain fabric rectangles on large piece of fabric with matching colors diagonally opposite each other (Diagram 1). Baste.

2. Baste narrower trimming tape horizontally across center of pieces, covering raw edges of rectangles. Baste wider tape vertically across center, covering raw edges of rectangles.

3. From each print fabric cut 12 triangles (Diagram 2). Turn in about ¼ inch all around each triangle. Check amount of turn-in so that triangles will just fit

in rectangular space as in photograph. Baste edges then baste all triangles in place.

4. Center the polyester padding on back of large piece of fabric. Baste diagonally from center out to each corner, then around edges.

5. Stitch along both edges of trimming tapes. Stitch outer edges of smaller rectangles, then stitch each triangle.

6. Center hardboard on back of piece. Draw extra fabric to back of hardboard and glue in place.

7. You can take the backgammon board to a picture framer and have it framed with glass. Or you can lay a piece of plate glass cut to size (with finished edges) over the backgammon board for a smooth playing surface.

8. You will need a set of commercial chips and dice.

THE BEST OF BITS

⑨ Mini-pouch

Wear this around your neck or over your shoulder. Make them in multiples, and wear them that way. Size: 5 inches wide x 5½ inches high.

You'll need: Fabric scraps large enough to accommodate patterns in Diagrams 1 and 2 (2 prints were used—a plaid and a stripe). ½ yard fusible stiffening. 2¼ yards fold-over braid. 1 inch piece of nylon tape fastener.

1. Cut out 2 pieces fabric and 2 pieces stiffening, following measurements in Diagram 1. From contrasting fabric cut out 2 pieces and 2 pieces stiffening following measurements in Diagram 2.

2. On the back of all fabric pieces fuse a piece of stiffening.

3. Baste pieces in Diagram 1 wrong sides together. Repeat with pieces in Diagram 2.

4. Place front and back of bag as in Diagram 3.

5. Fold braid over all outer edges of bag. Turn in raw end. Baste; stitch.

6. Cut 48 inches of braid. Stitch open edges together down the length of braid. Stitch center of braid to bag under top of flap (see Diagram 3). Knot ends of strap to desired length.

7. For closing bag stitch small piece nylon tape fastener inside flap, its connecting section on front of bag.

FABRICKED FRAME

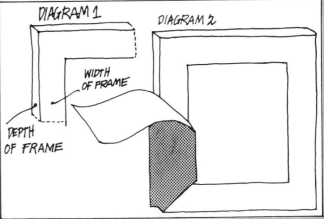

DIAGRAM 1   DIAGRAM 2

WIDTH OF FRAME

DEPTH OF FRAME

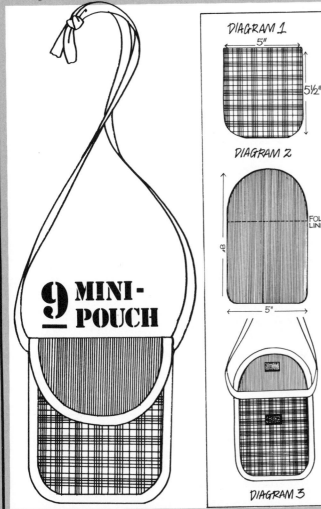

DIAGRAM 1
5"
5½"

DIAGRAM 2
FOLD LINE.
8"
5"

9 MINI-POUCH

DIAGRAM 3

⑩ Frame

You'll need: Open-back picture frame. Scraps of printed fabric. White glue. Paint brush. 1 yard ¼ inch wide velvet ribbon (or enough to fit around inside of frame).

1. Remove backing and glass from frame.

2. Measure width of frame and depth of frame (see Diagram 1). Add these measurements plus ½ inch. Cut a strip of fabric this width and 2 inches longer than distance around frame. If you must piece fabric, be sure the seams will be hidden in the corners.

3. In a small disposable container dilute 2 parts glue with 1 part water. Brush glue on frame a section at a time. Starting in a corner, attach fabric flush with inner edge of frame. Miter corners (Diagram 2) as you proceed around frame. Fold in end on the diagonal as you reach the final corner.

4. Now turn fabric sides over sides of frame, folding in excess at corners. Finish by gluing the extra fabric on back of frame all around.

2 YDS. FABRIC + 2½ HRS. = WRAP PANTS

⑪ Wrap Pants

You'll need: Opaque cotton fabric 36 inches wide (45 inches wide if you need extra width). Length is twice the desired length of pants from waist to lower edge plus 12 inches. For example, if length is 38 inches, use 88 inches of fabric or 2½ yards.

1. Lay out fabric as in Diagram 1. Cut 4 inches from each end for ties. Cut fabric in half crosswise.

2. Lay 1 piece on the other, right sides together; pin. Mark center from waistline down.

3. Use a pair of your own pants as a pattern to mark crotch (Diagram 2). Turn pants inside out, legs together, place front crotch seam of pants on left side of center line so that bottom edge of pants waistband is ½ inch below raw waistband of fabric and inseam of pants lies against center seam of fabric. With pencil or chalk trace pants crotch outline on fabric. Turn pants over to reveal back crotch seam and trace as before on right side of fabric's center line. (Front curve will be narrower than back.)

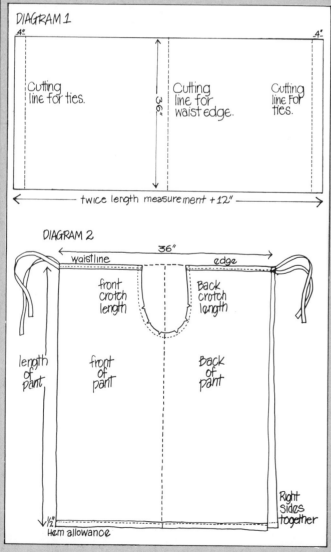

DIAGRAM 1

Cutting line for ties. Cutting line for waist edge. Cutting line for ties.

4" 36" 4"

← twice length measurement + 12" →

DIAGRAM 2

waistline   36"   edge

front crotch length   Back crotch length

length of pant   front of pant   Back of pant

½" Hem allowance   Right sides together

DIAGRAM 3

front view

4. Cut along traced curves, leaving ⅝ inch seam allowance. Stitch seam, clip curves and press seam open.

5. Turn under and stitch all non-selvage edges around fabric.

6. Hem bottoms at desired length.

7. For 4 ties cut tie strips in half crosswise. Fold each in half lengthwise; press. Turn in raw edges as far as fold line; press. Stitch open edge. Turn in raw ends; stitch. At each upper corner of pants overlap a tie for 1 inch. Stitch securely.

Wearing Pants: Straddle the crotch. Tie back ties around front of waist (Diagram 3), front ties around back.

wind sewing machine bobbin—by hand, if necessary. Use mercerized thread in top of machine. Use a 10-12 stitch length. Starting along top of dress (skirt), stitch parallel rows from raw edge to raw edge, making the rows about the width of the presser foot apart. In stitching the second and all following rows, stretch elastic in preceding rows (see Diagram 3, page 62). Make 2 inches of shirring on the skirt, 6 inches on the dress. At each end of stitching tie elastic and needle threads together. Set knot close to fabric.

3. Right sides together, stitch (with regular thread) raw edges with 1 inch seam, leaving 2 inches open at top, 12 inches open at bottom. Press seam open including seam openings at top and bottom.

4. Finish raw edges of seam openings by turning under ¼ inch and stitching. Stitch around openings ¼ inch from pressed edge to keep flat.

5. Make 2 buttonholes on right side of top opening. Try on garment and pin where buttons should be sewn at opening. Sew on buttons.

6. For dress, if desired cut two 1½ x 30 inch straps from scrap pieces. Wrong sides together, fold in thirds. Turn in raw edges. Stitch. Sew to top of dress as in photograph. Tie at back neck.

1½ YDS. FABRIC + 2 HRS. = SUMMER DRESS OR SKIRT

⑫ Summer dress or skirt

Sizes: Will fit 8-12.

You'll need: 1¼ yards 44 inch wide fabric for midi dress, 1½ yards 36 inch fabric for skirt. Elastic thread. Mercerized thread. 2 buttons.

1. Using the width of fabric as the length of the dress (skirt), fold over ¼ inch at top, 1 inch along bottom; stitch.

2. Following directions on elastic thread package,

MAKING THE BEST OF EMBROIDERY FLOSS

Jacobean Carnation

⑬ Espadrilles

Embroidering is a nice way to special-up espadrilles or any other fabric shoe. The four designs here have been chosen because they are easy to do on a curved surface. Because you're working in tight space, it's important to keep your designs as simple as possible.

You'll need: 1 pair canvas espadrilles. Dressmakers' carbon paper. 6-strand embroidery floss. Small curved needle.

1. For espadrilles in photograph trace design. Transfer design to shoes with dressmakers' carbon paper. **Note:** On other designs if the design faces one way, be sure to flop it before applying to second shoe.

2. With curved needle and 3 strands of floss work design on shoes. For stitches see page 126. Shoes in photograph were worked entirely in stem stitch. **Note:** It is difficult to finish off a thread inside the shoe so knot the ends on top and clip close to knot.

Mademoiselle editors' tip

Use a curved needle for the spots on the espadrille where you can't draw a straight needle through and a straight needle where you can. It's also easier working in tight corners if you wear a thimble. Remember canvas is a tough, closely woven fabric—you need to push!

Tyrolean Birds

13 FLOWER YOUR ESPADRILLES

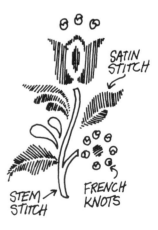

Pennsylvania Dutch Tulip

MAKING THE BEST OF YARN

⑭ Cardigan

You'll need: A ready-made cardigan. Dressmakers' carbon paper. Scraps of cotton organdy. Scraps of yarn. Size 0 crochet hook. Tapestry needle.

1. To trim edges, attach matching yarn at bottom of right front edge. Work sc loosely every ¼ inch up right front, around neck and down left front. Fasten off. Attach yarn at bottom of right front again.
* Ch 3, (dc in base of ch 3) twice; skip 2 sc, sl st in next sc. Repeat from * all around right front, neck and left front. Fasten off.

2. For embroidery trace design and work out pattern to fit one side of your cardigan. Transfer design with dressmakers' carbon paper to organdy. Flop design for other side of cardigan.

3. Baste organdy to sweater.

4. Embroider flowers in satin stitch. Work 3 French knots in center of each flower. Work leaves in 2 large chain stitches. (See page 126 for stitches.)

5. Carefully snip away organdy and pull out any visible threads with tweezers.

15 SNAP UP YOUR SOCKS

14 GARLAND CARDIGAN

⑮ Socks

You'll need: 1 pair knee socks with fold-over cuff. Dressmakers' carbon paper. Small piece cotton organdy. Scraps of knitting yarn. Tapestry needle.

1. Trace design and work out pattern to fit your socks. Transfer design with dressmakers' carbon paper to organdy. Repeat for other sock.

2. Baste organdy around cuffs of socks.

3. Embroider flowers in lazy-daisy stitch, stems and leaves in stem stitch (see page 126 for stitches).

4. Carefully cut away organdy from around stitches. Pull out extra threads with tweezers.

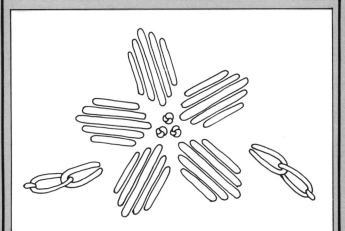

STITCHES: THE BEST BASICS

Here are all the embroidery stitches you'll need for every embroidery project in this book.

Backstitch:

Work from right to left. Bring needle through at A; insert back the width of a stitch —B. Then bring needle through one stitch width ahead of A—at C. Repeat across row, keeping stitches evenly spaced.

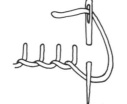

Blanket Stitch:

Work from left to right. Bring thread out at A. Hold it in place with left thumb. Insert needle to right above at B and bring out below at C, drawing it over the loop of thread.

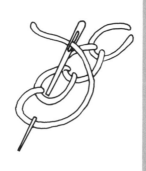

Chain Stitch:

Hold piece so that you can work from the top down. Bring needle out at A. Form loop and hold with left thumb. Insert needle at A and bring it out below at B. Draw it out over the loop and continue with next stitch. At end of a line of stitches, fasten last loop with a little stitch.

Cross-stitch:

Work from either direction. If started from left as in diagram, make a row of small diagonal stitches starting at lower left of stitch and going to upper right. At end of row go back over each diagonal stitch and cross it by going from lower right to upper left. Each cross-stitch can be worked separately or in rows as shown. **Note:** All cross-stitches in a given piece must always cross in the same direction.

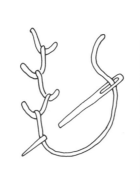

Feather Stitch:

Hold piece so that you can work from the top down. Baste or draw a guide line. Bring needle up slightly to the left of guide line. Hold thread with left thumb. With needle pointing to the left, make a slanting stitch on the right as in diagram. Bring needle out over the thread loop. Just slightly below make a slanting stitch on the left with needle pointing to the right. Bring needle out over the loop.

French knot:

Bring needle up where knot is to be made. Wrap thread around point of needle 2 or 3 times. Insert needle a couple of threads away from where working thread emerged and draw to back of work, holding the stitch in place with left thumb.

Lazy-daisy stitch:

Bring thread through at A. Hold thread loop down with left thumb and insert needle back at A. Bring needle out at B (the length of "petal" desired), drawing through over loop. Now tie down with a tiny stitch at C.

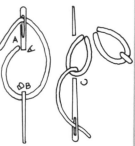

Running Stitch:

Work from right to left, taking one stitch at a time—not a number of stitches as in sewing. The stitch on top of fabric should be same length as stitch on wrong side.

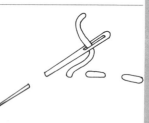

Satin Stitch:

Use this stitch when you want to cover an entire area. Bring needle up at one side of area and insert at opposite side. Carry thread under fabric and return to starting side. Although the stitching may go up and down or crosswise or on the diagonal, the stitches should always be close together and parallel.

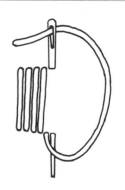

Stem Stitch:

Work from left to right. Bring needle out on line, insert a short distance to right and bring it out a smidgen to the left. Note that needle is at a slight angle. Thread should always be *below* the needle.

Straight Stitch:

Make a single stitch. Keep it well separated from the next one. These can form a precise pattern or just be scattered.

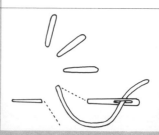

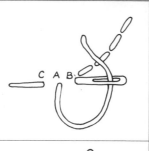

MAKING THE BEST OF KNITTING WORSTED

GAUGE: 5 sts = 1 inch;
7 rnds = 1 inch.

See page 135 for abbreviations.

Beg at top of cuff, cast on 60 sts. **1st Rnd:** * K 1, p 1. Repeat from * around. Repeat first rnd until length is 9 inches. **Next Rnd:** * K 2 tog, k 13. Repeat from * 3 more times (56 sts). **Following Rnd:** * K 2 tog, k 12. Repeat from * 3 more times (52 sts). **Next Rnd:** * K 2 tog, k 11. Repeat from * 3 more times (48 sts). Work even (k each row) until length is 11 inches. Bind off. Make 2nd Boot Top to match.

16 MAKE A FAKE:

16 Boot tops that look like socks

These were invented by a Mademoiselle Guest Editor who lived in California and wanted the look of heavy socks without heating up her feet. Don't try and make them longer than the directions given or they will wiggle out of your boots. It's better to fatten up your yarns and needles than to lengthen them.

MATERIALS: 1 (4 oz.) skein 4-ply knitting worsted. Knitting needle, No. 10 circular (smallest circumference).

17 Make a really crazy rug

This old-fashioned way of rug-making really works. One Mademoiselle editor began with a bedside rug and several years later ended up with a room-sized one! Size: From bath mat to room size rug.
You'll need: Horse reins spool (knitting knobby). Worsted weight yarn. Crochet hook. Heavy duty thread. Tapestry needle.

1. Following directions with your spool and using a crochet hook to lift yarn, make a 22 inch length of horse reins for each spiral on rug. Break off.

2. Work loose yarn back in at each end.

3. With needle and thread whip together each length into a spiral, starting at center.

4. Whip together spirals in a random color pattern or plan a specific arrangement.

17 MAKE A REALLY CRAZY RUG

MAKING THE BEST OF NEEDLEPOINT YARN

⑱ How to needle up a belt

This Indian design is terrific for working odd amounts of scrap yarn because you can do each section in a different color. You could also, in the center back panel, spell out a name. Use the graphed alphabet below.

Size: About 1½ inches wide.

You'll need: ¼ yard 36 inch wide canvas with 16 holes per inch. Masking tape. Persian yarn in red, white, black, blue, yellow and green. Tapestry needle. 1 yard 12½ inch wide grosgrain ribbon. Slide buckle.

1. Bind raw edges of canvas with masking tape.

2. Mark center of back of belt and plot out the placement of initials, using 20-22 spaces on each side of center. Working with 2 strands of yarn and tent stitch throughout, needlepoint initials. (For tent stitch, see below.)

3. Starting in center at A on chart, work design to B, then work backward to C. Continue to B, then back to C again until belt is half the length desired. Repeat on other half of belt. Finish belt in a point at 1 end, a straight edge on the other end.

4. Block needlepoint, then trim canvas, leaving ½ inch all around. Fold under canvas and baste. Slipstitch ribbon to back of belt.

5. Fold straight end of belt over bar of buckle and sew securely.

CHART FOR NEEDLEPOINT BELT   ALPHABET

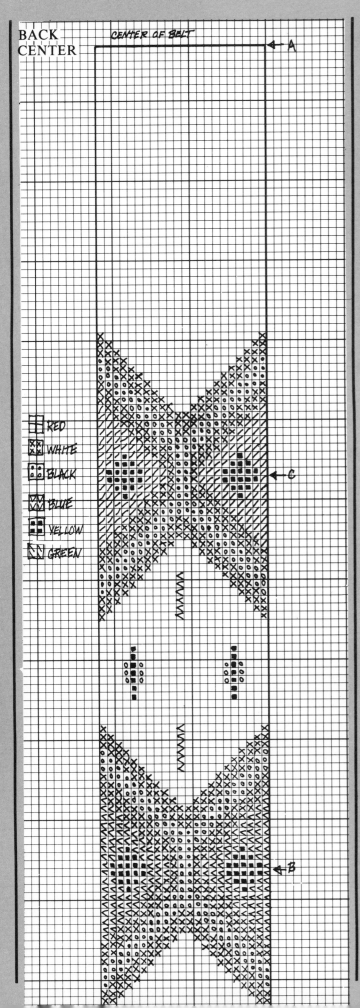

BACK CENTER

CENTER OF BELT

← A

← C

← B

RED
WHITE
BLACK
BLUE
YELLOW
GREEN

⑲ How to needle up a watchband

This works best on a large watch—like a man's. Don't try it on a tiny one. Because it's done in bargello, you can color it any way you want to. Bargello looks best in close color combinations—like pink, red, garnet.

Size: About ½ inch wide.

You'll need: scrap of canvas with 12 holes per inch. Masking tape. Scraps of Persian or tapestry yarn in 3 colors. Tapestry needle. ¼ yard ½ inch wide grosgrain ribbon. Findings from an old watchstrap.

1. Bind canvas edges with masking tape.

2. On canvas, with pencil, outline areas needed for the 2 sections of watchstrap using an old strap for pattern.

3. Following chart, work bargello design, using 2 strands of Persian or 1 strand of tapestry yarn.

4. Trim canvas, leaving ⅜ inch all around. Fold under canvas and baste.

5. Slipstitch ribbon to back of each piece, leaving small openings to attach findings.

6. Attach findings.

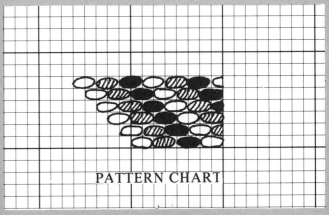

PATTERN CHART

129

MAKING THE BEST OF CROCHET THREAD

⑳ A. Solid Color Belts

SIZE: 1 x 72 inches plus fringe.

MATERIALS: 6 balls of pearl cotton.
Aluminum crochet hook, size E.

GAUGE: 5 sc = 1 inch;
7 rows = 1 inch.

WORK WITH 2 STRANDS OF SAME COLOR
HELD TOGETHER THROUGHOUT.
With 2 strands held together, make a chain about 73
inches long, or 1 inch longer than desired length of
belt. **Row 1:** Sc in 2nd chain from hook and in each ch
across. Ch 1, turn. **Row 2:** Sc in each sc across. Ch 1,
turn. Repeat last row 5 more times. At end of last row,
break off and fasten. Block to measurements.
FRINGE: With 2 strands held together, wind thread
15 times around a 3½ inch square of cardboard; cut
at one edge, making 7-inch strands. Hold 6 single
strands together and fold in half to form a loop.
Working along one end of belt, insert hook from back
to front in end sc of first row and draw loop through;
draw loose ends through loop on hook and pull tightly
to form a knot. Tie 4 more groups of 6 strands evenly
spaced along end of belt in same way. Tie fringe across
opposite end in same manner. Trim.

⑳ B. Striped Belts

SIZE: 1 x 72 inches plus fringe.

MATERIALS: 4 balls pearl cotton 1 color; 1 ball each
of any 2 other colors.
Crochet hook, size E.

GAUGE: 5 sc = 1 inch;
7 rows = 1 inch.

We used red for our main color, brown and pale blue
for the contrasting. For the lighter belt we used yellow
with orange and navy as contrast.

USE TWO STRANDS OF SAME COLOR HELD
TOGETHER THROUGHOUT.
With 2 strands held together of Red, make a chain
about 73 inches long or 1 inch longer than desired
length of belt. **Row 1:** Sc in 2nd ch from hook, sc in
each ch across. Break off and fasten; attach double
strand of first contrasting color to end of row. Ch 1,

turn. **Row 2:** With contrasting color, sc in each sc
across. Break off and fasten; attach double strand of
Red. Ch 1, turn. **Row 3:** With Red, sc in each sc across.
Ch 1, turn. **Row 4:** Repeat last row. At end of row,
break off and fasten; attach double strand of second
contrasting color. Ch 1, turn. **Rows 5, 6, 7:** Using
second contrasting color in place of first contrasting
color, repeat Rows 2, 3, 4. Break off and fasten.
FRINGE: With 2 strands held together, wind Red 3
times around a 3½ inch square of cardboard; cut at
one edge, making 7-inch strands. Hold the 6 strands
together and fold in half to form a loop. Working
along one end of belt, insert hook from back to front
in end of sc of first row and draw loop through; draw
loose ends through loop on hook and pull tightly to
form a knot. Matching color of each stripe, tie a group
of 6 strands in same way to end of each of next 4
stripes. Tie fringe across opposite end in same way.
Trim evenly.

㉑ A. Black Stripey Pouch

SIZE: 6¼ x 8½ inches.

MATERIALS: 1 (2 oz.) skein sock and sweater yarn.
1 ball each of pearl cotton in 4 different contrast colors.
Aluminum crochet hook, size E.

GAUGE: 5 sc = 1 inch;
7 rows = 1 inch.

We used black yarn and turquoise, red, violet and
orange pearl cotton for contrast.

USE 2 STRANDS OF SAME COLOR PEARL
COTTON HELD TOGETHER THROUGHOUT.
USE SINGLE STRAND OF BLACK.
FRONT: Starting at lower edge with a single strand
of black, ch 33. **Row 1:** Sc in 2nd ch from hook, sc in
each ch across—32 sc. Ch 1, turn. **Rows 2 through 5:** Sc
in each sc across. Ch 1, turn. At end of last row, break
off and fasten; attach double strand of turquoise. Ch 1,
turn. **Row 6:** With turquoise, work same as Row 2.
Break off, and fasten; attach black. Ch 1, turn. **Rows
7 through 10:** With black repeat Row 2. At end of last
row, break off and fasten; attach double strand of red.
Ch 1, turn. **Rows 11-12:** Working same as for Row 2,
make 1 row red, and 1 row violet. Break off and fasten;
attach black. Ch 1, turn. **Rows 13 through 17:** With
black repeat Row 2. At end of last row, break off and
fasten; attach double strand of orange. Ch 1, turn.
Row 18: With orange, work same as Row 2. Break off
and fasten; attach black. Ch 1, turn. **Row 19:** With
black, sc in each sc across. Ch 1, turn. Repeat last 18
rows (Rows 2 through 19) for stripe pattern. Work in
stripe pattern until total length is 8½ inches. Break
off and fasten. **BACK AND FLAP:** Work same as
front until total length is 8½ inches, having same
number of rows as on Front. Mark both ends of last
row to indicate beg of flap. **For Flap:** Continue to
work in pattern until length from markers is about 5
inches. Break off and fasten. Matching starting chains,

sew Back and Front together along side and bottom edges. **EDGING:** Using a double strand of black and a darning needle, embroider 1 row of Satin Stitch (see page 126) closely over entire outer edge of purse and flap and across top edge of front. Fold flap over front. **CORD:** Cut 10 single strands of black, each 3¼ yards long. Hold strands evenly together and twist tightly in one direction; fold in half and twist in the opposite direction. Sew ends neatly together. Sew first 8½ inches of cord across top edge of Front, under flap.

㉑ B. Turquoise Stripey Pouch

SIZE: 6¼ x 8½ inches.

MATERIALS: 9 balls main color pearl cotton, 1 ball each of 2 other contrast colors.
Aluminum crochet hook, size E.

GAUGE: 5 sc = 1 inch;
7 rows = 1 inch.

We used turquoise for the main color; red and black for contrast.

USE 2 STRANDS OF THE SAME COLOR HELD TOGETHER THROUGHOUT.
FRONT: Starting at lower edge with 2 strands of turquoise held together, ch 33. **Row 1:** Sc in 2nd ch from hook, sc in each ch across—32 sc. Ch 1, turn. **Rows 2-3:** Sc in each sc across. Ch 1, turn. At end of last row, break off and fasten; attach double strand of red. Ch 1, turn. **Row 4:** With red, sc in each sc across. Break off and fasten; attach double strand of turquoise. Ch 1, turn. **Rows 5 through 9:** With turquoise, work same as Row 2. At end of last row, break off and fasten; attach double strand of black. Ch 1, turn. **Row 10:** With black, work same as Row 4. Break off

and fasten; attach double strand of turquoise. Ch 1, turn. **Rows 11 through 15:** With turquoise, work same as Row 2. At end of last row, break off and fasten; attach double strand of red. Ch 1, turn. Repeat last 12 rows (Rows 4 through 15) for stripe pattern. Work in stripe pattern until total length is 8½ inches. Break off and fasten. **BACK AND FLAP:** Work same as front until total length is 8½ inches, having same number of rows as on front. Mark both ends of last row to indicate beg of flap. **For Flap:** Continue to work in pattern until length from markers is about 5 inches. Break off and fasten. Matching starting chains, sew back and front together along side and bottom edges. **EDGING:** Using double strand of turquoise and a darning needle, embroider 1 row of Satin Stitch (see page 126) closely together over entire outer edge of purse and flap and across top edge of front. Fold flap over front. **CORD:** Cut 13 single strands of turquoise, each 3¼ yards long. Hold strands evenly together and twist tightly in one direction, fold in half and twist in the opposite direction. Sew ends neatly together. Sew first 8½ inches of cord across top edge of front, under flap.

㉕ HOW TO MAKE SKINNY BELTS

㉑ HOW TO MAKE STRIPEY POUCHES

LAROUSSE DE POCH

MAKING THE BEST OF WHAT YOU'VE GOT ALREADY

DIAGRAM 1

22 FROM CLASSIC TO WESTERN

23 FROM MAN'S SHIRT TO CHINESE JACKET

You'll need: A classic tailored shirt. Scraps of cotton fabric. 1½ yards flat braid ½ inch wide.

1. Make paper patterns for front and back yokes and cuffs. Following patterns, cut 2 front yokes, 1 back yoke and 2 cuffs from fabric, adding ½ inch on all except lower edges of yokes.

2. With ½ inch seams, join front and back yokes at shoulders. Press seams open.

3. Turn under ½ inch on outer shoulder and front edges of yokes; press. Place yokes on shirt; baste. Stitch around yokes.

4. Band lower edge of yokes with braid, turning in raw ends; stitch.

5. Remove sleeve buttons from shirt.

6. Turn under ½ inch all around on cuffs; press. Place cuffs on shirt; baste. Stitch around.

7. Trim cuffs with braid as desired.

8. Work new cuff buttonholes over the old ones. Replace buttons.

You'll need: A man's medium weight outer shirt (we used a navy brushed cotton). 2 packages 1 inch wide contrasting bias tape (we used brown). Five ½ inch toggles.

1. Following dotted lines on Diagram 1, cut off collar (at top of collar band): buttons, front placket, shirttails and cuffs (just above cuff openings).

2. Hem lower edge of shirt and sleeves.

3. Pin in place 5 bias tape loops to fit toggles, putting them at 3½ inch intervals on right shirt front, starting ½ inch from top. Loops should be on wrong side of shirt front ¼ inch from edge.

4. Stitch bias tape over all raw edges, stitching over loops as you go.

5. Sew on toggles.

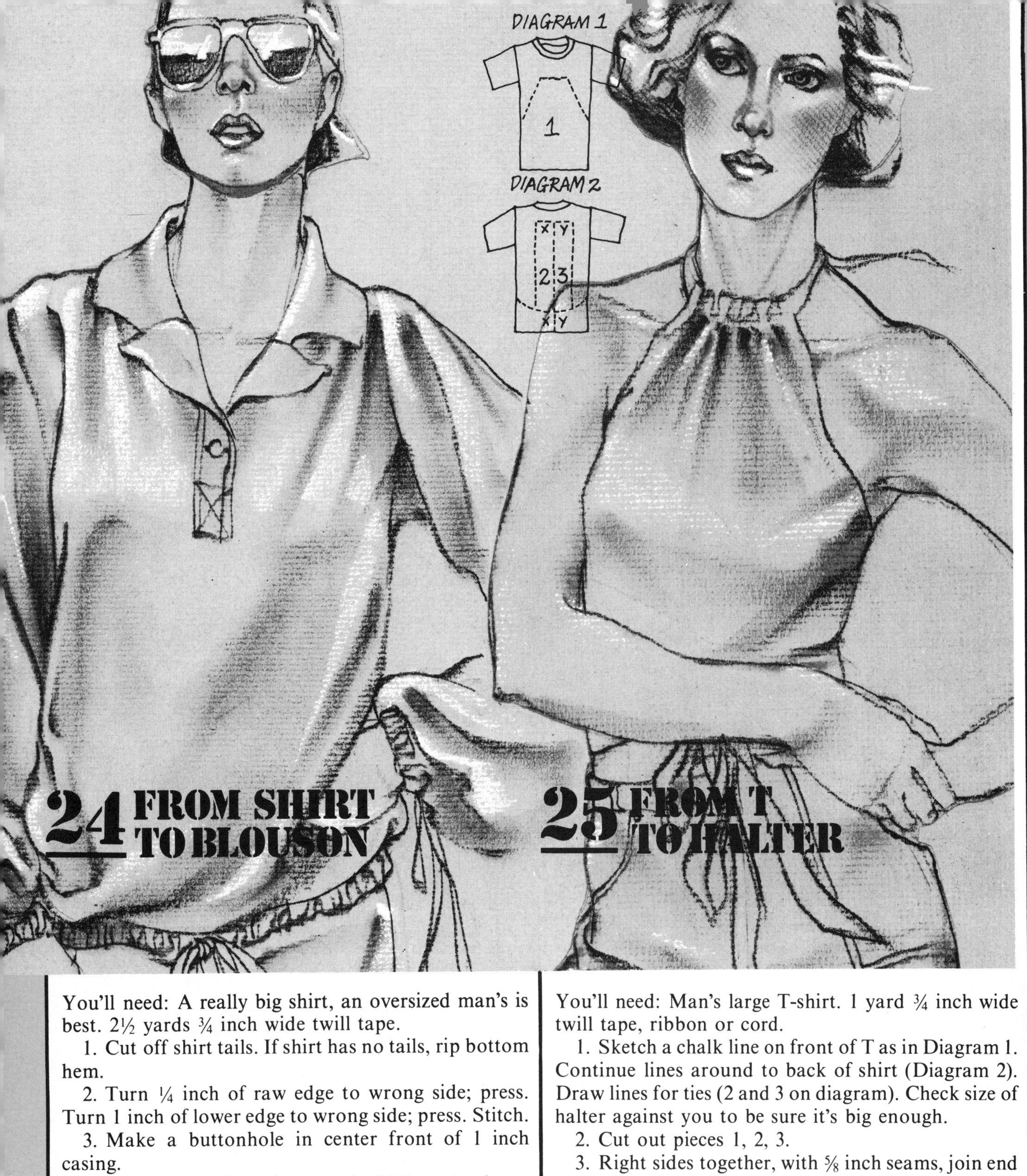

DIAGRAM 1

DIAGRAM 2

1

X Y
2 3
X Y

24 FROM SHIRT TO BLOUSON

25 FROM T TO HALTER

You'll need: A really big shirt, an oversized man's is best. 2½ yards ¾ inch wide twill tape.

1. Cut off shirt tails. If shirt has no tails, rip bottom hem.

2. Turn ¼ inch of raw edge to wrong side; press. Turn 1 inch of lower edge to wrong side; press. Stitch.

3. Make a buttonhole in center front of 1 inch casing.

4. Put a large safety pin on end of 1½ yards of tape and pull through casing, evening up ends.

5. Draw up tape to fit and tie ends in bow.

6. Cut off cuffs, leaving side slashes intact.

7. Turn to wrong side ¼ inch raw edge of sleeves; press. Turn to wrong side 1 inch of lower edge of sleeves; press. Stitch.

8. Make a buttonhole in center front of each casing.

9. Pull ½ yard length of tape through each sleeve casing. Draw up to fit and tie ends in bow.

Note: This can also be done using elastic threaded through the casings.

You'll need: Man's large T-shirt. 1 yard ¾ inch wide twill tape, ribbon or cord.

1. Sketch a chalk line on front of T as in Diagram 1. Continue lines around to back of shirt (Diagram 2). Draw lines for ties (2 and 3 on diagram). Check size of halter against you to be sure it's big enough.

2. Cut out pieces 1, 2, 3.

3. Right sides together, with ⅝ inch seams, join end X on piece 2 to end X on piece 1. Join end Y on piece 3 to end Y on piece 1.

4. Turn ¼ inch of all raw edges (except neck) to wrong side. Straight stitch or zigzag stitch, being careful not to stretch fabric.

5. Turn neck edge under 1 inch. Stitch.

6. Attach a large safety pin to tape and draw through neck casing. Center it and stitch back or knot ends.

Note: Halter can be tied at back waist or wrapped around to tie in front.

KNITTING AND CROCHETING

General Directions

Note: All directions are given for smallest size. Other sizes are given in parentheses.

GAUGE

Basic to good fit in both knitting and crochet is working to the gauge specified in the individual directions. Gauge is usually indicated by the exact number of stitches that must be worked in the space of 1 or 2 inches. The number of rows that must be worked in 1 or 2 inches may also be indicated.

To check your gauge use the needles and the yarn called for and make a practice piece about 4 inches square. Count the number of stitches and rows. If you have fewer stitches and rows, use smaller needles or hook; if you have more stitches than specified, use larger needles or hook. Experiment until your gauge is exact.

ABBREVIATIONS

beg	beginning
ch	chain
dc	double crochet
dec	decrease
dp	double-pointed (needles)
d tr	double treble
grp	group
hdc	half double crochet
inc	increase
lp(s)	loop(s)
k	knit
p	purl
psso	pass slip st over last st as if binding off
rnd	round
sc	single crochet
SKP	sl 1 st, k next st, psso k st
sl	slip
sp(s)	space(s)
st(s)	stitch(es)
tog	together
tr	treble
yo	yarn over needle or hook

TERMINOLOGY

Work even	continue without further increases or decreases
*	repeat whatever follows the asterisk as many times as specified
( )	do what is in parentheses as many times as indicated

READING CHARTS

Charts are used when elaborate knit-in patterns are called for. Usually they are used when more that one color is required. Each little square on the chart represents one stitch. When reading the chart (unless specified otherwise), start at lower right corner and read the lowest row across from right to left; that is a knit row. The next row, starting at the left and reading left to right is a purl row. Alternate rows all the way to the top of chart or repeat sections of chart as indicated.

BLOCKING

You will note that many directions give the Blocking Measurements for your garment. Blocking will often give a garment a professional finish. First check your yarn label; it may tell how to block that particular yarn. If not, block pieces before sewing them together. Two similar pieces, such as two fronts, can be blocked together. Place pieces, wrong side up, on a padded board. Pin with rustproof pins ½ inch apart, gently stretching and shaping each piece to the exact measurements needed. Place a damp cloth over piece and press with a hot iron, being careful not to let the weight of the iron rest on piece. Allow work to dry thoroughly before removing pins. After the garment is assembled, it may require a light steaming along the seams.

SCARVES:

everything you need to know about making a great one

Often it's something as simple as a scarf that can make the difference between plain and perfect. If you're making the kind of sweater or vest that will take a scarf (and most of them will) be sure to buy enough yarn at the beginning to make one. If the sweater is plain, using more intricate stitches — like cabling or pointelle — will make a good go-with scarf. A scarf is super simple to make — the fun is in the stitch-mix and the fringing.

Basic Crochet Scarf

SIZES: Directions are given for 8 x 36 inch scarf, excluding fringe. Changes for 8 x 60 and 8 x 72 inch scarf are in parentheses.

MATERIALS: Coats & Clark's Red Heart Wintuk® 4 Ply (4 oz. skeins): 8 (10, 12) ounces. Crochet Hook, Size H.

GAUGE: 4 dc = 1 inch; 4 rows = 2 inches.

Starting at narrow edge, ch 34. Row 1: Dc in 4th ch from hook and in each ch across—32 dc, counting ch-3 as 1 dc. Ch 3, turn. Row 2: Skip first dc, dc in next dc and in each dc across. Ch 3, turn. Repeat rows 1 and 2 for pattern until total length is 36 (60, 72) inches. Break off and fasten.

Basic Knit Scarf

SIZES: Directions are given for 8 x 36 inch scarf, excluding fringe. Changes for 8 x 60 inch and 8 x 72 inch scarf are in parentheses.

MATERIALS: Coats & Clark's Red Heart Wintuk® 4 Ply knitting worsted weight yarn (4 oz. skeins): 6 (8, 10) ounces. Knitting Needles, 1 pair No. 10.

GAUGE: 4 sts = 1 inch; 11 rows = 2 inches.

Starting at narrow edge, cast on 32 sts. K 3 rows. Row 4 (wrong side): K 2, p across to within last 2 sts, k 2. Row 5: K across. Repeat last 2 rows for pattern. Work in pattern until total length is 35½ (59½, 71½) inches, ending with a wrong side row. Next 3 rows: K across. Bind off.

136

Long Narrow Scarf

SIZE: 4 x 72 inches, excluding fringe.

MATERIALS: Coats & Clark's Red Heart Wintuk® Sport Yarn, 2 Ply (2 oz. skeins), 12 ounces. Knitting Needles, 1 pair No. 5.

GAUGE: 11 sts = 2 inches; 9 rows = 1 inch.

Starting at narrow edge, cast on 22 sts. Work in garter st (k each row) for 9 rows (border). Now work as follows: Next row: K. Following row: K 4, p to within last 4 sts, k 4. Repeat last 2 rows for pattern. Work in pattern until total length is 71 inches, ending with a k row. Work 9 rows in garter st for border. Bind off.

Fair Isle Border Scarf

SIZE: Approximately 8 x 72 inches, excluding fringe. To add Fair Isle borders to the Basic Knit Scarf, you will need one ounce each of two contrasting colors (Color A and Color B) in addition to the main color. Pattern is worked in stockinette st (k 1 row, p 1 row). When changing colors always twist the color not in use around the other once to prevent making holes; carry the unused color loosely along wrong side of work. When a color is no longer in use, break off. Follow first and all even rows from left to right and 2nd row and all uneven rows from right to left.
Follow Basic Knit Scarf instructions through Row 5. Starting with Row 1, follow Chart as directed until Row 29 is completed. Now repeat last 2 rows of Basic Knit Scarf instructions until total length measures 69 inches. Following Chart in reverse, work border design. Repeat Rows 4 and 5 of Basic Knit Scarf. K 3 rows. Bind off.

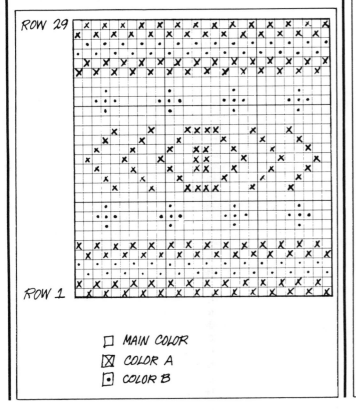

☐ MAIN COLOR
☒ COLOR A
⊡ COLOR B

Fringes

Basic Fringe

Cut one strand of yarn 10 inches long. Double this strand to form a loop. Insert crochet hook in first st at narrow edge and draw loop through. Draw ends through loop and pull up tightly to form a knot. Knot one strand in each st across. Trim evenly. Repeat for other edge.

Tassels

Wind yarn 20 times around an 8-inch piece of cardboard. Break off yarn. Draw a 10-inch length under strands at one end and tie securely; slip from cardboard and wind another strand around tassel, ¾ inch below tied end and fasten; cut strands at opposite end and trim evenly.

Knotted Fringe

Cut 8 strands of yarn, each 26 inches long. Double these strands to form a loop (Diagram 1). With right side facing, insert hook (Diagram 2) from back to front through the first st at narrow edge and draw loop through (Diagram 3). Draw loose ends through loop (Diagram 4) and pull up tightly to form a knot (Diagram 5). Make a fringe in every other st across. Pick up half the strands of the first fringe and half the second fringe and make a knot (Diagram 6) one inch down and in the center between 2 previous knots. *Pick up remaining strands of previous fringe and first half of the next fringe and knot as before. Repeat from * across. Make another row of knots as before. Trim evenly.

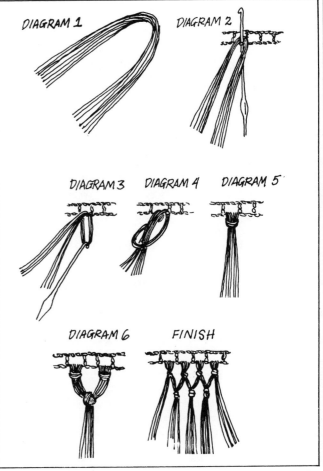

137

1 ⊗
Long, slouchy, in a color that's nature's own

SIZES: Small (8-10), Medium (12-14), Large (16-18).

MATERIALS: Bernat Scandia, (2 oz. skein) 13 (14,15) skeins.
Knitting Needles, 1 pair each No. 10 and No. 13.
6 buttons.
1 yard 1½ inch grosgrain ribbon.
Seam binding.

GAUGE: 5 sts = 2 inches;
7 rows = 2 inches.

Back: Using No. 10 needles, cast on 40 (44, 48) sts. K 1, p 1 in ribbing for 2 inches. Change to No. 13 needles and work even in stockinette st until piece measures 20½ inches. **SHAPE ARMHOLES:** At the beg of each of next 2 rows bind off 3 sts. Dec 1 st each end of needle every other row twice. Work even on 30 (34, 38) sts until armholes measure 7½ (8, 8½) inches. **SHAPE SHOULDERS:** At the beg of each of next 2 rows bind off 5 (5, 6) sts. At the beg of each of next 2 rows bind off 5 (6, 6) sts. Bind off remaining 10 (12, 14) sts. **POCKET LININGS** (Make 2): Using No. 13 needles, cast on 12 sts. Work even in stockinette st until piece measures 4 inches, ending on a p row. Slip sts onto holder. **RIGHT FRONT:** Using No. 10 needles, cast on 23 (25, 27) sts. Row 1: K 4 (front band), p 1, * k 1, p 1; repeat from * across row. Row 2: K 1, * p 1, k 1; repeat from * to last 4 sts, k 4. Repeat these 2 rows for 2 inches, ending with Row 2. Change to No. 13 needles. Row 1: Knit. Row 2: P 19 (21, 23), k 4 (front band). Repeat last 2 rows until piece measures 4½ inches, ending with Row 1. **POCKET BAND:** Row 1: P 5 (6, 6), k 12 (pocket band), work to end of row. Row 2: Knit. Repeat Rows 1 and 2 once. **POCKET OPENING:** P to pocket band, bind off next 12 sts, work to end of row. On next row k to pocket opening, k 12 sts of one pocket lining onto same needle, k to end of row. Then, keeping 4 sts of front band in garter st, work even in stockinette st on remaining sts until piece measures 11½ (13, 14) inches, ending at front edge. **SHAPE COLLAR:** Rows 1 and 3: K 2, inc 1 st in next st, k to end of row. Row 2: P 19 (21, 23), k 2, inc 1 st in next st, k 2. Row 4: P 18 (20, 22), k 5, inc 1 st in next st, k 2. Continue in this manner to inc 1 st in 3rd st from front edge EVERY ROW 4 times more and to work 1 st more in garter st at front edge every 4th row until 16 (18, 18) sts are worked in garter st at front edge, and AT THE SAME TIME, when piece measures 20½ inches **SHAPE ARMHOLE:** At arm edge bind off 3 sts. Dec 1 st at same edge every other row twice. Work even on 26 (28, 30) sts until armhole measures 7½ (8, 8½) inches. **SHAPE SHOULDER:** At arm edge bind off 5 (5, 6) sts once and 5 (6, 6) sts once ending at neck edge. **SHAPE BACK COLLAR:** Short rows: Work as follows on remaining 16 (17, 18) sts of collar: K 16 (17, 18) (outer edge); k 13 (neck edge), turn; k to outer edge, k 12, turn, k to outer edge, k 7, turn, k to outer edge, k 12, turn, k to outer edge, k 13, k to outer edge, k 16 (17, 18). Continue in garter st for 2½ inches more. Bind off. **LEFT FRONT:** Using No. 10 needles, cast on 23 (25, 27) sts. Row 1: P 1, * k 1, p 1; repeat from * to last 4 sts, k 4 (front band). Row 2: K 5, * p 1, k 1; repeat from * across row. Finish to correspond to right front, reversing placing of pocket and all shaping and forming first buttonhole when piece measures 1 inch. **BUTTONHOLE:** Starting at front edge, k 1, bind off the next 2 sts, work to end of row. On next row cast on 2 sts over those

bound off previous row. Make 5 more buttonholes, evenly spaced—the last one made ½ inch below start of collar shaping. **SLEEVES:** Using No. 10 needles, cast on 20 (22, 24) sts. K 1, p 1 in ribbing for 2 inches. Change to No. 13 needles and work in stockinette st, inc 1 st each end of needle every 2½ inches, 5 times. Work even on 30 (32, 34) sts until piece measures 17½ (18, 18) inches. **SHAPE CAP:** At the beg of each of next 2 rows bind off 3 sts. Dec 1 st each end of needle every other row for 4½ (5, 5½) inches. At the beg of each of next 2 rows bind off 2 sts. Bind off remaining sts. **FINISHING:** Sew underarm, shoulder and sleeve seams. Seam collar and sew to back of neck. Sew pocket linings in place. Steam. If desired, with ribbon face each front to start of collar shaping. It is wise to shrink ribbon first. Finish buttonholes. Sew on buttons. Bind shoulders and back of neck with seam binding.

2 ⊗
A quick little crewneck

SIZES: 8, 10, 12, 14, 16, 18.

MATERIALS: Reynolds Lopi (100 gram skeins) 4 (5, 5, 6, 6, 7) skeins.
Knitting Needles, 1 pair each No. 9 and No. 11.
Set of dp needles No. 10.
2 stitch holders.

GAUGE: On No. 11 needles,
3 sts = 1 inch;
4 rows = 1 inch.

Blocking Measurements						
Sizes	8	10	12	14	16	18
Body Bust Size (In Inches)						
	31½	32½	34	36	38	40
Actual Knitting Measurements Bust						
	34	35½	37½	39½	41½	43½
Width across back at underarms						
	16½	17½	18	19½	20	21½
Width across front at underarms						
	17½	18	19½	20	21½	22
Width of sleeve at upperarm						
	12½	13¼	14	14	14½	15½

BACK: With No. 9 needles, cast on loosely 44 (46, 48, 52, 54, 58) sts. Work in k 1, p 1 ribbing for 3½ inches. Change to No. 11 needles. Work in stockinette st (k on right side, p on wrong side), inc 6 sts evenly spaced across first row—50 (52, 54, 58, 60, 64) sts. Work even until piece measures 12½ (12½, 13, 13, 13½, 13½) inches from beg, or desired length to underarm. Mark last row. **ARMHOLES:** Bind off 3 (3, 3, 4, 4, 5) sts at beg of next 2 rows. Dec 1 st each edge every other row 3 times—38 (40, 42, 44, 46, 48) sts. Work even until armholes measure 7 (7¼, 7½, 7¾, 8, 8) inches above marked row. **SHOULDERS:** Bind off 5 (5, 5, 5, 6, 6) sts at beg of next 2 rows, then 4 (5, 6, 6, 6, 7) sts at beg of next 2 rows. Sl remaining 20 (20, 20, 22, 22, 22) sts on st holder for neckband. **FRONT:** With No. 9 needles, cast on loosely 46 (48, 52, 54, 58, 60) sts. Work in k 1, p 1 ribbing for 3½ inches. Change to No. 11 needles. Work in stockinette st, inc 6 sts evenly spaced across first row—52 (54, 58, 60, 64, 66) sts. Work even until piece measures same as back to underarm. Mark last row. **ARMHOLES:** Bind off 4 (4, 4, 4, 5, 5) sts at beg of next 2 rows. Dec 1 st each edge every other row 3 (3, 4, 4, 4, 4) times—38 (40, 42, 44, 46, 48) sts. Work even until armholes measure 4 (4¼, 4½, 4¾, 5, 5) inches above marked row, ending right side. **NECK:** Next Row (wrong side): P 13 (14, 15, 15, 16, 17) sts, join another ball of yarn and p next 12 (12, 12, 14, 14, 14) sts and sl them on a holder, p remaining sts. Working on both sides at once, dec 1 st at neck edge every other row 4 times—9 (10, 11, 11, 12, 13) sts each side. Work even until armholes measure 7 (7¼, 7½, 7¾, 8, 8) inches above marked row. **SHOULDERS:** Bind off 5 (5, 5, 5, 6, 6) sts at beg of each armhole edge once, then 4 (5, 6, 6, 6, 7) sts once. **SLEEVES:** With No. 9 needles, cast on loosely 24 (24, 26, 26, 28, 28) sts. Work in k 1, p 1 ribbing for 3½ inches. Change to No. 11 needles. K next row, inc 6 sts evenly spaced across—30 (30, 32, 32, 34, 34) sts. Continue in stockinette st, inc 1 st each edge every 6th row 4 (5, 5, 5, 5, 6) times—38 (40, 42, 42, 44, 46) sts. Work even until total sleeve length is 16 (16½, 16½, 17, 17, 17) inches or desired length to underarm. **TOP SHAPING:** Bind off 4 sts at beg of next 2 rows. Dec 1 st each edge every other row 10 (11, 11, 11, 12, 13) times. Bind off remaining 10 (10, 12, 12, 12, 12) sts. **FINISHING:** Sew shoulder seams. Sew side and sleeve seams. Sew in sleeves. **NECKBAND:** Beg at right shoulder and right side of work, with dp needles (divide sts on 3 dp needles) k sts from back holder, pick up and k 10 (10, 11, 11, 12, 12) sts along side of left front neck, k sts from front holder, pick up and k 10 (10, 11, 11, 12, 12) sts along side of right front neck—52 (52, 54, 58, 60, 60) sts. Join, working around in k 1, p 1 ribbing for 2 inches. Bind off loosely in ribbing.

3 ⊗
Hooded, belted, crunchy as cereal

SIZES: Small (8-10), Medium (12-14), Large (16-18).

MATERIALS: Bernat Krysta, a bulky yarn, (2 oz. skeins), 16 (17-18) skeins.
Knitting Needles, 1 pair No. 10.
Aluminum Crochet Hook, Size I.
Stitch Holder.

GAUGE: 7 sts = 2 inches;
         5 rows = 1 inch

PATTERN STITCH: Work in stockinette st for 14 rows, ending with a p row, starting with a p row work in reverse stockinette st for 14 rows, ending with a k row. Repeat these 28 rows for pattern stitch. **BACK:** Cast on 60 (66, 74) sts. K 1, p 1 in ribbing for 2½ inches. Then work even in pattern st until piece measures 20 inches. Put a marker in work to mark start of armhole. Continue in pattern st until armholes measure 8 (8½, 9) inches above marker in work. **SHAPE SHOULDERS:** At the beg of each of the next 4 rows bind off 10 (11, 12) sts. Sl remaining 20 (22, 26) sts onto a holder. **LEFT FRONT:** Cast on 30 (34, 38) sts. K 1, p 1 in ribbing for 2½ inches. Then work in pattern st until piece measures 20 inches. Put a marker in work to mark start of armhole. Continue in pattern st until armhole measures 5 (5½, 6) inches above marker in work, ending at front edge. **SHAPE NECK:** At front edge bind off 6 (7, 8) sts, work to end of row. At

edge dec 1 st every other row 4 (5, 6) times. Work even on remaining 20 (22, 24) sts until armhole measures 8 (8½, 9) inches. **SHAPE SHOULDER:** At arm edge bind off 10 (11, 12) sts twice. **RIGHT FRONT:** Work to correspond to left front, reversing all shaping. **SLEEVES:** Sew shoulder seams. With right side facing you and starting at marker, pick up 60 (66, 74) sts around arm edge to other marker. Working in pattern st, dec 1 st each end of needle every 4th row 15 (17, 20) times. Work even on 30 (32, 34) sts until piece measures 14 (14½, 15) inches. Then k 1, p 1 in ribbing for 4 inches. Bind off. **HOOD:** With wrong side facing you pick up 60 (66, 74) sts around neck edge, including sts from holder. Starting with a p row work in reverse stockinette st for 11 inches. Bind off. **BELT:** Cast on 12 sts. K 1, p 1 in ribbing until piece measures 40 inches or desired finished length. Bind off. **POCKETS:** (Make 2): Cast on 20 sts. Work in stockinette st for 14 rows, ending with a p row. P the next row and continue in reverse stockinette st for 7 rows more. Then work in garter st until piece measures 6 inches. Bind off. **FINISHING:** Sew underarm and sleeve seams. Seam hood. Sew pockets in place above ribbing, 1 inch from each underarm seam. With right side facing you work 1 row s c around entire front and hood. Steam seams.

4 ⊗
A long lean line of ribs

SIZES: Petite (6-8), Small (10-12), Medium (14-16).

MATERIALS: Columbia-Minerva Bulky Nantuk®, (2 oz. skeins), 11 (13, 15) skeins.
Knitting Needles, 1 pair each No. 9 and No. 11.

GAUGE: When slightly stretched
         3 sts = 1 inch;
         4 rows = 1 inch.

BACK: With No. 9 needles cast on 51 (55, 61) sts. **Row 1 — Right side:** K 1, * p 1, k 1, repeat from * across. **Row 2:** P 1, * k 1, p 1, repeat from * across. Repeat Rows 1 and 2 to 2 inches from beg. Change to No. 11 needles. Continue in ribbing to 20 inches from beg. Width is 17 (18, 20) inches. **RAGLAN ARMHOLES:** Bind off 4 (4, 5) sts at beg of next 2 rows. Dec 1 st each side every other row until 23 (25, 27) sts remain then every 4th row until 17 (19, 21) sts remain. Bind off. **FRONT:** Work same as back to 1 inch below underarm, ending on wrong side. **NECK AND RAGLAN ARMHOLES:** Next row: Work 21 (23, 26) sts and sl them to a holder, bind off center 9 sts for neck, work to end-21 (23, 26) sts remain. Dec 1 st at neck edge every 8th (8th, 6th) row 3 (4, 5) times **And At The Same Time** when side edge matches back to underarm, bind off 4 (4, 5) sts at side edge once to start raglan armhole then dec 1 st at raglan every other row 10 (11, 12) times then every 4th row 3 times. Bind off remaining st. Starting at opposite neck edge, work other side. **SLEEVES:** With No. 9 needles, cast on 31 (33, 37) sts. Work in ribbing same as on back for 3 inches. Change to No. 11 needles. Continue in ribbing to 7 inches. Inc 1 st each side on next row then every 10th row 2 more times working the added sts in pattern. Work on the 37 (39, 43) sts to 17 inches from beg. Width is 12¼ (13, 14¼) inches. **RAGLAN SLEEVE CAP:** Bind off 4 (4, 5) sts at beg of next 2 rows. Dec 1 st each side every other row until 9 sts remain then every 4th row until 3 sts remain. Bind off. Sew raglan seams joining sleeves to back and front, then sew side and sleeve seams. **COLLAR:** With No. 9 needles cast on

9 sts. Work 2 rows in ribbing same as on Back. Mark **end** of Row 2 for outer edge of collar. Keeping marked edge straight, continue in ribbing inc'ing 1 st at **other edge every row** until there are 21 sts on needle, then inc 1 at same edge every other row until there are 35 (35, 37) sts on needle. Continue in ribbing on the 35 (35, 37) sts until collar fits to center back of neck. Mark for center back of collar. Continue on the 35 (35, 37) sts to match other side of collar to last inc worked. Keeping marked outer edge of collar straight, dec 1 st at **other edge** every other row until 21 sts remain then **every row** until 9 sts remain. Work 2 rows on the 9 sts. Bind off. Pin shaped edge of collar to neck edge with the 9 cast-on sts across the 9 bound-off sts at center front. Pin the 9 bound-off sts of collar underneath at center front as shown. Sew collar neatly in place with a weaving st.

5 ⦰ A pull of a vest

SIZES: 8, 10, 12, 14, 16.

MATERIALS: Reynolds Velourette, a chenille-type yarn, (30 gram ball), 8 (8, 8, 9, 9) balls red.
Aluminum Crochet Hook Size F.

GAUGE: 11 hdc = 3 inches;
        5 rows = 2 inches.

Blocking Measurements

Sizes	8	10	12	14	16
Body Bust Size (In Inches)					
	31½	32½	34	36	38
Actual Knitting Measurements					
	33¼	35¾	37½	40	42
Width of back at underarms					
	15¾	17	18	19¼	20¼
Width of front at underarms					
	17½	18½	19½	20¾	21¾

For longer length vest more yarn may be needed.
PATTERN: (Half double crochet): **Row 1:** Hdc in 3rd ch from hook and in each ch across. Turn. **Row 2:** Ch 2 (counts as 1 hdc), skip first hdc, hdc in each hdc across, hdc in top of turning-ch. Turn. Repeat row 2 for pattern. **To Inc 1 Hdc:** Work 2 hdc in same hdc. **To Dec 1 Hdc:** Pull up a lp in each of 2 dc, yo and through 3 lps on hook. **TO BIND OFF: At beg of row,** sl st across specified number of hdc, then sl st in next hdc, ch 2, work in pattern across. **At end of row,** leave specified number of hdc unworked. **BACK:** Ch 57 (61, 65, 69, 73) loosely to measure 15¼ (16½, 17½, 18½, 19½) inches. Work in pattern on 56 (60, 64, 68, 72) hdc. Dec 1 hdc each edge every 3rd row 3 times—50 (54, 58, 62, 66) hdc. Work even until piece measures 5½ inches from beg. Inc 1 hdc each edge every 3rd row 4 times—58 (62, 66, 70, 74) hdc. Work even until piece measures 13½ inches from beg or desired length to underarm. Mark last row. **ARMHOLES:** Bind off 4 (4, 5, 5, 6) hdc (see To Bind Off) each edge of next row, then dec 1 hdc each edge every other row 3 (4, 4, 5, 5) times—44 (46, 48, 50, 52) hdc. Work even until armholes measure 7 (7¼, 7½, 7¾, 8) inches above marked row. **SHOULDERS:** Bind off 5 hdc each edge of next 2 rows, then 3 (4, 5, 6, 7) hdc each edge of next row— 18 hdc remain for back neck. Fasten off. **FRONT:** Ch 63 (67, 71, 75, 79) loosely to measure 17¼ (18¼, 19½, 20½, 21½) inches.

Work in pattern on 62 (66, 70, 74, 78) hdc. Dec 1 hdc each edge every 3rd row 3 times—56 (60, 64, 68, 72) hdc. Work even until piece measures 5½ inches from beg. Inc 1 hdc each edge every 3rd row 4 times—64 (68, 72, 76, 80) hdc. Work even until piece measures 1 row less than back to underarm. **Divide for Neck: Next Row:** Work 32 (34, 36, 38, 40) hdc, drop yarn. With another ball of yarn make a sl knot on hook, hdc in next hdc and each hdc across. Mark last row. **ARMHOLES AND NECK: At same time** working both sides at once, bind off 4 (4, 5, 5, 6) hdc at beg of each side edge once, then dec 1 hdc at same edges every other row 3 (4, 4, 5, 5) times; **and at the same time,** * dec 1 hdc at each neck edge every row twice, work 1 row even. Repeat from * until 12 hdc have been decreased—13 (14, 15, 16, 17) hdc each side. Work even until armholes measure 7 (7¼, 7½, 7¾, 8) inches above marked row. **SHOULDERS:** Bind off 5 hdc at beg of each armhole edge twice, then 3 (4, 5, 6, 7) hdc once. **FINISHING:** Sew shoulder seams. Sew side seams leaving 4 inches open from each lower edge for side slits. If desired, steam vest lightly over a dry cloth on wrong side. Have the steam penetrate but do not let the weight of the iron touch the vest. Steam press seams open flat on wrong side.

6 ⊗ Shoulder buttoned basic

SIZES: Small (6-8), Medium (10-12), Large (14-16).

MATERIALS: Coats & Clark's Red Heart® Fabulend, a knitting worsted type yarn, Art. E. 235, 4 ply (4 oz. skein), 5 (5, 6) skeins No. 909 Scarlet.
Knitting needles, 1 pair each No. 6 and No. 9.
4 buttons, ½ inch in diameter.

GAUGE: 4 sts = 1 inch;
        13 rows = 2 inches.

Blocking Measurements

Sizes	Small (6-8)	Medium (10-12)	Large (14-16)
Body Bust Size (In Inches)			
	30½-31½	32½-34	36-38
Actual Knitting Measurements			
Bust	33	35	39
Width across back or front at underarm			
	16½	17½	19½
Length from shoulder to lower edge			
	22½	24	25
Length of side seam			
	16	16½	17
Length of sleeve seam			
	17½	18	18½
Width across sleeve at upper arm			
	12	13	14

BACK: Starting at lower edge with No. 6 needles, cast on 65 (69, 77) sts. **Row 1 (wrong side):** P 1, * k 1, p 1. Repeat from * across. **Row 2:** K 1, * p 1, k 1. Repeat from * across. Repeat Rows 1 and 2 alternately for ribbing for 3 inches, ending with Row 1, increasing one st at each end on last row - 67 (71, 79) sts. Change to No. 9 needles and work in seed st pattern as follows: **Next Row:** K 1, * p 1, k 1. Repeat from * across. Repeat last row for seed st pattern. Work in seed stitch pattern until total length is 16 (16½, 17) inches, ending with a row on wrong side. **Armhole Shaping:** Continuing in seed st pattern, bind off 5 (5, 6) sts at beg of next 2 rows. Dec one st at each end every other row 4 (4, 5) times-49 (53, 57) sts. Work even until length from first row of armhole shaping is 5¾ (6¾, 7¼) inches, ending with a row on wrong side. **Neck Shaping: Row 1:** Work in seed st across first 18 (19, 20) sts; place remaining 31 (34, 37) sts on a stitch holder. Turn. **Row 2:** Bind off at neck edge first 5 sts, complete row in pattern. **Row 3:** Work in pattern across. **Row 4:** Bind off 5 sts, complete row. Place remaining 8 (9, 10) sts on another stitch holder. Leaving center 13 (15, 17) sts on stitch holder, slip remaining 18 (19, 20) sts onto free needle, attach yarn at neck edge and work to correspond with opposite side, reversing shaping. **Back Neckband:** With right side facing, using No. 6 needles, work in seed st across sts on first stitch holder, (pick up and k 10 sts along neck edge to next stitch holder, work in seed st across sts on stitch holder) twice - 49 (53, 57) sts. Starting with Row 1 of ribbing, work ribbing for 5 rows. Bind off in ribbing. **FRONT:** Work same as Back until length from first row of armhole shaping is 5¼ (6¼, 6¾) inches, ending with a row on wrong side. **Neck Shaping: Row 1:** Work in pattern across first 20 (21, 22) sts; place remaining 29 (32, 35) sts on a stitch holder. Turn. **Row 2:** Bind off 4 sts at neck edge, work in pattern across. **Row 3:** Work across. Repeat last 2 rows alternately 2 more times. Work even until length of armhole is same as Back, ending with a row on wrong side. Place remaining 8 (9, 10) sts on another stitch holder. Leaving center 9 (11, 13) sts on stitch holder, slip remaining sts onto free needle; attach yarn at neck edge and complete to correspond with opposite side, reversing shaping. **Front Neckband:** With right side facing, using No. 6 needles, work in seed st across sts on first stitch holder; (pick up and k 12 sts along neck edge to next stitch holder, work in seed st across sts on stitch holder) twice - 49 (53, 57) sts. Work in ribbing same as for Back Neckband for 2 rows. **Next Row:** Work in ribbing across first 2 (3, 4) sts; ** bind off next 2 sts for buttonhole, work in ribbing until there are 2 sts on right-hand needle following bound-off sts, bind off next 2 sts **, work in ribbing across to last 8 (9, 10) sts. Repeat directions from ** to ** once, complete row. **Following Row:** Casting on 2 sts over each set of bound-off sts, work in ribbing across. **Next Row:** Work in ribbing across. Bind off loosely in ribbing. **SLEEVES:** Starting at lower edge with No. 6 needles, cast on 35 (39, 43) sts. Work ribbing same as on Back for 3 inches, ending with Row 2 of ribbing. **Next Row:** Increasing 13 sts evenly spaced, work in ribbing across - 48 (52, 56) sts. Change to No. 9 needles and work in seed st pattern until total length is 17½ (18, 18½) inches, ending with a row on wrong side. **Top Shaping:** Continuing in seed st pattern, bind off 5 (5, 6) sts at beg of next 2 rows. Dec one st at each end on every other row until 20 (20, 24) sts remain, then dec one st at each end every 4th row until 16 sts remain. Bind off 2 sts at beg of next 4 rows. Bind off remaining 8 sts. Pin pieces to measurements on a padded surface; cover with a damp cloth and allow to dry; **do not press.** Sew side and sleeve seams. Fold front neckband over back neckband and stitch at shoulder edge. Sew in sleeves. Sew buttons on back neckband.

MATERIALS: Lion Brand 100% Virgin Wool Knitting worsted, (4 oz. skein), 6 (7, 7) skeins.
Knitting Needles, 1 pair No. 10.
Aluminum Crochet Hook, Size G.

GAUGE: With double yarn: 4 sts = 1 inch.

Note: Yarn is used double throughout and purl side is right side of work.

BACK: With 2 strands of yarn, cast on 54 (58, 62) sts. Work in stockinette st. Work even until 17 (17½, 18) inches from beg or desired length to underarm. **SHAPE DROPPED SHOULDERS:** Cast on 12 (14, 16) sts at beg of next 2 rows. Work even until 7 (7¼, 7½) inches from cast-on sts. Bind off all sts. **FRONT:** Work as for back until ½ inch less to underarm. **SHAPE NECK:** Work across 27 (29, 31) sts; sl remaining sts on holder. Working on one side only, dec 1 st at center edge every other row until 30 (32, 34) sts remain; *at the same time,* casting on 12 (14, 16) sts at outside edge when same length as back to beg of dropped shoulder. Work even until same length as back to shoulder. Bind off all sts. Work other side to correspond. **SLEEVES:** Sew shoulder seams. With purl side facing, pick up 48 (50, 52) sts around arm edges. Work in st st. Work even until 17 inches from beg or desired length to wrist. Work even for 4 inches more for turn-back cuff, reversing pattern. Bind off all sts. **COLLAR:** Starting at back, with double strand of yarn, cast on 54 sts. Work in st st. Work even for 8 inches, ending with k row. **Next row:** Work across 18 sts; bind off center 18 sts; sl remaining 18 sts on holder to be worked later. Working on left side only, dec 1 st at neck edge. Work even for 4 rows. Dec 1 st at same edge every 4th row until 12 sts remain. Work even for 8 (10, 10) rows. Dec 1 st at center edge (11 sts). Dec 1 st each row at center edge until 3 sts remain. Work even for 2 rows. Bind off. **RIGHT SIDE:** Work as for left side until 11 sts remain. Dec 1 st at same edge every other row until 7 sts remain. Working 1 st more at center edge in reverse st st every row, work in this manner until all 7 sts are reversed. Bind off 2 sts at center edge (5 sts). **TAB:** Work even for 9 rows. Bind off. **FINISHING:** Block. With p sides facing, sew side and sleeve seams, leaving 4 inches free at each lower edge for slits. Pin collar in place, having left front slightly under right front cross-over. Baste collar in position and try on to be sure that tab will be in center of sweater. Sew on collar. With p side facing, work 1 row of sc on cuff edges, 2 rows around lower edge, working in slip st around slit openings and having 3 sc in corner sts for turning.

8 ◖◗
A fluff of a dress, cowled & cozy

SIZES: Small, Medium, Large, Extra Large.

MATERIALS: Spinnerin Genie, (1 oz. ball), 26 (28, 30, 32) balls Red (MC) and Spinnerin Aladdin, (1 oz. ball), 19 (21, 23, 25) balls Red (CC).
Aluminum Crochet Hook, Size I.

GAUGE: 3 sts = 1 inch;
        3 rows = 1 inch.

Blocking Measurements Sizes	Small	Medium	Large	Extra Large
Bust (In Inches)	32	34½	37¼	40

7 ⊗
New over-alling: the middy

SIZES: 10, 12, 14.

Length to underarm

	30	30	30	30

STRIPE PATTERN—Row 1: With MC, sc in 2nd ch from hook and each ch to end, join CC draw through last MC lp on hook. Ch 1, turn. **Row 2:** With CC, sc in first sc and each sc to end. Ch 1, turn. **Row 3:** Repeat Row 2, ending pick up MC, draw through last CC lp on hook (always change yarns in this manner). Ch 1, turn. **Row 4:** With MC, repeat Row 2. **Row 5:** With MC, repeat Row 3, ending pick up CC. Repeat Rows 2 through 5 for pattern. **BACK (worked vertically):** Ch 91 or desired length having a multiple of 10. Beg with Row 1, work in stripe pattern on 90 sts until 12 (13, 14, 15) CC stripes are completed. Work 1 row MC. Mark end of this row for top edge. **Side Shaping—Short Row 1:** With MC, sl st in first 10 sts, sc in each of remaining sts, pick up CC. Ch 1, turn. **Row 2:** With CC, sc in each of first 70 sc, turn. **Row 3:** Skip 1 st, sl st in next 9 sts, sc in each of remaining sts, pick up MC. Ch 1, turn. **Row 4:** With MC, sc in each of first 50 sc, turn. **Row 5:** With MC, repeat Row 3, ending pick up CC. Ch 1, turn. **Row 6:** With CC, sc in each of first 30 sc, turn. **Row 7:** Repeat Row 3 of shaping. **Row 8:** With MC, sc in each of first 10 sts. Fasten off. Along other side of foundation ch, join MC in first ch at top corner. **Row 1:** Sl st in first ch and in next 9 chs, sc in each remaining ch to lower edge, join CC. Ch 1, turn. Beg with Row 2, work short rows as on other side. Fasten off. **FRONT:** Work same as Back. **FRONT YOKE—Row 1:** From right side join CC in first row at top front, sc in same row, work 1 sc in each row to other corner. Ch 1, turn-48 (52, 56, 60) sts. **Row 2:** With CC, sc in each sc to end, fasten off CC, join MC. Ch 1, turn. **Row 3:** With MC, sc in each sc to end. Ch 1, turn. Repeat Row 3 until 8 (8, 8¾, 8¾) inches, ending ready for a right side row. **LEFT FRONT AND NECK—Row 1:** Sc in each of first 17 (18, 20, 21) sts. Ch 1, turn. Do NOT work over remaining sts. **Row 2:** Decrease 1 sc, sc in each sc to end-16 (17, 19, 20) sts. Continue to dec 1 sc at neck edge every other row 2 times more. Work to 10 (10, 10¾, 10¾) inches from beg of yoke. Fasten off. **RIGHT FRONT:** On last full yoke skip center 14 (16, 16, 18) sts, join MC in next st, sc in same st and each st across. Work as Left Front reversing all shaping. **Back Yoke:** Omitting neck shaping work same as Front to 10 (10, 10¾, 10¾) inches. Fasten off. **SLEEVES (worked from 1 seam edge to other seam edge):** With MC, ch 51 or desired length having a multiple of 10. Beg with Row 1 of Stripe Pattern work on 50 sts until there are 13 (13, 14, 14) CC Stripes. With MC work 1 row. Mark end of this row for cap edge of sleeves. **Underarm Short Row 1:** Sl st in first 10 sts, sc in remaining sts, pick up CC. Ch 1, turn. **Row 2:** With CC, sc in each of first sts, turn. **Row 3:** Skip first st, sl st in next 9 sts, sc in each of remaining sts, pick up MC, ch 1, turn. **Row 4:** With MC, sc in each of first 10 sts. Fasten off. At cap along other side of foundation ch join MC in first ch. **Row 1:** Sl st in first st and in next 9 sts, sc in each remaining st, pick up CC. Ch 1, turn. Beg with Row 2, work short rows as on other side. Fasten off. Sew shoulder seams. **COWL COLLAR:** With MC ch 51. Beg with Row 1, work in stripe pattern as on back on 50 sts until collar is wide enough to fit smoothly around entire neck edge. **FINISHING:** Sew collar tog at center back forming a tube. Sew to neck edge. Sew side seams to beg of yoke sections. Sew sleeve seams. **Upper Sleeve Edging:** From right side, join CC to underarm seam at top of sleeve, work 1 sc in each row around entire edge. **Armhole Edging:** Work same as Sleeve Edging. Sew sleeve to armholes. **Lower Border:** From right side, join CC at seam edge and work 1 sc in row around entire lower edge, join to first sc with a sl st. Ch 1, turn. Work in sc for 5 rows more. Fasten off. **Sleeve Border:** Work same as Lower Border.

9 ⊗ ⏀
Drop-shouldered boatneck & brimmed hat

SIZES: Small (6-8), Medium (10-12), Large (14-16).

MATERIALS: American Thread Dawn Sayelle® knitting worsted weight 8 (8, 8) 4 oz. skeins camel.
Knitting needles, one pair No. 13.
One crochet hook size K.
2 large buttons.

GAUGE: 8 sts = 3 inches;
7 rows = 2 inches.

Blocking Measurements

Sizes	Small (6-8)	Medium (10-12)	Large (14-16)
Actual Knitting Measurements			
Bust (In Inches)			
	35¼	37½	41¼
Back Length			
	22¼	23½	24½
Sleeve underarm (with cuff rolled)			
	15½	16	16

Boatneck

Notes: Entire garment is worked in reverse stockinette st: p 1 row, k 1 row. Work with double strand of yarn throughout. **BODY (Make 2):** Beg at hem with No. 13 needles, cast on 49 (52, 57) sts. **ROWS 1 through 77 (81, 85):** Work even in reverse stockinette st. **ROW 78 (82, 86):** Bind off. **SLEEVE (Make 2):** Beg at cuff edge with No. 13 needles, cast on 46 (46, 50) sts. **ROWS 1 through 95 (97, 97):** Work even in reverse stockinette st. **ROW 96 (98, 98):** Bind off, leaving yarn end about 2 yds. long for sl st. **FINISHING:** Steam all pieces lightly. Right shoulder: Join body pieces tog at bound-off rows for 4¼ (4¼, 4½) inches from right edge with size K crochet hook and sl st. Fasten off. Left shoulder: Work as for right shoulder for 1 (1, 1¼) inch. Work remaining 2 inches with button lps on one bound-off edge as follows: * Ch 3, skip 2 bound-off sts, sl st in next 2 sts; repeat from * once more; continue by working 1 row sc around neck edge. Fasten off. Join sleeves to body with sl st by overlapping edges and working through front lp of bound-off row, matching center of each sleeve to corresponding shoulder. Sew sleeve and body tog at side and underarm, working bottom 12 inches of sleeve seam with wrong sides tog. Work 1 row sc around hem edges. Double roll a 6 inch cuff on each sleeve. Sew on buttons.

Brimmed hat

SIZE: Brim is approximately 4 inches wide.

MATERIALS: Tahki Donegal Heavy Homespun Tweed (4 oz. skein), 1 skein main color, small amount contrasting color. Aluminum crochet hook, size I.

GAUGE: With 1 strand of yarn
3 sc = 1 inch;
3 rnds = 1 inch.

CROWN: Starting at center with 1 strand of main color, ch 3, sl st in first ch to form ring. **Rnd 1:** Work 6 sc in ring. Mark end of rnd and all succeeding rnds. **Rnd 2:** Work 2 sc in each sc around (12 sc). **Rnd 3:** * Sc in next sc, 2 sc in next sc; repeat from * around (18 sc). **Rnd 4:** * Sc in each of next 2 sc, 2 sc in next sc; repeat from * around (24 sc). Continue working making 1 more sc in sc before incs until there are 7 sc between incs (54 sc). Continue even until piece measures 6½ inches from center. **BRIM: Rnd 1:** Working with 2 strands of main color, sc around, inc'ing in every 6th sc around (63 sc). **Rnds 2, 4, 6:** Sc around. **Rnd 3:** Sc around, inc'ing in every 7th sc around (72 sc). **Rnd 5:** Sc around, inc'ing in every 8th sc around (81 sc). **Rnd 7:** Sc around, inc'ing in every 9th sc around (90 sc). Break off 1 strand main color, add contrasting color. **BORDER:** Working loosely, 2 sc in first sc, * ch 1, skip next sc, 2 sc in next sc; repeat from * around. Fasten off.   Designed by Joan Vass for Tahki Yarns

10 ⊗ ◑
Tweedy, hooded sweaterjack & big beret

SIZES: 10-12, 14-16.

MATERIALS: Bucilla Fingering Yarn (1 oz. skeins) 5 (6) skeins each of 2 contrasting colors for A, 3 (4) skeins each of 2 contrasting colors for B; Bear Brand, Fleisher's or Botany Win-Knit knitting worsted weight yarn, Color C, 16 (20) oz; Color D, 8 (12) oz.
Knitting Needles, 1 pair No. 10.

GAUGE: St st—3 sts = 1 inch;
        5 rows = 1 inch.

Blocking Measurements

Sizes	10-12	14-16
Actual Knitting Measurements		
Bust (In Inches)	36	40
Back at underarm	18	20
Each front, including facing	10½	11½
Length of sleeve at underarm	12½	13½

BACK: With one strand each of A (2 contrasting colors of fingering yarn) and D, cast on 54 (60) sts. Work in garter st—k all rows—until 4 inches from beg; ending even-numbered-wrongside row. Drop D only; join C. Note: First row on all pieces is right side row. **Next Row:** With A and C, k across. Continue in st st—p 1 row, k 1 row until piece measures 17½ inches from beg; ending with p row. Mark for underarm. **ARMHOLE SHAPING:** Bind off 4 sts at beg of next 2 rows. Dec 1 st each edge on next row, then every right side row 2 (3) times more—40 (44) sts. Work even in st st until 7 (7½) inches above beg of armhole shaping; ending with p row. **SHOULDER SHAPING:** Bind off 6 (7) sts at beg of next 4 rows—16 sts. Bind off. **LEFT FRONT:** With A (2 contrasting colors of fingering yarn) and D, cast on 31 (34) sts. Work in garter st as for Back for 4 inches; ending wrong side row. Drop D; join C. **Next Row:** Right side—K across 23 (26) sts; sl remaining 8 sts to holder for border. Continue in st st—p 1 row, k 1 row—until same as back to underarm; ending with a p row. Mark for underarm. **ARMHOLE SHAPING:** Bind off 4 sts at beg of next row. Work 1 row even. Dec 1 st at armhole edge on next row, then every right side row 2 (3) times more—16 (18) sts.

Work even until 6 inches above underarm marker. Mark for neck. **NECK AND SHOULDER SHAPING:** Dec 1 st at neck edge every row twice, then every other row twice more—12 (14) sts. At the same time, when same length as back to shoulder, bind off as for right back shoulder. **FRONT BAND:** With A and D, sl sts from holder to needle and work in garter st until same length as front to neck marker. Bind off. Sew band to front edge, with bound-off row at first neck dec. Mark for 7 buttons evenly spaced, with the first about 1 inch from lower edge, and the last about ¾ inch from neck edge. **RIGHT FRONT:** Work as for left front, reversing band placement and shaping, and working buttonholes in front band, opposite markers, as follows: k 3, bind off 2 sts, k 3. In next row, cast on 2 sts over bound-off sts of previous row. **SLEEVES:** With 1 strand each of B (2 contrasting colors of fingering yarn) and C, cast on 38 (42) sts. Work even in garter st until 8 inches from beg; ending wrong side row. Drop C; join D. Continue in garter st until 13 inches from beg, ending wrong side row. Drop B; join A. Continue in garter st until 18 inches from beg, ending wrong side row. Drop B; join C. Continue in garter st until 20 inches from beg, ending wrong side row. **CAP SHAPING:** Bind off 4 sts at beg of next 2 rows—30 (34) sts. Dec 1 st each edge on next row, then every 4th row 7 (8) times more—14 (16) sts. Bind off 5 sts at beg of next 2 rows. Bind off remaining 4 (6) sts. **HOOD:** With No. 10 needles and A and D, cast on 74 sts. Work in garter st for 4 inches, ending wrong side row. Drop A; join B. K across first 37 sts; sl remaining sts to holder for other half of hood. Continuing in garter st, dec 1 st at beg of next row—seam edge—then 1 st at same edge every 3rd row 6 times—31 sts. Drop D; join C. Working in garter st, continue dec as before until 26 sts remain. Bind off. Sl sts from holder to needle and work as for first side, reversing shaping. **FINISHING:** Block. Sew shoulder seams. Sew bands to fronts. Sew back seam of hood; sew hood to sweater with front edges at front band seam, easing fullness. Sew in sleeves, sew side and sleeve seams, sewing last 4 inches of sleeve seam on wrong side of sleeve—right side for cuff. **BELT:** With B and D, cast on 9 sts. **Row 1:** Sl 1 as if to p, * k 1, p 1; repeat from * across. **Row 2:** Sl 1 as if to p, * p 1, k 1; repeat from * across. Repeat Rows 1 and 2 until 52 inches from beg. Bind off loosely in ribbing. Steam lightly.

Big beret

SIZE: 10 inches in diameter.

MATERIALS: Tahki Donegal Knitting Worsted (2 oz. skeins) 2 skeins.
Aluminum Crochet Hook, Size I.

GAUGE: 3½ sc = 1 inch;
        3 rnds = 1 inch.

Work as for small beret, page 153, but continue inc rnds until there are 14 sc between incs (96 sc). Work even for 3 rnds or until piece measures slightly more than 10 inches in diameter. NEXT 8 RNDS: Sc around, dec'ing 6 sc evenly around—to dec (draw up a loop in next sc) twice; yo, draw through 3 loops on hook (48 sc). Next Rnd: Sc around, dec'ing 4 sc evenly around (44 sc). Work even for 1 rnd. Finish as for small beret.
Designed by Joan Vass for Tahki Yarns

11 ⊗ ⦶
Hooded, cabled, handy as a parka & baby cap

SIZES: Small (6-8), Medium (10-12), Large (14-16).

MATERIALS: Columbia-Minerva Nantuk® Bulky, (2 oz. skein), 18 (19, 20) skeins.
Knitting Needles, Circular needle No. 11 and 1 pair straight needles No. 11 and 1 double-pointed needle.
Crochet Hook, Size H.

GAUGE: 3 sts = 1 inch;
         4 rows = 1 inch.

Blocking Measurements

Sizes	6-8	10-12	14-16
Actual Knitting Measurements (In Inches)			
Bust			
	35	38	42
Sleeves at upperarm			
	14	14¾	15

BACK: Beg at lower edge, cast on 50 (54, 60) sts. Work in garter st (k each row) for 8 rows. Beg on the wrong side work in st st (p 1 row, k 1 row) until piece measures 14 inches or 2½ inches less than desired length to underarm, ending on the right side. Beg working in garter st and work for 10 rows. SHAPE ARM-HOLES: Working in garter st bind off 3 sts at beg of next 2 rows. Dec 1 st at each end every other row twice. Place remaining 40 (44, 50) sts on a holder. Fasten off. FRONT: Beg at lower edge, cast on 56 (60, 66) sts. Row 1 (right side): K 6 (8, 11), (p 1, k 6, p 1, k 10) twice; p 1, k 6, p 1, k 6 (8, 11) - 3 Cable panels. Row 2: K 7 (9, 12), p 6, (k 12, p 6) twice; k 7 (9, 12). Row 3 (Cable Row): K 6 (8, 11), (p 1, place 3 sts on dpn, hold in back, k next 3 sts, k 3 sts from dpn (Cable made), p 1, k 10) twice; p 1, Cable, p 1, k 6 (8, 11). Rows 4 through 9: Repeat Rows 2 and 1. Row 10: P 6 (8, 11), (k 1, p 6, k 1, p 10) twice; k 1, p 6, k 1, p 6 (8, 11). Row 11: Repeat Row 1. Row 12: Repeat Row 10. Row 13: Repeat Row 3. Keeping panels between Cables in st st (k on right side, p on wrong side), repeat Cable Row every 10th row until piece measures 5 inches, ending on the wrong side. POCKET OPENINGS: K 5 (7, 10), inc 1 st in next st, join another skein of yarn to left-hand needle, cast on 2 sts for pocket border, k these 2 sts, work in pattern as established to within last 8 (10, 13) sts, (inc 1 st next st) twice (end of center panel and beg of pocket border); join another skein of yarn, inc 1 st in next st, k next 5 (7, 10) sts. Row 2: P 6 (8, 11) sts, k 1, with next skein of yarn k 2, work in pattern as established to within last 2 sts of center panel, k 2, with next skein of yarn, k 1, p 6 (8, 11). Keeping all inc sts in garter st work in pattern as established until opening is 6½ inches, ending on the wrong side. JOINING: K 5 (7, 10) sts, skip next st, sl next st over skip st, with this st still on left-hand needle k this st, fasten off yarn, with next skein of yarn bind off next 2 sts, work pattern to within 2 sts of pocket border, bind off next 2 sts, k 1 st remaining from bind-off and next st tog, fasten off yarn, with remaining yarn k 6 (8, 11). Work in pattern as established until piece measures 2½ inches less than Back to underarm, ending on the right side. Keeping cable panels as established work st st panels in garter st until piece measures same as Back to underarm, ending on the wrong side. SHAPE ARMHOLES: Keeping continuity of

pattern bind off 3 sts at beg of next 2 rows. Dec 1 st at each end every other row twice. Place remaining 46 (50, 56) sts on a holder. Fasten off. SLEEVES: Beg at lower edge, cast on 42 (44, 46) sts. Work in garter st for 5½ inches. Row 1: K 17 (18, 19), p 1, k 6, p 1, k 17 (18, 19) - 1 Cable panel. Row 2: P 17 (18, 19), k 1, p 6, k 1, p 17 (18, 19). Row 3 (Cable Row): K 17 (18, 19), p 1, Cable, p 1, k 17 (18, 19). Work in pattern as established working Cable row every 10th row until piece measures 15 inches, or 2½ less than desired length, ending on the right side. Keeping Cable panel as established work st st panels in garter st for 10 rows, ending on the wrong side. SHAPE ARMHOLES: Bind off 3 sts at beg of next 2 rows. Dec 1 st at each end every other row twice. Place remaining 32 (34, 36) sts on holder. Fasten off. YOKE: Row 1: With right side facing divide Front evenly in half. With circular needle beg at last 3 sts of center cable twist, join yarn and k next 3 sts, work garter st panel, p 1, k 6, p 1, work garter st panel, place marker, work in pattern across one Sleeve, place marker, k across sts for Back, place marker, work in pattern across 2nd Sleeve, place marker, work in pattern across Front to beg, do not join - 150 (162, 178) sts. Working back and forth, work in pattern as established for 1 row. Dec Row: Work to within first marker, * sl marker, k 2 tog, work to within 2 sts of next marker, k 2 tog *, (2 sts dec on sleeve), repeat between *s twice, ending sl marker, work to end (6 sts dec). Repeat Dec Row every 4th row 7 times, then every other row 4 (6, 6) times, and at the same time, 2 sts from front edge dec 1 every 4th row 5 times. On next row work in pattern as established to beg of Back sts, k 2 tog across Back only 8 (8, 11) times; then work in pattern as established across remaining sts. HOOD: Working on 60 (60, 73) sts work garter st between Front and Sleeve Cables and keeping continuity of Cable and garter st panels work for 4 rows. Next row (inc row): Work in pattern as established inc'ing 1 st after first cable, 1 st at center back and 1 st after 3rd cable. Repeat Inc Row every 6th row twice. Work in pattern on 69 (69, 82) sts until hood measures 17 inches. Fold in half, weave remaining sts tog. POCKETS: Beg at lower edge, cast on 31 sts. Row 1 (Wrong Side): K 15, sl 1, k 15. Row 2: K 1, p 29, k 1. Repeat last 2 rows 7 times. Row 17 (Dec Row): K 13, k 2 tog, k 1, k 2 tog, k 13. Row 18: K 1, p to within last st, k 1. Repeat Dec Row every other row 7 times always knitting 1 less at beg of row before dec'ing - 15 sts. Next row: K 8, fold work in half, * with dpn take 2 sts from right-hand needle and 1 st from left-hand needle, k these 3 tog, take remaining st and 1 st from left-hand needle, k these 2 tog, repeat from * across. On wrong side sew pocket along straight edge for 2 inches. FINISHING: On wrong side, sew pockets to pocket openings on Front. Sew side and sleeve seams. Sew bound-off edges of sleeves to bound-off edges of underarm. Sew pocket borders to sweater. EDGING: With right side facing, sc evenly around lower edge, join with sl st to first sc. Working from left to right for reverse sc, sc in each sc around, join to first sc. Fasten off. Repeat edging along pocket openings, Sleeve and Hood edges.
Designed by Viola Sylbert for Columbia-Minerva

Baby cap

MATERIALS: Tahki Donegal Knitting Worsted (2 oz. skein) 2 skeins.
Aluminum crochet hook, size I.

GAUGE: 3 dc = 1 inch;
         3 dc rnds = 1¾ inches.

Starting at center, ch 3. Join with sl st to form ring. Rnd 1: Ch 3, 7 dc in ring; join with sl st (8 dc, counting ch 3 as 1 st). Rnd 2: Ch 3, dc in sl st, 2 dc in each dc around; join (16 dc). Rnd 3: Ch 3, * 2 dc in next dc, dc in next dc; repeat from * around, ending 2 dc in last dc; join (24 dc). Rnd 4: Ch 3, dc in next dc, * 2 dc in next dc, 1 dc in each of next 2 dc; repeat from * around, ending 2 dc in last dc; join (32 dc). Rnds 5 and 6: Continue in pattern as established, making 1 more dc between incs on each rnd (48 dc at end of 6th rnd). Rnd 7: * Sc in next dc, ch 1, skip next dc; repeat from * around, join to first sc. Rnd 8: Sc in first sc, * dc OVER ch-1 going into next st of rnd below - Rnd 6, sc in next sc of Rnd 7; repeat from * around, ending dc over last ch-1 going into last st

of rnd below; join. **Rnd 9:** Sc around; join. Work rnds 7, 8, and 9 four more times. **At the same time** inc 6 sts evenly around on rnd 12 (54 sts). Fasten off. **FLAPS:** Hold cap with first st of last rnd facing you. Attach yarn 8 sts to left and work in sc in each of next 9 sts, ch 1. Turn. **Next (dec) Row:** Sc across, dec'ing 1 st at beg and end of rnd, ch 1. Turn. Repeat Dec Row until 1 sc remains, ch 25. Fasten off. Attach yarn 17 sts to the right of first st of last rnd of cap. Work 2nd flap to correspond with first flap. **FINISHING:** Attach yarn at center back (first st of last rnd of cap). Sc in each st to flap, sc in ends of rows of flap, sc in each ch of ch 25, working 3 sc in last ch; sc in opposite side of each ch and continue around entire cap in this manner. Fasten off.
Designed by Joan Vass for Tahki Yarns

12 ⊙ ⊙
Chunky, crunchy sweaterjack & cap

SIZE: Sweaterjack: Small (8-10), Medium (12-14), Large (16-18)
Cap: One size fits all.

MATERIALS: Coats & Clark's Red Heart Wintuk® 4 Ply, a knitting worsted weight yarn, Art. E. 267, (4 oz. skeins): 8 (9, 10) skeins No. 688 Forest Green
Red Heart Wintuk® Clansman Sport Yarn, Art. E. 281-C, 2 Ply (1¾ oz. skeins): 8 (9, 10) skeins No. 926 Dundee.
Crochet Hook, Size I.

GAUGE: 11 sts = 4 inches;
         2 rows = 1 inch.
Use 1 strand of Green and 1 strand of Dundee held together throughout.

Blocking Measurements

Sizes	Small (8-10)	Medium (12-14)	Large (16-18)
Body Bust Size (In Inches)	31½-32½	34-36	38-40
Actual Crocheting Measurements Bust (Sweaterjack wrapped)	34	38	42
Width across back at lower edge	21½	22	24
Width across back at underarm	16½	18	20
Width across each front below neck shaping	12	13	14
Length from shoulder to lower edge	29	30½	31½
Length of side seam	22	22½	23
Length of sleeve seam (excluding cuff)	17½	18	18½
Width across sleeve at upper arm	13½	14	14½

Sweaterjack

BACK: Starting at lower edge with 1 strand each of Green and Dundee held together, ch 59 (62, 67) to measure 22½ (23, 25) inches. **Row 1 (right side):** H dc in 3rd ch from hook and in each

ch across—57 (60, 65) h dc; **do not count chain at beg of row as one st.** Ch 2, turn. **Row 2:** H dc in first h dc and in each h dc across—57 (60, 65) h dc. **Do not count turning chain as one st.** Ch 2, turn. Repeat last row until total length is 6 (6, 7) inches. Ch 2, turn. **Side Shaping: Row 1:** *Yarn over hook and draw up a loop in each of first 2 sts, yarn over hook and draw through all 4 loops on hook—dec made;* h dc in each st across to within last 2 h dc, *yarn over hook, draw up a loop in each of next 2 sts, yarn over hook and draw through all 4 loops on hook—dec made at end of row.* Ch 2, turn. **Rows 2, 3 and 4:** Work 3 rows even (no decs) in h dc. Repeat last 4 rows (Rows 1 through 4) 4 more times—47 (50, 55) h dc. Work even in h dc until total length is 22 (22½, 23) inches. At end of last row, ch 1, turn. **Armhole Shaping: Row 1:** Sl st in each of first 4 (4, 5) sts, ch 2, h dc in next st and in each st across to within last 4 (4, 5) h dc; do not work over remaining sts. Ch 2, turn. Repeat Row 1 of Side Shaping 4 (4, 5) times—31 (34, 35) h dc. Ch 2, turn. Work even in h dc over these sts for 2 (2, 4) rows. Ch 2, turn. **Next row:** *2 h dc in first h dc—inc made;* h dc in each h dc across to last h dc, *2 h dc in last h dc—inc made at end of row.* Ch 2, turn. **Following row:** H dc in each h dc across. Repeat last 2 rows 2 more times—37 (40, 41) h dc. Ch 2, turn. If necessary, work even in h dc until length is 7 (8, 8½) inches from first row of armhole shaping. Ch 1, turn. **Neck and Shoulder Shaping: Row 1:** Sl st in each of first 4 (5, 5) sts; ch 2, h dc in each of next 7 h dc, dec 1 h dc over next 2 h dc; do not work over remaining sts. Ch 2, turn. **Row 2:** H dc in each of first 3 h dc, sl st in next h dc. Break off and fasten. Skip next 10 (11, 12) h dc on last row made before neck shaping, using 1 strand each of Green and Dundee held together, attach yarn to next st, ch 2, dec 1 h dc over next 2 h dc; complete to correspond with opposite side, reversing shaping. **LEFT FRONT:** Starting at lower edge with 1 strand each of Green and Dundee held together, ch 40 (43, 46) to measure 14½ (15½, 16½) inches. Having 38 (41, 44) h dc on each row, work same as for Back until total length is 6 (6, 7) inches, ending with a row on wrong side. Ch 2, turn. **Side Shaping: Row 1:** Dec 1 h dc at beg of row—side edge; h dc in each h dc across. Ch 2, turn. Continuing in h dc, dec 1 h dc at side edge every 4th row 4 more times—33 (36, 39) h dc. Work even (no more decs) until total length is 16 (16½, 17) inches, ending at front edge. **Front Shaping:** Keeping side edge straight and continuing in h dc, dec 1 h dc at front edge every other row until total length is 22 (22½, 23) inches, ending at side edge. Ch 1, turn. **Armhole Shaping: Row 1:** Sl st in each of first 4 (4, 5) sts, work in h dc across to within last 2 sts, dec one st over last 2 sts. Ch 2, turn. **Row 2:** Decreasing one st at each end, work in pattern across. Ch 2, turn. Repeat last row 3 (3, 4) more times. Keeping armhole edge straight, continue in h dc, decreasing one st at neck edge on each of next 2 (3, 3) rows—12 (14, 14) h dc. Work even for 0 (0, 1) more row. Ch 2, turn. **Next row:** Working in h dc, inc 1 h dc at armhole edge and dec 1 h dc at neck edge. Ch 2, turn. **Following row:** Work even in pattern, Ch 2, turn. Repeat last 2 rows alternately 2 more times—12 (14, 14) sts. If necessary, work even until length of armhole is same as on Back, ending at armhole edge. Ch 1, turn. **Shoulder Shaping: Row 1:** Sl st in each of first 4 (4, 5) sts; work in pattern across, dec 1 h dc at end of row. Ch 2, turn. **Row 2:** H dc in each of first 3 h dc, sl st in next st. Break off and fasten. **RIGHT FRONT:** Work to correspond with Left Front, reversing shaping. **SLEEVES:** Starting at lower edge (excluding cuff) with 1 strand each of Green and Dundee held together, ch 29 (31, 33). Having 27 (29, 31) sts in each row, work in h dc same as for Back until total length is 4 inches. Ch 2, turn. Continuing in h dc as before, inc one st at each end of next row and every 5th row thereafter 5 times in all—37 (39, 41) h dc. Work even in h dc until total length is 17½ (18, 18½) inches. Ch 1, turn. **Top Shaping: Row 1:** Work same as Row 1 of Back Armhole Shaping. Work 0 (1, 2) rows even. Continuing in h dc, dec one st at each end every row until 13 sts remain. Ch 2, turn. **Next row:** *Yarn over hook, skip first st, draw up a loop in each of next 2 sts, yarn over hook and draw through all 4 loops on hook—2 sts decreased;* work in pattern across to within last 3 sts, skip next st, dec over next 2 sts. Ch 2, turn. Repeat last row once—5 h dc remain. Break off and fasten. **CUFF (Make 2):** Starting at side edge with 1 strand each of Green and Dundee held together, ch 10.

Row 1: Sc in 2nd ch from hook and in each ch across—9 sc. Ch 1, turn. **Row 2:** Working in the **back** loop only of each sc, sc in each sc across. Ch 1, turn. Repeat Row 2 until total length is 12 (12½, 13) inches. Break off and fasten. With a single strand of Green and a large darning needle, working through back loops only of sts, sew last row to starting chain. **Left Half of Collar:** Starting at lower edge with 1 strand each of Green and Dundee held together, ch 2. **Row 1 (right side):** 3 sc in 2nd ch from hook. Ch 1, turn. **Row 2:** Working in the **back** loop only of each sc, sc in each sc across. Mark last sc made for outer edge of collar. Ch 1, turn. **Row 3:** Working in **back** loop of each sc, make *2 sc in first sc—1 sc increased at outer edge;* sc in each of next 2 sc. Ch 1, turn. **Note:** Work in back loop only of each sc throughout collar. **Row 4:** Sc in each sc across. Ch 1, turn. **Row 5:** 2 sc in first sc, sc in each sc across. Ch 1, turn. Repeat last 2 rows alternately until there are 17 sc in row. Ch 1, turn. Now repeat Row 4 only over these sts until total length is (when slightly stretched) same as length of left front edge from first dec of front shaping, plus half of back of neck. Break off and fasten. **Right Half of Collar:** Work same as Left Half of Collar until Row 2 has been completed. Ch 1, turn. Mark first sc on last row for outer edge of collar. **Row 3:** Working in **back** loop only of each sc throughout, sc in each of first 2 sc, 2 sc in last sc. Ch 1, turn. **Row 4:** Sc in **back** loop of each sc across. Ch 1, turn. **Row 5:** Sc in **back** loop of each sc to within last sc, 2 sc in last sc. Repeat last 2 rows alternately until there are 17 sc. Work even until total length is same as left half of collar. Break off and fasten. **BELT:** Starting at one end with 1 strand each of Green and Dundee held together, ch 9. **Row 1:** Sc in 2nd ch from hook and in each ch across—8 sc. Ch 1, turn. Repeat Row 2 of Cuff until total length is 56 (60, 64) inches. Break off and fasten. **FINISHING:** To block, pin pieces to measurements on a padded surface; cover with a damp cloth and allow to dry; **do not press.** Using a large darning needle and Green only, sew side, shoulder and sleeve seams. Adjusting to fit, sew one edge of cuff to lower edge of sleeve, matching seams. Sew in sleeves. With right side facing, sew halves of collar together for center back seam. Starting at first dec row at front edge, sew straight edge of collar along shaped front edges of jacket and across back of neck, adjusting to fit and being careful to have seam of collar at center back of neck. Turn collar to right side. **EDGING:** With right side facing, using 1 strand each of Green and Dundee held together, attach yarn to end of first free row below collar on left front edge, ch 1, sc in same st where yarn was attached, sc evenly along left front edge, along lower edge and up right front edge to beg of collar, making 3 sc in same st at each corner. Break off and fasten. Turn cuffs to right side. Overlap right front over left front, adjusting to fit and tie belt at waist.

Cap

RIBBED CUFF: Starting at back edge, with one strand each of Green and Dundee held together, ch 22. Having 21 sc on each row, work same as for Cuff of Jacket until total length is about 23 inches, without stretching or 1 inch longer than head measurement. Break off and fasten. With Green, sew back loops of sts across last row to starting chain. **CROWN:** Starting at center top with 1 strand each of Green and Dundee held together, ch 4. Join with sl st to form ring. **Rnd 1:** Ch 2, 8 h dc in ring. Join with sl st to top back loop of first h dc. **Do not count ch-2 at beg of each rnd as one st. Rnd 2:** Ch 2, working in **back** loop only of each h dc, 2 h dc in same st used for joining, 2 h dc in each st around. Join as before—16 h dc. **Rnd 3:** Ch 2, working in **back** loop only of each h dc, h dc in same st used for joining, 2 h dc in next st, (h dc in next st, 2 h dc in next st) 7 times. Join as before—8 sts increased. **Work in back loop of each st throughout. Rnd 4:** Ch 2, h dc in same st as joining, h dc in next st, * 2 h dc in next st, h dc in each of next 2 sts. Repeat from * around, ending with 2 h dc in last st. Join as before—32 h dc. **Rnd 5:** Ch 2, increasing 8 h dc evenly spaced around (having 1 more h dc before each inc than previous rnd), h dc in next st. Join as before—40 h dc. Repeat last rnd 2 more times—56 h dc in last rnd. **Next rnd:** Ch 2, h dc in same st as joining, h dc in back loop of h dc around. Join as before. Repeat last rnd until length is 6½ inches from starting ring. Break off and fasten. Holding in cuff to fit, with a darning

needle and Green, sew one edge of cuff to lower edge of crown, allowing for stretching. Fold 2/3 of ribbed cuff to right side.

13⊕
"Tweed" cardigan margined with satin stitch

SIZES: Small (32-34), Medium (36-38), Large (40-42).

MATERIALS: Brunswick Germantown Knitting Worsted, (4 oz. skein), No. 444 Dartmouth Green 5 (5, 6) skeins, No. 4321 Russet 5 (5, 6) skeins and No. 474 Brick 1 skein for trim. Aluminum Crochet Hook, Size H.

GAUGE: 2½ hdc = 1 inch.

Note: The green and russet yarn is worked double throughout the entire cardigan and allowance has been made for style and bulkiness of this garment.

BODY OF CARDIGAN: Beg at bottom, using 1 strand each of green and russet. Chain loosely 112 (118, 124) sts. Turn, hdc in 3rd st from hook, then hdc in each st across 110 (116, 122) sts. Always chaining 2 sts to beg of each row and always being careful to hdc in 2nd st of turning ch at end of each row, work even in hdc until piece measures from beg 19 (19, 19½) inches. **SHAPE RIGHT FRONT:** Counting beg ch 2 as 1 st, hdc across 28 (30, 32) sts, turn, ch 1, then pull this st tight as to almost disappear, sl st in next st, ch 2, then work hdc across to front edge (1 dec made at arm edge). Ch 2, then work hdc back to within 1 st of arm edge (another dec made at arm edge). Repeat the first dec row 1 more time, then work even until armhole measures 6 (6¼, 6½) inches. **SHAPE NECK:** If work ended at arm edge, ch 2 then work hdc across to within 12 (13, 14) sts of end. If work ended at neck edge, sl st across first 12 (13, 14) sts, ch 2, then hdc to arm edge. Now working dec as before at neck edge, dec 1 st every row 3 times. When armhole measures 8 (8¼, 8½) inches, **SHAPE SHOULDER:** If work ended at arm edge, sl st across 4 (5, 6) sts, sc in next st, hdc across to neck edge. If work ended at neck edge, ch 2, then hdc across next 4 (4, 5) sts, sc in next st. Fasten off. **BACK:** Beg at arm edge of right front, skip 6 sts, attach yarn in next st, ch 2, then work hdc across back to within 34 (36, 38) sts of other end leaving 6 sts for other underarm and 28 (30, 32) sts for left front. Now working only on the 42 (44, 46) sts of back, dec 1 st each side (as for front) 3 times when armhole measures same as front, **SHAPE SHOULDER:** Sl st across 4 (5, 5) sts, sc in next st, hdc across to within 5 (6, 6) sts of other end, then sc in next st. Fasten off. **LEFT FRONT:** Skip the 6 sts of underarm, attach yarn in next st, ch 2, then hdc across to front edge. Work same as for right front, reversing shaping. **SLEEVES:** Ch loosely 39 (41, 43) sts, turn, hdc in 3rd st from hook, then hdc in each st across. Work even until sleeve measures 8 inches from beg. Inc 1 st each side of next row, then every following 3 inches 2 more times. When sleeve measures from beg 21 (21, 21½) inches; **SHAPE SLEEVE CAP:** Sl st across 3 sts, ch 2, then hdc across to within 3 sts of other end. Now dec 1 st each side (as for cardigan) every row 5 (6, 7) times. Sl st across 2 sts, ch 2, hdc to within 2 sts of other end. Repeat this row 1 more time then fasten off. **BELT:** Ch loosely 101 (103, 105) sts and work 5 rows hdc as for bottom of cardigan. Fasten off. Belt will measure approximately 44 (44½,

45) inches. **FINISHING:** Weave shoulder and sleeve seams. Sew sleeves in place. Work row sc up right front, then work hdc around neck edge, then row sc down left front. Fasten off. **SATIN STITCH TRIM:** Thread 2 strands of brick yarn into large needle. Mark center down each sleeve to use as guide. Work about ½ inch wide satin st (see page 126) down each sleeve center to within about 4 inches of bottom, around neck edge and each armhole. Press satin st with damp cloth and warm iron. Turn cuff back as shown.

14 ◐◐
Sweaterjack & cap—terribly tweedy

SIZES: 6, 8, 10, 12.

MATERIALS: Brunswick Germantown Knitting Worsted or Windrush (4 oz. skeins), Light Navy and Parchment: 1 skein each for cap, 4 (4, 5, 5) skeins each for sweaterjack.
Aluminum Crochet Hook, Size K.

GAUGE: 2 dc = 1 inch;
　　　　1 row = ⅞ inch.

Note 1: Use 2 strands throughout. Note 2: This coat should be worked with a big, fat, loose stitch which must be maintained or garment will not be correct size.

Sweaterjack

Using 1 strand of each color, chain 104 (106, 108, 112) sts loosely, turn and dc in 3rd ch from hook. Work dc in each chain across. Work even in this manner for 4 rows, chaining 3 each time to turn. Piece should measure approximately 51 (52, 53, 55) inches across. Place piece on flat surface and overlap each end (front edges) 7 inches. Pin in place. Center this overlap in front and mark each side edge. With safety pins that can be moved up as you work, mark a dec line half-way between center and side edge on each side of back and front (4 dec marks). Skip 1 dc at each pin in next, then every following 4th row, 5 times. Piece should measure approximately 39 (40, 41, 43) inches across. Remember overlap. When piece measures approximately 24 inches or desired length to underarm; **SHAPE ARMHOLE:** Right side: At front edge ch 2, dec 1 st, work to within 3 dc of mark at side edge or underarm, turn. **NOTE:** A ch-2 instead of ch-3 will begin to curve your neck a little. To dec, yo, insert hook in next st, pull up loop, yo, insert hook in next st, pull up loop, yo, pull yarn through half the loops, then yo and pull yarn through remaining loops. This may be done at either end of row. Sometimes you will have to work a hdc at end to keep slant or curve the same at either end. If one type dec does not look right, try another. You want to have an even slant or rounded curve. Make each side identical as possible. At arm edge ch 2, dec 1 st, work to end. At neck edge ch 2, dec 1 st, work to end. At armhole ch 2, work to end. Now dec neck edge only every other row until armhole measures 6¾ (7, 7¼, 7½) inches. **SHAPE SHOULDER:** Keeping neck edge even, at arm edge sc across 3¼ (3½, 3¾, 4) inches of shoulder, hdc in next st, dc to end. Do not break yarn. With another skein of each color, work other front the same, reversing the shaping. **BACK:** Tie in yarn 3 dc from underarm mark, ch 2, work dc across to within 3 dc of other mark at underarm. Turn, ch 2, dec 1 st, work across to last 2 sts, dec in last 2 sts, ch 2, work dc to other end, turn ch 2, then work dc even, chaining 3 as usual to turn until

armhole measures same as front. Weave or sew shoulder seam. Beg at right front edge work dc, chaining 2 to turn each time, work across lapel, on around neck edge, then across other lapel. Work 5 rows even, then dec 1 st each end of next 3 rows. Check to see that collar lies smoothly in a shawl, and that dec edges curve smoothly. **SLEEVES:** Chain loosely 20 (22, 24, 26) sts, working dc with a ch 3 to turn each time, inc 1 st every 2 rows (alternate incs, first one side of needle, then next one at other side) 6 times. When sleeve measures approximately 20 inches or 2½ inches longer than desired length to underarm, **SHAPE CAP:** Slip st across 3 dc, hdc in next st, dc across to last 4 sts, hdc in last st, ch 2. Dec 1 st each end every row 6 (6, 7, 7) times. Fasten off. Weave or sew sleeve seams. Turn up cuff 2½ inches. Sew sleeve in place. If desired sc around entire neckline and bottom. **BELT:** Using 1 strand of each color ch 130 sts loosely. Work 3 rows dc, chaining 3 to turn each time. Fasten off.

Cap:

Using 1 strand of each color, chain loosely 23 sts, then sc in 2nd ch from hook, then sc in back loop only of each ch across, ch 1. Work ribbing pattern in this manner until piece measures 25 inches in length. Ribbing should be 9 inches wide. Bring ends together and sl st to join. Do not break yarn, but working now in rounds on the ribbed band, sc 50 sts, evenly spaced around ring. Work even, maintaining a gauge to measure 10 inches across when laid flat, until hat measures 13 inches from bottom of ribbing. **1st dec rnd:** Sc in next 5 sts, skip 1 sc, repeat around to beg. **2nd dec rnd:** Sc in next 4 sts, skip 1 sc, repeat around to beg. Now, working in continuous rnds, skip every 4th sc until ½ inch hole remains. Break the yarn, leaving the end to thread in needle and finish off on wrong side. Turn the brim as shown.

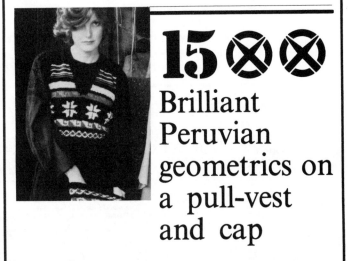

15 ⊗⊗
Brilliant Peruvian geometrics on a pull-vest and cap

SIZES: Pullover: 8, 10, 12, 14;
Cap: One size fits all.

MATERIALS: Coats & Clark's Red Heart Wintuk® knitting worsted weight yarn, Art. E. 267, 4 Ply (4 oz. skeins): 8 (9, 10, 11) ounces No. 12 Black, ½ ounce each No. 230 Yellow, No. 686 Paddy Green, No. 848 Skipper Blue, No. 737 Pink, No. 111 Eggshell, No. 902 Jockey Red and No. 515 Dk. Turquoise.
Knitting Needles, 1 pair each No. 5 and No. 7.
4 bobbins.

GAUGE: 5 sts = 1 inch;
　　　　6 rows = 1 inch.

Blocking Measurements Sizes	8	10	12	14
Body Bust Size (In Inches)	31½	32½	34	36
Actual Knitting Measurements Bust	32½	33½	35	37
Width across back or front at underarm	16¼	16¾	17½	18½

Length from shoulder to lower edge

17½	18	19	19½

Length of side seam (excluding armhole band)

10½	10½	11	11

Pull-vest

BACK: Starting at lower edge with black and No. 5 needles, cast on 74 (78, 82, 86) sts. **1st row:** K 1, * p 2, k 2. Repeat from * across, ending with p 2, k 1. **2nd row:** P 1, * k 2, p 2. Repeat from * across, ending with k 2, p 1. Repeat first and 2nd rows alternately for ribbing until total length is 3 (3, 3½, 3½) inches. **For Size 8 Only:** Inc one st at each end of last row. **For All Sizes:** Work pattern over 76 (78, 82, 86) sts as follows: Break off black and attach again when needed. Wind 4 bobbins with eggshell. Change to No. 7 needles. **Note: If 2 colors are used in same row, when changing color, always twist color not in use around the other once to prevent making holes in work. Carry color not in use loosely along wrong side of work. When strand not in use is carried across 4 or more sts, twist around strand being used, once every 4th st to hold in place. Use a separate bobbin for each of the 4 star motifs; do not carry eggshell from star to star. Pattern is worked in stockinette st (k 1 row, p 1 row). When a color is no longer in use, break off and attach next color or colors as needed.** **1st row:** With green, k 2 (3, 0, 2); attach yellow, * with yellow k 2, with green k 3. Repeat from * across, ending with k 2 yellow, with green k 2 (3, 0, 2). **2nd row:** With green p 1 (0, 2, 1), with yellow

p 1, with green p 2 (1, 2, 1), * with yellow p 1, with green p 1, with yellow p 1, with green p 2. Repeat from * across, ending last repeat with yellow p 1, with green p 1 (0, 2, 1). Starting with 3rd row, follow Chart back and forth between lines indicating desired size until the 8th row has been completed, working knitted rows from right to left and purled rows from left to right. **9th row:** Follow Chart, increasing one st at each end as indicated on Chart. Continue to follow Chart as directed, increasing one st at each end every 9th row 2 more times as indicated on Chart and attaching a separate bobbin for each star motif on the 18th row—82 (84, 88, 92) sts. Follow Chart to end of 44th row. **Armhole Shaping:** Continuing to follow Chart to end of top row for design, bind off 5 (5, 6, 6) sts at beg of next 2 rows. Dec one st at each end of next row and every other row thereafter 7 (7, 7, 8) times in all—58 (60, 62, 64) sts. With black only, work even (no more decs) in stockinette st until length is 7 (7½, 8, 8½) inches from first row of armhole shaping, ending with a p row. **Shoulder Shaping:** Bind off 8 sts at beg of next 2 rows. Bind off 7 (8, 8, 9) sts at beg of following 2 rows. Place remaining 28 (28, 30, 30) sts on a stitch holder for neckband. **FRONT:** Work same as for back until the 36th row of pattern (above ribbing) has been completed, thus ending with a wrong-side row. **Neck Shaping: 1st row:** Continuing to follow Chart for design throughout, work across first 40 (41, 43, 45) sts; place next 2 sts on a safety pin; place remaining sts on a stitch holder. Working over sts on needle only and following Chart for design, work 3 rows even. Dec one st at neck edge on next row. Work 3 rows even, ending with a p row. **Armhole Shaping: 1st row:** Continuing to follow Chart for design,

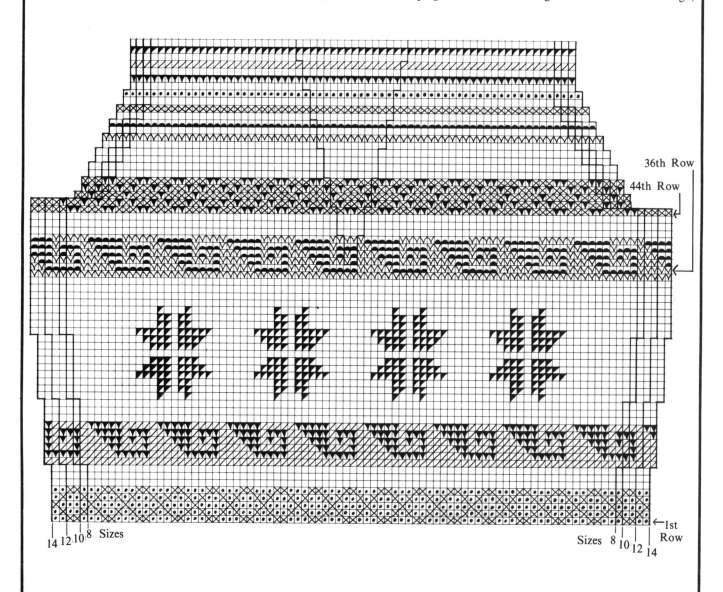

36th Row

44th Row

14 12 10 8 Sizes

Sizes 8 10 12 14

1st Row

bind off 5 (5, 6, 6) sts at beg of row, work in pattern across to within last 2 sts; *k 2 tog*-dec made at neck edge. **Note: When last row on Chart has been completed, continue with black only.** Now shape both edges as follows: Dec one st at armhole edge every other row 6 (6, 6, 7) more times, **AT THE SAME TIME,** continue to dec one st at neck edge every 4th row 7 (7, 8, 8) more times; then keeping armhole edge straight, dec at neck edge every other row 5 times—15 (16, 16, 17) sts. If necessary, work even until length of armhole is same as on Back, ending at armhole edge. **Shoulder Shaping: 1st row:** At armhole edge, bind off 8 sts; complete row. **2nd row:** P across. Bind off remaining 7 (8, 8, 9) sts. Place sts from holder on a No. 7 needle; attach yarn at neck edge and work to correspond with opposite side, reversing shaping. Block to measurements. Sew left shoulder seam. **NECKBAND:** With right side facing, using black and No. 5 needles, k sts on back holder; pick up and k 45 (49, 51, 55) sts along left front edge of neck, place a marker on needle; k the 2 center sts on safety pin, place a marker on needle; pick up and k 45 (49, 53, 57) sts along right front edge of neck—120 (128, 136, 144) sts. **1st row (wrong side):** K 1, starting with p 2, work in p 2, k 2 ribbing across to within 2 sts before next marker; k 2 tog, slip marker, p 2 for center sts, slip marker; k 2 tog, starting with p 2, work in p 2, k 2 ribbing across to end of row, ending with k 1. **2nd row:** Work in ribbing as established across to within 2 sts before next marker; p 2 tog, slip marker, k the 2 center sts, slip marker, p 2 tog, complete row in ribbing as established. Repeat 1st and 2nd rows alternately 2 more times. Bind off in ribbing, decreasing before and after the 2 center sts as before. Sew right

shoulder seam including neckband. **ARMHOLE BANDS:** With right side facing, using black and No. 5 needles, pick up and k 80 (84, 92, 96) sts evenly along entire armhole edge. Work in k 2, p 2 ribbing for 6 rows. Bind off in ribbing. Sew side seams, including armhole bands, matching rows.

Cap

Starting at lower edge with black and No. 5 needles, cast on 92 sts. Work in k 2, p 2 ribbing for 6 rows. Break off black; attach green. **1st row:** With green, k 3; attach yellow, * with yellow k 2, with green k 3. Repeat from * across, ending with k 2 green. Starting with 2nd row on Chart for Cap and working as for Pull-vest, follow Chart, increasing one st at each end of 15th row as indicated on Chart; then, continue over 94 sts until the 30th row on Chart has been completed, ending with a wrong-side row. Continuing in stockinette st and following Chart for design, work top shaping as follows: **Top Shaping: 1st row:** K 2 tog, k 20, sl 1, k 1, psso, place a marker on needle; (k 2 tog, k 19, sl 1, k 1, psso) twice; k 2 tog, k 20, sl 1, k 1, psso—8 sts decreased. **2nd row:** Slipping markers, p across. **Note: Always slip markers. 3rd row:** * K 2 tog, k to within 2 sts before next marker, sl 1, k 1, psso. Repeat from * 3 more times. Following Chart for placement of colors, repeat 2nd and 3rd rows alternately until 14 sts in all remain, ending with a p row. Break off, leaving a 12-inch length of yarn. Using a darning needle, draw this end through remaining sts, pull tightly and sew back seam. Steam lightly.

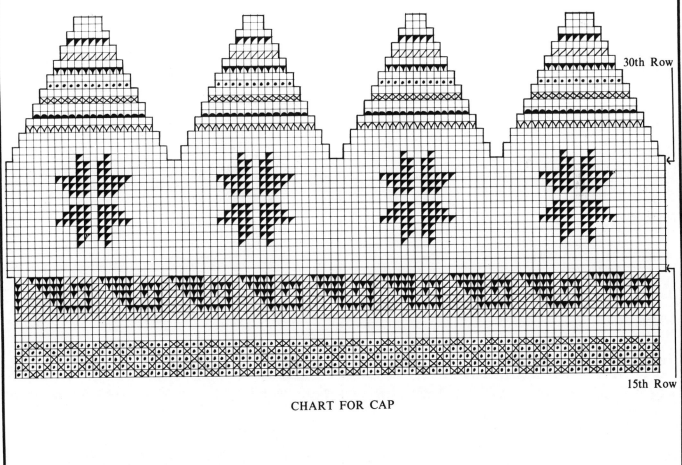

30th Row

15th Row

CHART FOR CAP

COLOR KEY

⊠ = YELLOW   ⊿ = BLUE   ◪ = EGGSHELL   ⊡ = RED

⊡ = GREEN   ▼ = PINK   ◩ = TURQUOISE   ☐ = BLACK

16 ⊗

Icelandia—a long wrappy cardigan trekked with zigzags

SIZES: Small (10-12), Medium (14-16), Large (18-20).

MATERIALS: Reynolds Lopi, 6 (7, 8) skeins Grey #56 (color A), and 1 skein each Natural White #51 (color B) and Dark Brown #52 (color C).
Knitting Needles, Circular needles (29 inch), 1 each No. 9 and No. 11, 1 pair each straight needles No. 9 and No. 11.
Steel Crochet Hook, Size 0.

GAUGE: On No. 11 needles,
3 sts = 1 inch;
4 rows = 1 inch.

Blocking Measurements

Sizes	10-12	14-16	18-20
Body Bust Size (In Inches)			
	32¼-34	36-38	40-42
Actual Knitting Measurements			
Bust with border (closed)			
	37	41	45
Width of sleeve at upperarm			
	14	15	16
Length of body to underarm			
	20½	20½	20½

SPECIAL NOTES: Body and yoke are worked back and forth on circular needle. **To Follow Chart: Odd Rows** (right side): Knit from right to left on chart; on **Even Rows:** Purl from left to right on chart. Do not use bobbins for color changes; wind pattern colors into small balls. Change color on wrong side, lock strands by picking up new color from under dropped color. Carry colors not being used loosely across back of work. Cut and join colors as needed. Run in all yarn ends. **BODY:** Beg at lower edge of front and back, with No. 9 circular needle and A, cast on 111 (123, 135) sts. Do not join. Work in k 1, p 1 ribbing for 3 inches. Change to No. 11 circular needle. Work in stockinette st (k 1 row, p 1 row) for 2 rows. **PATTERN:** (see Special Notes): Following chart, work in stockinette st, beg at arrow on row 1. Work pattern repeat across row ending as indicated by arrow. Work to top of chart. Work in stockinette st with A only for 4 inches. Following chart work 26 rows same as before. Break off B and C. With A k 1 row, knitting tog the 58th and 59th (64th and 65th, 70th and 71st) sts—110 (122, 134) sts. **Divide Work: Next Row** (wrong side): P 26 (28, 30) sts for left front, bind off next 3 (5, 7) sts for underarm, p until 52 (56, 60) sts beyond bound-off sts for back, bind off next 3 (5, 7) sts for underarm, p remaining sts for right front. Lay work aside. **SLEEVES:** With No. 9 straight needles and A, cast on 28 (32, 34) sts. Work in k 1, p 1 ribbing for 2½ inches. Change to No. 11 straight needles. K 1 row, inc 4 (3, 4) sts evenly spaced across row)—32 (35, 38) sts. P next row. Continue in stockinette st inc 1 st each edge of next row, then every 4th row 4 times more—42 (45, 48) sts. Work even until sleeve measures 9 inches from beg (note: sleeve length is planned for 17 inches, make any adjustments here before starting pattern), ending on

wrong side. **PATTERN:** Following chart, work in stockinette st, beg at arrow on row 1. **For Small and Large Sizes:** Work pattern repeat only. **For Medium Size:** Work pattern repeat across row ending as indicated by arrow as on body. Work to top of chart. Break off B and C. With A bind off 2 (3, 3) sts at beg of next row. Then bind off 2 (2, 3) sts at beg of next row. Put remaining 38 (40, 42) sts on a colored strand of yarn. Work 2nd sleeve. **YOKE:** From right side, put on No. 11 circular needle sts of right front, place a marker on needle, one sleeve, place a marker on needle, back, place a marker on needle, other sleeve, place a marker on needle, left front—180 (192, 204) sts. **Shape Raglan and Neck** (at same time): Work with A only hereafter. **Next Row** (right side): * K to within 2 sts of marker, k 2 tog, sl marker, sl 1, k 1, psso; repeat from * across all markers, finish row (8 decs made). **Next Row:** Purl. Repeat these 2 rows 16 (17, 18) times in all; **and at the same time,** dec 1 st at each neck edge every 3rd row 10 (11, 12) times. Bind off remaining 32 (34, 36) sts. **RIGHT COLLAR AND FRONT BAND:** With No. 9 straight needles and A, cast on 6 sts. Work in garter st (k each row) for 23 inches. Inc 1 st at end of next row, then every other row at same edge until there are 22 sts. Continue in garter st until piece reaches from lower right front edge of cardigan to center back of neck. Slip sts on st holder, break yarn (leave an 18 inch end for weaving on right front band). **LEFT COLLAR AND FRONT BAND:** Work same as right collar and front band; garter stitch is reversible. Weave the 2 bands tog at back of neck, making an invisible seam (see Diagram). Fasten securely and weave in ends. **FINISHING:** Steam press pieces lightly. Weave bound-off underarm sts tog. Weave sleeve seams. **Join Front Bands and Collar:** Beg at lower right front edge and holding inc edge of band piece toward front edge of cardigan, with crochet hook and A, * work a sl st on front edge and then a sl st on band piece. Repeat from * around fronts and neck edges, keeping joining edge flat. **BELT:** With No. 9 straight needles and A, cast on 12 sts. Work in k 1, p 1 ribbing for 56 inches or desired belt length. Bind off loosely in ribbing.

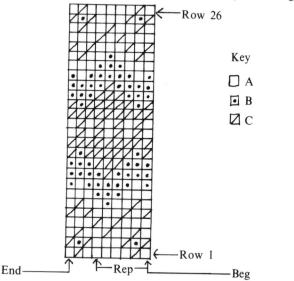

Key
□ A
⊡ B
⬓ C

←Row 26

←Row 1

End———— ⌐Rep⌐ ————Beg

TO MAKE AN INVISIBLE SEAM: The stitches are held facing each other and must be slipped off the holders a few at a time, and taken alternately as in the diagram. The first as is shown by the needle in the diagram, and the second and third by two arrows.

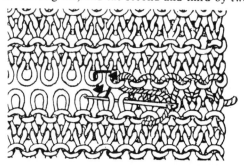

17 ⊗
Fair Islanders: pull/beret mittens

SIZES: 8, 10, 12.

MATERIALS: Knitting Worsted, (4 oz. skeins), 4 (4, 5) skeins Main Color (MC), 1 skein each Olive Green (A) and Brick (B), 1 oz. each Burgundy (C), Blue (D) and Rose (E).
Knitting Needles, Circular needles 16 inch and 29 inch, 1 each No. 5 and No. 8.
Double-pointed Needles, 1 set each No. 5 and No. 8.

GAUGE: On No. 8 needles:
    5 sts = 1 inch;
    6 rows = 1 inch.

Pullover

Knitted in one piece to underarm. With No. 5 29 inch circular needle and MC, cast on 152 (160, 172) sts. Join, being careful not to twist sts. Work in k 2, p 2 ribbing for 2 inches, inc or dec on last row to 153 (162, 171) sts. Change to No. 8 needle and st st (k every rnd). Working from chart 1, repeat the 9 sts across rnd for 8 rnds. K even for 1 (2, 3) rnds. Working from chart 2, repeat the 9 sts on next 8 rnds; then repeat the 9 sts of chart 3 on next 7 rnds. With C, k 2 rnds; with MC, k 18 rnds; with C, k 2 rnds. Repeat from chart 1 through chart 3 once more. **DIVIDE AND SHAPE ARMHOLES:** With MC, work across 73 (77, 82) sts; bind off next 8 sts; work across 68 (73, 77) sts of back; bind off next 8 sts. Working on remaining 69 (73, 78) sts of front, dec 1 st each end every other row 3 times. Work 2 rows even. With A, work 1 row. With MC, work 4 rows. **Next row:** * With MC, work 4 sts; with E, k 1 st; repeat from * across row. With MC, work even for 4 rows; with A, work 1 row. With MC, work until armholes are 4¾ (5, 5¼) inches. **SHAPE NECK:** Work across 22 (24, 26) sts; sl next 19 (19, 20) sts on holder; attach another skein of yarn and work across to end. Using 2 skeins, at each neck edge, dec 1 st every other row 3 times—19 (21, 23) sts. Work even until armholes are 6¾ (7, 7¼) inches. **SHAPE SHOULDERS:** At each arm edge, bind off 6 (7, 8) sts every other row twice; then 7 sts once. **BACK:** With MC, dec 1 st each end every other row 3 times. Work 2 rows even. Finish as for front, omitting neck shaping and slipping remaining 24 (25, 25) sts of back neck on holder. **SLEEVES:** With No. 5 circular needle, cast on with MC, 36 (36, 40) sts. Work back and forth as on straight needles. Work in k 2, p 2 ribbing for 2 inches increasing 8 (10, 8) sts evenly on last row. Change to No. 8 needle and repeat the 4 sts of chart 4 across row on next 7 rows. Work with MC only. Inc 1 st each end every 6th row until there are 58 (60, 62) sts. Work even until 14½ (15½, 16½) inches from beg or desired length to underarm. **SHAPE CAP:** Bind off 4 sts at beg of next 2 rows. Dec 1 st each end every other row 8 (9, 10) times. Bind off 3 sts at beg of next 6 rows. Bind off remaining 16 sts. **FINISHING:** Sew seams. Sew in sleeves. **NECKBAND:** With No. 5 circular needle (16 inch) and MC, pick up and k 24 (25, 25) sts from back holder; pick up and k 13 (14, 15) sts along side of neck; pick up and k sts from front holder, increasing 1 (0, 1) sts; pick up and k 13 (14, 15) sts along other side of neck. Join. Work around in k 1, p 1 ribbing for 8 rnds—70 (72, 76) sts. Bind off in ribbing loosely.

Sweater Charts

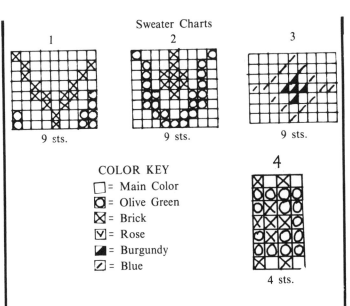

1 — 9 sts.
2 — 9 sts.
3 — 9 sts.

COLOR KEY
☐ = Main Color
◯ = Olive Green
⊗ = Brick
☑ = Rose
◣ = Burgundy
◿ = Blue

4 — 4 sts.

Beret

With No. 5 circular needle or dp needle, with MC, cast on 100 sts. Join, being careful not to twist sts. Work around in k 1, p 1 ribbing for 8 rnds. Change to No. 8 needle. **Next rnd:** * K 4, inc 1 st in next st; repeat from * around—120 sts. Work 1 rnd even. Now work the 12 sts from chart 1 across on next 9 rnds. With MC, work 1 rnd. Repeat the 4 sts of chart 2 for next 3 rnds. With MC, work 1 rnd. Repeat the 12 sts of chart 3 on next 9 rnds. With MC, work 1 rnd even. **Dec rnd:** * K 1, k 2 tog; repeat from * around (80 sts). Work 1 rnd even. **CENTER OF BERET:** Work the 16 sts of chart 4, dec 1 st each side of **center stitch of each 16 st repeat,** beg with 3rd row; then every other row until 10 sts remain. **Rnd 16:** K 2 tog around. Break yarn, leaving a length to run through remaining sts. End off on wrong side. Cut a 10 inch wide circle from cardboard and insert into beret and press. Remove cardboard.

Beret Chart 1

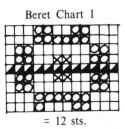

= 12 sts.

Beret Chart 2

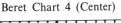

= 4 sts.

Beret Chart 3

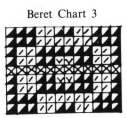

= 12 sts.

Beret Chart 4 (Center)

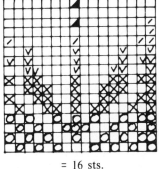

= 16 sts.

Mitten Chart

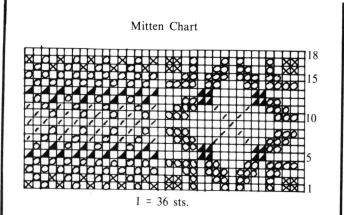

1 = 36 sts.

Mittens

RIGHT MITTEN: With No. 5 dp needles and MC, cast on 36 sts. Divide evenly on 3 needles. Work around in k 2, p 2 ribbing for 2 inches. Change to No. 8 needles. Follow chart 1 from rnd 1 through 15. **Next rnd: THUMB POSITION:** Work first 18 sts of rnd 16 for right hand and 31 sts of rnd 16 for left hand; then using a color yarn that is not in the color sequence k 5 sts and sl these 5 sts back on left hand needle and k them again from chart. When rnd 18 is completed, repeat from rnd 1 until 6 inches from end of cuff. **SHAPE TOP:** Continuing to work in color pattern, work as follows. **Next rnd:** K 1, k 2 tog through back loop only (TBL); work 12 sts; k 2 tog, k 1, k 1, k 2 tog TBL; work next 12 sts; k 2 tog, k 1. **Next rnd:** K 1, k 2 tog TBL; work next 10 sts, k 2 tog; k 1, k 1, k 2 tog TBL; work next 10 sts, k 2 tog, k 1. Continue in this manner, dec 4 sts each rnd until 12 sts remain. Break yarn, leaving a length to weave the 6 sts of front and back tog. **THUMB:** Remove the yarn from the 5 sts of thumb opening and sl them onto No. 5 dp needle for lower edge of thumb. Turn mitten upside down and sl the 4 loops onto another dp needle, picking up 1 more st at each end. Change to No. 8 needles and MC. K even for 7 rnds. Change to No. 5 dp needles and work around until thumb is 2 inches. **Next rnd:** * K 1, k 2 tog; repeat from * around. **Next rnd:** K 2 tog, ending k 1. Break yarn, leaving an end to fasten off on wrong side. **LEFT MITTEN:** Work as for right mitten, placing thumb at other side of palm. Insert mitten shaped cardboard and press. Remove cardboard.

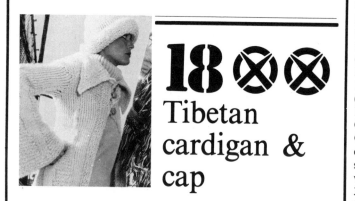

18 ⊗⊗ Tibetan cardigan & cap

SIZES: Cardigan: Small, Medium, Large; Cap: One size fits all.

MATERIALS: Spinnerin Susi, a heavy boucle-type yarn, (100 gram balls) 9 (10, 11) balls Main Yarn (MC); Germantown Deluxe or Marvel Twist Deluxe Knitting Worsted, (4 oz. balls) 4 (5, 5) balls Contrasting Yarn (CC).
Knitting Needles, 1 pair No. 10½.
Aluminum Crochet Hook, Size J.

GAUGE: 3 sts = 1 inch;
5 rows = 1 inch.

Blocking Measurements			
Sizes	Small	Medium	Large
Actual knitting measurements (In Inches)			
Bust			
	33½	37½	41½
Sleeve at upperarm			
	12½	14	15½

NOTE 1: Carry Yarn not in use loosely in back of work, taking care to maintain gauge and have MC strands lie on top of CC strands. **NOTE 2:** All MC sts are worked in Garter St (k every row). All CC sts are worked in Twist Knit (knit st through back loop, twisting it). Purl sts are worked as usual. **BACK:** With No. 10½ needles and MC cast on 68 (76, 84) sts. Work in Garter St for 1 inch. **GORE PATTERN—Row 1:** With MC k 12 (13, 14), attach CC, with CC k 2, * with MC, k 12 (14, 16), with CC k 2; repeat from * 2 times more, ending with MC k 12 (13, 14). **Row 2:** With MC k 12 (13, 14), with CC p 2, * with MC k 12 (14, 16), with CC p 2; repeat from * 2 times more, ending with MC k 12 (13, 14). **Rows 3 and 4:** Repeat Rows 1 and 2. **Row 5:** With MC, k 2 tog, k 9 (10, 11), with CC k 4, * with MC k 10 (12, 14), with CC k 4; repeat from * 2 times more, ending with MC k 9 (10, 11), k 2 tog—66 (74, 82) sts. **Row 6:** With MC k 10 (11, 12), with CC p 4, * with MC k 10 (12, 14), with CC p 4; repeat from * 2 times more, ending with MC k 10 (11, 12). Work in pattern for 12 (10, 8) rows, **and at the same time** dec 1 st each side every 8th row 7 (8, 9) times. **Row 19 (17, 15):** With MC k 7 (8, 9), with CC k 6, * with MC k 8 (10, 12), with CC k 6; repeat from * 2 times more, ending with MC k 7 (8, 9). Continue working Gore pattern working 2 sts more in each CC gore every 16 (14, 12) rows until there are 12 (14, 16) sts in each CC gore and 2 sts in each of remaining 3 MC gores. Work in pattern on 52 (58, 64) sts to 18 (19½, 19½) inches from beg or desired length to underarm, ending on wrong side. **ARMHOLES—Row 1:** With CC bind off 3 (4, 5) sts, k 21 (23, 25), with MC k 4, with CC k to end. **Row 2:** With CC bind off 3 (4, 5) sts, p 20 (22, 24), with MC k 6, with CC, p to end. **Row 3:** With CC, k 2 tog, k 18 (20, 22), with MC k 8, with CC k to last 2 sts, k 2 tog. **Row 4:** With CC p 17 (19, 21), with MC k 10, with CC p to end. Continue to dec 1 st each side every other row 2 times more **and at the same time** work 2 sts more in MC every row until all sts are worked in MC. Break CC. Continue with MC on 40 (44, 48) sts until armhole measures 7½ (8, 8½) inches. **SHOULDERS:** Bind off 4 sts beg of next 4 rows, 4 (5, 6) sts next 2 rows. Bind off remaining 16 (18, 20) for back of neck. **LEFT FRONT:** With No. 10½ needles and MC cast on 30 (34, 38) sts. Work in Garter St for 1 inch. **GORE PATTERN— Row 1:** With MC, k 12 (13, 14), with CC k 2, with MC k 12 (14, 16), with CC k 4 (5, 6). **Row 2:** With CC p 4 (5, 6), with MC k 12 (14, 16), with CC p 2, with MC k 12 (13, 14). **Rows 3 and 4:** Repeat Rows 1 and 2. **Row 5:** With MC k 2 tog, k 9 (10, 11), with CC k 4, with MC k 10 (12, 14), with CC k 5 (6, 7). Continue in Gore Pattern as for back **and at the same time** dec 1 st at side edge every 8th row 7 (8, 9) times. Work on 22 (25, 28) sts (having one 2-st MC gore), to same length as back to underarm, ending on wrong side. **ARMHOLE—Row 1:** At side edge, with CC bind off 3 (4, 5) sts, k to end. **Row 2:** With CC, p. **Row 3:** With CC k 2 tog, k to end. **Row 4:** With MC k 1, with CC p to end. **Row 5:** With CC k 2 tog, k to last 2 sts, with MC k 2. **Row 6:** With MC k 3, with CC p to end. **Row 7:** With CC k 2 tog, k to last 4 sts, with MC k 4. Continue on 16 (18, 20) sts, working 1 st more MC every row as established until all sts are worked in MC. Break off CC and continue with MC only. Work until armhole measures 5½ (6, 6½) inches, ending on right side. **NECK:** At front edge bind off 2 (3, 4) sts. Dec 1 st every other row 2 times. Work on 12 (13, 14) sts until armhole measures same as back to shoulder. **SHOULDER:** At side edge bind off 4 sts every other row 2 times, 4 (5, 6) sts once. **RIGHT FRONT:** Work same as Left Front, reversing all shaping. Work Row 1 of Gore Pattern as follows: With CC k 4 (5,

6), with MC k 12 (14, 16), with CC k 2, with MC k 12 (13, 14).
SLEEVES: With No. 10½ needles and MC cast on 54 (60, 66) sts. Work in Garter st for 1 inch. **GORE PATTERN—Row 1:** With MC k 5, with CC k 2, * with MC k 12 (14, 16), with CC k 2; repeat from * 2 times more, ending with MC k 5. **Row 2:** With MC k 5, with CC p 2, * with MC k 12 (14, 16), with CC p 2; repeat from * 2 times more, ending with MC k 5. **Rows 3 and 4:** Repeat Rows 1 and 2. **Row 5:** With MC k 2 tog, k 2, with CC k 4, * with MC k 10 (12, 14), with CC k 4; repeat from * 2 times more, ending with MC k 2, k 2 tog. Continue in Gore Pattern same as for back **and at the same time** dec 1 st each side every 1½ (1½, 1¼) inches 8 (9, 10) times. Work on 38 (42, 46) to 17 inches from beg or desired length to underarm ending on wrong side. **CAP—Row 1:** With CC bind off 3 (4, 5) sts, k 14 (15, 16), with MC k 4, with CC k to end. **Row 2:** With CC bind off 3 (4,5) sts, p 13 (14, 15), with MC k 6, with CC p to end. Dec 1 st each side every 4th row 2 times, every other row 10 (11, 12) times **and at the same time** work 2 sts more in MC every row until all sts are worked in MC. Break off CC. Bind off 2 sts beg of next 2 rows. Bind off remaining sts.
FINISHING: Sew shoulder, side and sleeve seams. Set in sleeves. **COLLAR:** With MC from right side, beg at right front neck edge pick up 42 (46, 50) sts around entire neck edge. Work in Garter St for 5 inches, inc 1 st each side every other row. Bind off loosely. **RIGHT FRONT BAND:** With MC from right side, beg at right lower edge, pick up 1 st in every other row along front and collar edge. **Row 1—(Collar edge):** Inc 1 st in first st, k to end. **Row 2:** Knit. Repeat these 2 rows for 1½ inches. Bind off. **LEFT FRONT BAND:** Work same as Right Front Band, reversing all shaping and beg at top of collar. On Left Front Band, sew on 3 buttons, having top button ½ inch below neck edge, 2nd button 6 inches below and 3rd button evenly spaced. **BUTTONHOLE LOOPS (Make 3):** With Crochet Hook and MC, work a chain 2 inches long. Fasten off. Sew on opposite buttons. If desired, on wrong side of work, work zigzag running sts, tacking down loose strands of work.

Cap

BRIM: With No. 10½ needles and MC cast on 60 sts. Work in Garter st for 9 inches. **CROWN—Row 1:** * With MC k 2, with CC k 13; repeat from * to end. **Row 2:** * With CC p 13, with MC k 2; repeat from * to end. Repeat these 2 rows for 4½ inches above brim. **Dec Row 1:** With MC k 1, k 2 tog (1 MC and 1 CC k tog), * with CC k 11, with MC k 2 tog 2 times; repeat from * 2 times more, ending with CC k 10, k 2 tog. **Next Row:** * With CC p 11, with MC k 2; repeat from * to end. **Dec Row 2:** With MC k 1, k 2 tog, * with CC k 9, with MC k 2 tog, 2 times; repeat from * 2 times more, ending with CC k 8, k 2 tog—44 sts. Continue in this manner, dec 2 sts in each CC gore every other row until 12 sts remain. **Last Dec Row:** With MC k 2 tog 6 times. Knit one row. Bind off. **FINISHING:** Sew back seam.

19⊕⊕
Guatemalan brights on black; cardigan & small beret

SIZES: Small (8-10), Medium (12-14), Large (16).

MATERIALS: Coats & Clark's Red Heart Wintuk®, 4 Ply, Art. E. 267, knitting worsted weight yarn, (4 oz. Skeins): 13 (13, 14) skeins No. 12 Black; 3 (3, 4) skeins No. 929 Mood Indigo; Red Heart Wintuk® Clansman Sport Yarn, Art. E. 281-C, 2 Ply (1¾ oz. Skeins): 1 skein No. 938 Montrose for each size. Crochet Hook, Size K.

GAUGE: 3 sts = 1 inch;
          6 rows of pattern = 3 inches.
Use 2 strands of same color held together throughout.

Blocking Measurements

Sizes	Small (8-10)	Medium (12-14)	Large (16)
Body Bust Size (In Inches)			
	31½-32½	34-36	38
Actual Crocheting Measurements			
Bust (Jacket wrapped)			
	33½	37	39
Width across back at underarm			
	16½	18½	19½
Width across each front at underarm (excluding border)			
	11	12	12½
Length from shoulder to lower edge			
	28	29	31
Length of side seam (excluding border)			
	21	21	22
Length of sleeve seam (including cuff, but excluding border)			
	18	18	19
Width across sleeve at upper arm			
	12	13	14

BACK: Starting at lower edge, excluding border, with 2 strands of black held together, ch 51 (57, 60) to measure 17½ (19½, 20½) inches. **Foundation Row:** Sc in 2nd ch from hook, sc in each ch across—50 (56, 59) sc. Ch 3, turn. Work in pattern as follows: **Row 1 (right side):** With black, skip first sc, dc in each remaining sc—50 (56, 59) dc, counting turning ch-3 as 1 dc. Ch 1, turn. **Row 2:** Sc in each dc across, sc in top of ch-3. Ch 3, turn. Always count ch-3 as 1 dc. **Rows 3-4:** Repeat Rows 1-2. Ch 3, turn. **Row 5:** Repeat Row 1. At end of row, break off and fasten; with 2 strands held together, attach mood indigo to end of row and ch 1, turn. **Row 6:** With mood indigo, work same as for Row 2. Break off and fasten; attach double strand of black and ch 3, turn. Repeat last 6 rows (Rows 1 through 6) for pattern. Work in pattern until total length is about 21 (21, 22) inches, ending with a wrong-side row. Turn. **Armhole Shaping: Row 1:** Keeping in pattern throughout, sl st in each of first 4 sc, ch 3, dc in each sc across to within last 3 sc; do not work over remaining sts. Ch 1, turn. **Row 2:** *Draw up a loop in each of first 2 dc, yarn over hook and draw through all 3 loops on hook—dec made;* sc in each dc across to within last dc and ch-3, dec over remaining 2 sts. Ch 3, turn. **Row 3:** Skip first st, *holding back on hook last loop of each dc, dc in each of next 2 sc, yarn over hook and draw through all 3 loops on hook—another dec made;* dc in each sc to within last 3 sc, dec over next 2 sc, dc in last sc—dec made at each end. Ch 1, turn. Keeping in pattern, repeat last 2 rows (Rows 2-3) 0 (1, 1) more time—40 (42, 45) sts. Ch 1, turn. Work even (no more decs) in pattern until length is about 7 (8, 9) inches from first row of armhole shaping, ending with a wrong-side row. Turn. **Shoulder Shaping: Row 1:** Sl st in each of first 3 sts, sc in next sc, dc in each sc across to within last 4 sc, sc in next sc; do not work over remaining sts. Ch 1, turn. **Row 2:** Skip first sc, sl st in each of next 4 (5, 6) dc, ch 1, sc in each dc across to within last 4 (5, 6) dc and end sc. Turn. **Row 3:** Sl st in first 3 sts, sc in next st, dc in each of next 16 (16, 17) sc for back of neck, sc in next sc. Break off and fasten. **LEFT FRONT:** Starting at lower edge with 2 strands of black held together, ch 34 (37, 39) to measure 12 (13, 13½) inches. Having 33 (36, 38) sts on each row, work same as for Back until total length is about 21 (21, 22) inches, ending with same pattern row as on Back to underarm. Turn. **Armhole Shaping: Row 1:** Sl st in each of first 4 sts, ch 3, dc in each sc across to end of row. Ch 1, turn. **Row 2:** Sc in each dc across to last dc and ch-3, dec over last 2 sts. Ch 3, turn. **Row 3:** Skip first st, *holding back on hook last loop of each dc, dc in each of next 2 sc, yarn over hook and draw through all 3 loops on hook—dec made at armhole edge;* dc in each sc across. Ch 1, turn. Keeping in pattern, repeat last 2 rows (Rows 2-3) 0 (1, 1) more time—28 (29, 31) sts. Ch 1, turn. Work even in pattern over these sts until length is about 5 (6, 7) inches, ending at armhole edge with a wrong-side row. **Neck Shaping: Row 1:** Work in pattern across to within last 14 (14, 15) sts, dec over next 2 sts; do not work over remaining sts—neck edge. Turn. Keeping armhole edge straight, work in pattern, decreasing one st at neck edge every row 3 times—12 (13, 14) sts remain. Turn. **Shoulder Shaping: Row 1:** From armhole edge, sl st in each of first 3 sts, sc in next sc, dc in each sc across. Ch 1, turn. **Row 2:** Work in pattern across to within last 4 (5, 6) dc and end sc; do not work over remaining sts. Break off and fasten. **RIGHT FRONT:** Work to correspond with Left Front, reversing shaping. **SLEEVES:** Starting at outer edge of cuff with 2 strands of black held together, ch 47 (50, 53) to measure 16 (17, 18) inches, Having 46 (49, 52) sts on each row, work same as for Back until Row 6 of pattern has been completed. Break off and fasten; attach double strand of black and ch 3, turn. **Row 7:** Skip first st, dec over next 2 sc (same as on Row 3 of Back Armhole Shaping); dc in each sc to within last 3 sc, dec over next 2 sc, dc in last sc—dec made at each end. Ch 1, turn. **Rows 8 through 12:** Repeat Rows 2 through 6 of Back pattern. Break off and fasten; attach double strand of black and ch 3, turn. Repeat last 6 rows (Rows 7 through 12) 4 more times—36 (39, 42) sts. Work even in pattern over these sts until total length is about 18 (18, 19) inches, ending with same pattern row as on Back to underarm. At end of last row, turn. **Top Shaping: Rows 1, 2 and 3:** Work same as for Rows 1, 2 and 3 of Back Armhole Shaping. Repeat Rows 2-3 of Armhole Shaping 4 (5, 6) more times. Break off and fasten. **BELT:** Starting at a narrow edge with 2 strands of black held together, ch 9. Having 8 sts on each row, work same as for Back until Row 2 of pattern has been completed. Repeat Rows 1-2 of pattern alternately until total length is about 64 (66, 68) inches, ending with a sc row. Break off and fasten. To block, pin pieces to measurements on a padded surface; cover with a damp cloth and allow to dry; **Do not press.** Sew side, shoulder and sleeve seams, matching rows. Sew in sleeves. **BORDER:** With right side facing, using 2 strands of black held together, attach yarn to lower end of a side seam; being careful to keep work flat, sc evenly along entire outer edge of cardigan, making 3 sc in same st at each corner. Join with sl st to first sc. Break off and fasten. **Satin Stitch Embroidery:** Thread a large-eyed darning needle with a long, double strand of mood indigo. Working over sc round just made, embroider a row of satin stitch (see page 126) over entire outer edge, placing sts close together. Fasten off at end of each strand and start again with a new double strand. Fasten off at end of rnd. Using a single strand of macduff, embroider a row of satin stitch over previous row of embroidery, placing sts slightly apart and covering sc rnd completely. Fasten off at end of rnd. **Sleeve Borders:** Working along opposite side of starting chain and starting at end of seam, work Border same as for outer edge of cardigan at lower edge of each sleeve. Turn back 2½-inch cuff at end of each sleeve. **Armhole Borders:** With right side facing, working along armhole seam, attach double strand of black at underarm and sc evenly along armhole seam, being careful to keep work flat. Join. Break off and fasten. Embroider satin stitch rows same as for cardigan.. Work Border across each short edge of belt in same manner. **CORD (May be used in place of belt):** Cut 7 strands of mood indigo and 7 strands of macduff, each 4½ (4¾, 5) yards long. Holding all strands evenly together, twist tightly in one direction; fold in half and twist in opposite direction. Tie 2 knots at each end. Trim loose ends evenly.

Small beret

SIZE: 8½ inches in diameter.

MATERIALS: Tahki Donegal Knitting Worsted (2 oz. skeins)

2 skeins. Aluminum crochet hook, size I.

GAUGE: 3½ sc = 1 inch; 3 rnds = 1 inch.

Starting at center, ch 3. Join with sl st to form ring. **Rnd 1:** 2 sc in each ch around (6 sc). Mark end of rnd and each succeeding rnd. **Rnd 2:** 2 sc in each sc around (12 sc). **Rnd 3:** * Sc in next sc, 2 sc in next sc; repeat from * around (18 sc). **Rnd 4:** * Sc in next 2 sc, 2 sc in next sc; repeat from * around (24 sc). **Rnds 5 through 12:** Repeat Rnd 4, making 1 more sc in sc before incs until there are 10 sc between incs (72 sc). Work even for 3 rnds or until piece measures slightly more than 8½ inches in diameter. **Next 4 Rnds:** Sc around, dec'ing 8 sc evenly around—to dec (draw up a loop in next sc) twice; yo, draw through 3 loops on hook (40 sc). Work even for 3 rnds. Now working backward—from left to right—work sl st in each sc around. Fasten off.
Designed by Joan Vass for Tahki Yarns

20 ⊗
Pleasant peasantry: a striated tie-vest

SIZES: 8, 10, 12, 14, 16.

MATERIALS: Reynolds Flamme (40 gram ball), 6 (7, 7, 7, 7) balls. (Knitted effect of variegated yarn may vary depending on your technique).
Knitting Needles, 1 pair each No. 8 and No. 10.
Steel Crochet Hook, Size 0.

GAUGE: 4 sts = 1 inch;
6 rows = 1 inch.

Blocking Measurements Sizes	8	10	12	14	16
Body Bust Size (In Inches)					
	31½	32½	34	36	38
Actual Knitting Measurements					
Bust (including front bands)					
	35	37	39	41	43
Width at back of underarms					
	17	18	19	20	21
Width of each front without front band					
	8½	9	9½	10	10½

BACK: With No. 8 needles, cast on 68 (72, 76, 80, 84) sts. Work in k 1, p 1 ribbing for 2 inches. Change to No. 10 needles and stockinette st (k on right side, p on wrong side). Work until 11 (11½, 12, 12½, 13) inches from beg. Mark last row. **ARMHOLES:** Bind off 5 (6, 6, 7, 7) sts at beg of next 2 rows. Dec 1 st each edge every other row 5 (5, 6, 6, 7) times—48 (50, 52, 54, 56) sts. Work even until armholes measure 7 (7¼, 7½, 7¾, 8) inches above marked row. **SHOULDERS:** Bind off 7 (7, 7, 7, 8) sts at beg of next 2 rows, then 7 (7, 7, 8, 8) sts at beg of next 2 rows. Bind off remaining 20 (22, 24, 24, 24) sts. **LEFT FRONT:** With No. 8 needles, cast on 34 (36, 38, 40, 42) sts. Work in k 1, p 1 ribbing for 2 inches. Change to No. 10 needles and stockinette st. Work until piece measures same as back to underarm, ending at side edge. Mark last row. **ARMHOLE AND NECK:** *Next row:* Bind off first 5 (6, 6, 7, 7) sts, finish row. *Next row:* P first 2 sts tog (neck edge), finish row. Dec 1 st at beg of armhole edge rows 5 (5, 6, 6, 7) times; **And at the same time,** continue to dec 1 st at neck edge every other row 4 times more, then every 4th row 5 (6, 7, 7, 7) times—14 (14, 14, 15, 16) sts. Work even until armhole measures 7 (7¼, 7½, 7¾, 8) inches above marked row. **SHOULDER:** Bind off at beg of armhole edge 7 (7, 7, 7, 8) sts once, then 7 (7, 7, 8, 8) sts once. **RIGHT FRONT:** Work to correspond to left front, reversing shaping. **FINISHING:** Steam press pieces lightly. Sew shoulder seams. **ARMHOLE BAND:** Beg at underarm, from right side, using No. 8 needles, pick up and k 1 st in each bound-off st at underarm, 1 st in every row to end of decs, 1 st in every 3 out of 4 rows to shoulder, then pick up other half of armhole to correspond. Work in k 1, p 1 ribbing for 5 rows. Bind off loosely in ribbing. Sew side seams. **FRONT BAND:** From right side, with No. 8 needles, starting at right front lower edge, pick up and k 1 st in every 3 out of 4 rows to V, 1 st in every row to shoulder having an even number of sts altogether, 1 st in each bound-off st on back of neck, then down left front to correspond to right front however having an uneven number of sts. *Row 1* (wrong side): P 1, * k 1, p 1. Repeat from *. *Row 2:* K 1, * p 1, k 1. Repeat from *. Repeat these 2 rows for ribbing for 5 rows. Bind off loosely in ribbing. **TIES:** With crochet hook and double strand of yarn, make a chain about 12″ long on each front edge at V-neck, then a 2nd pair of ties 5″ below first ties.

21 ⏾ Guatemalan brights on black; smock & big beret

SIZES: 8-10, 12, 14.
Note: Smock is designed to have a loose fit.

MATERIALS: Malina's Acrilan® Yarn, Knitting worsted weight yarn (4 oz. skeins): 5 (6, 6) skeins Black, 1 skein Snow, 1 skein Sapphire, 1 skein Cadet, 1 skein Daffodil, 1 skein Cranberry, 1 skein Pansy, 1 skein Lilac.
Knitting Needles, 1 pair No. 6.

GAUGE: Stockinette st—5 sts = 1 inch; 7 rows = 1 inch.
Garter stitch—5 sts = 1 inch; 10 rows = 1 inch.

Measurements:

Sizes	8-10	12	14
Body Bust Size (In Inches)	32½	34	36

BACK: Cast on 90 (94, 98) sts in black. Work in garter stitch (knit every row) for 1 inch. Change to stockinette st (k 1 row, p 1 row) and work till 3½ inches from the very beginning. On next row and then every 4 inches, dec 1 st each side 3 times in all–84 (88, 92) sts across. Work even till 18 (18, 18½) inches from beginning, or desired length to armhole, ending with a P row. **ARMHOLE SHAPING:** Bind off 4 sts at beg of next 2 rows. Then dec 1 st at each side on every other row 3 (3, 4) times in all. Work even on 70 (74, 76) sts till 7½ (7¾ 8) inches from first bound-off armhole sts. **SHOULDER SHAPING: ROWS 1 and 2:** Bind off 6 (7, 7) sts. Work across row. **ROWS 3 and 4:** Bind off 6 (6, 7) sts. Work across row. **ROWS 5 and 6:** Bind off 6 (6, 6) sts. Work across row. Bind off remaining 34 (36, 36) sts for back of neck. **FRONT:** Work same as for back till 1 inch from armhole shaping, ending with a P row. **Next Row:** Work across first 17 (18, 20) sts. Place remaining sts on holder. Work on 17 (18, 20) sts for 1 inch more, ending at side seam. Do armhole shaping as for back, then con-

tinue working even till front armhole measures same as back armhole, ending at armhole edge. **SHOULDER SHAPING: Row 1:** Bind off 6 (7, 7) sts. Work across row. **Row 2:** Work even. **Row 3:** Bind off remaining 4 (4, 5) sts. Bind off next 50 (52, 52) on stitch holder for center front. Then work on remaining 17 (18, 20) sts, doing shaping to correspond with other side. **SLEEVES:** With black, cast on 66 (68, 70) sts. Work in garter st for 1 inch, then work even in stockinette st till sleeve measures 20 (20, 21) inches from the very beginning. **ARMHOLE SHAPING:** Bind off 4 sts at beg of next 2 rows. Then dec 1 st each side *every other* row till there are 30 (32, 32) sts left. Then bind off 1 st each side on *every* row till there are 8 sts left. Bind off. **YOKE:** In snow, cast on 50 (52, 52) sts. Knit 2 rows, then continue in garter st pattern (knit every row) while working in the following stripe pattern: * 2 rows sapphire, 2 rows cadet, 2 rows sapphire, 2 rows daffodil, 2 rows cranberry, 2 rows pansy, 2 rows lilac, 2 rows snow. Repeat from * for stripe pattern and work even till 7 (7, 7½) inches are completed, ending with a "Row 2" of any color stripe. Continue stripe pattern while working the following neckline shaping. **NECKLINE SHAPING:** Knit across first 15 (16, 16) sts. Place remaining sts on holder. Turn. **Row 2:** Bind off 2 (3, 3) sts. Work across row. **Row 3:** Work even. **Row 4:** Bind off 2 sts. Work across row. **Row 5:** Work even. **Row 6:** K 2 tog at neckline. Work across row. **Row 7:** Work even. Repeat Rows 6 and 7 two more times till there are 8 sts left. Work even till yoke measures 9 (9½, 10) inches from the very beginning. Bind off. Bind off next 20 sts on holder for center front neckline. Work on remaining 15 (16, 16) sts, doing shaping to correspond with other side. Sew yoke into front opening. Sew shoulder, side, sleeve seams. Sew sleeves into armholes, easing in extra fullness at caps. Steam sweater lightly. Big beret see instructions on page 143.

Big beret

Size: 10 inches in diameter.

MATERIALS: Tahki Donegal Knitting Worsted (2 oz. skein), 2 skeins.
Aluminum Crochet Hook, Size I.

GAUGE: 3½ sc = 1 inch;
3 rnds = 1 inch.

Work as for Small Beret but continue inc rnds until there are 14 sc between incs (96 sc). Work even for 3 rnds or until piece measures slightly more than 10 inches in diameter. **Next 8 Rnds:** Sc around, dec'ing 6 sc evenly around—to dec (draw up a loop in next sc) twice; yo, draw through 2 lps on hook (48 sc). **Next Rnd:** Sc around, dec'ing 4 sc evenly around (44 sc). Work even for 1 rnd. Finish as for Small Beret.

22 ⏾ Romantic & lacy

MATERIALS: Bernat Carioca, a boucle-type yarn of sport weight, (1 oz. tube), 13 tubes.
Aluminum Crochet Hook, Size D.

GAUGE: 4 tr and 3 ch-3 sps = 2 inches.

NOTE: Always count ch as 1 tr.
Ch 4. **Row 1:** 10 tr in 4th ch from hook, ch 5, turn. **Row 2:** 1 tr in 2nd tr, (ch 2, 1 tr in next tr) 4 times; ch 5, 1 tr in same tr (center v sp), (ch 2, 1 tr in next tr) 5 times; ch 6, turn. **Row 3:** 1 tr in next tr, (ch 2, 1 tr in next tr) 4 times; ch 2, 1 tr-ch 5-1 tr in center v sp, (ch 2, 1 tr in next tr) 6 times; ch 6, turn. **Row 4:** (1 tr in next tr, ch 3) 6

times; 1 tr-ch 5-1 tr in center v sp, (ch 3, 1 tr in next tr) 7 times, ch 4, turn. **Row 5:** (3 tr in ch 3 sp, 1 tr in next tr) 7 times; 1 tr-ch 5-1 tr in center v sp, (1 tr in next tr, 3 tr in next sp) 7 times; 1 tr in 3rd st of turning ch, ch 6, turn. **Row 6:** 1 tr in first st, ch 3, skip 3 tr, (1 tr in next tr, ch 3, skip 3 tr) 5 times; 1 tr in each of next 4 tr, ch 3, skip 1 tr, 1 tr in next tr, ch 3, 1 tr-ch 5-1 tr in center v sp, ch 3, 1 tr in next tr, ch 3, skip 1 tr, 1 tr in each of next 4 tr, (ch 3, skip 3 tr, 1 tr in next tr) 6 times; ch 3, 1 tr in top of turning ch, ch 6, turn. **Row 7:** (1 tr in next tr, ch 3) 7 times; 1 tr in each of next 4 tr, (ch 3, 1 tr in next tr) twice; ch 3, 1 tr-ch 5-1 tr in center v sp, (ch 3, 1 tr in next tr) twice; ch 3, 1 tr in each of next 4 tr, (ch 3, 1 tr in next tr) 6 times; 1 tr in 3rd st of turning ch, ch 6, turn. **Row 8:** (1 tr in next tr, ch 3) 7 times; 1 tr in each of next 4 tr, (ch 3, 1 tr in next tr) 3 times; ch 3, 1 tr-ch 5-1 tr in center v sp, (ch 3, 1 tr in next tr) 3 times; ch 3, 1 tr in each of next 4 tr, (ch 3, 1 tr in next tr) 7 times; ch 3, 1 tr in 3rd st of turning ch, ch 6, turn. **Row 9:** (1 tr in next tr, ch 3) 8 times; 1 tr in each of next 4 tr, (ch 3, 1 tr in next tr) 4 times; ch 3, 1 tr-ch 5-1 tr in center v sp, (ch 3, 1 tr in next tr) 4 times; ch 3, 1 tr in each of next 4 tr, (ch 3, 1 tr in next tr) 7 times; ch 3, 1 tr in 3rd st of turning ch, ch 6, turn. **Row 10:** (1 tr in next tr, ch 3) 8 times; 1 tr in each of next 4 tr, (ch 3, 1 tr in next tr) 5 times; ch 3, 1 tr-ch 5-1 tr in center v sp, (ch 3, 1 tr in next tr) 5 times; ch 3, 1 tr in each of next 4 tr, (ch 3, 1 tr in next tr) 8 times; ch 3, 1 tr in 3rd st of turning ch, ch 6, turn. **Row 11:** (1 tr in next tr, ch 3) 9 times; 1 tr in each of next 4 tr, (ch 3, 1 tr in next tr) 6 times; ch 3, 1 tr-ch 5-1 tr in center v sp, (ch 3, 1 tr in next tr) 6 times; ch 3, 1 tr in each of next 4 tr, (ch 3, 1 tr in next tr) 8 times; ch 3, 1 tr in 3rd st of turning ch, ch 6, turn. **Row 12:** (1 tr in next tr, ch 3) 9 times; 1 tr in each of next 4 tr, (ch 3, 1 tr in next tr) 7 times; ch 3, 1 tr-ch 5-1 tr in center v sp (ch 3, 1 tr in next tr) 7 times; ch 3, 1 tr in each of next 4 tr, (ch 3, 1 tr in next tr) 9 times; ch 3, 1 tr in 3rd st of turning ch, ch 6, turn. **Row 13:** (1 tr in next tr, ch 3) 10 times; 1 tr in each of next 4 tr, (ch 3, 1 tr in next tr) 8 times; ch 3, 1 tr-ch 5-1 tr in center v sp, (ch 3, 1 tr in next tr) 8 times; ch 3, 1 tr in each of next 4 tr, (ch 3, 1 tr in next tr) 9 times; ch 3, 1 tr in 3rd st of turning ch, ch 6, turn. **Row 14:** (1 tr in next tr, 3 tr in next sp) 10 times; 1 tr in each of next 4 tr, (3 tr in next sp, 1 tr in next tr) 9 times; 1 tr-ch 5-1 tr in center v sp, (1 tr in next tr, 3 tr in next sp) 9 times; 1 tr in each of next 4 tr, (3 tr in next sp, 1 tr in next tr) 10 times; 3 tr in next sp, 1 tr in 3rd st of turning ch, ch 6, turn. **Row 15:** (1 tr in next tr, ch 3, skip 3 tr) twice; * 1 tr in each of next 4 tr, ch 3, skip next 4 tr, (1 tr in next tr, ch 3, skip 3 tr) 7 times ;* repeat between *'s once more, 1 tr in each of next 4 tr, ch 3, skip 1 tr, 1 tr in next tr, ch 3, 1 tr-ch 5-1 tr in center v sp, ch 3, 1 tr in next tr, ch 3, skip 1 tr, ** 1 tr in each of next 4 tr, (ch 3, skip 3 tr, 1 tr in next tr) 7 times; ch 3 **; repeat between **'s once more, ending skip 3 tr, 1 tr in each of next 4 tr, ch 3, skip 4 tr, 1 tr in next tr, ch 3, 1 tr in 4th st of turning ch, ch 6, turn. **Row 16:** (1 tr in next tr, ch 3) twice; * 1 tr in each of next 4 tr, (ch 3, 1 tr in next tr) 7 times ch 3 *; repeat between *'s once more, 1 tr in each of next 4 tr, (ch 3, 1 tr in next tr) twice; ch 3, 1 tr-ch 5-1 tr in center v sp, (ch 3,.1 tr in next tr) twice; ch 3, ** 1 tr in each of next 4 tr, (ch 3, 1 tr in next tr) 7 times; ch 3 **; repeat between **'s once more, 1 tr in each of next 4 tr, (ch 3, 1 tr in next tr) twice; 1 tr in 3rd st of turning ch, ch 6, turn. **Rows 17 through 22:** Repeat Row 16, having 1 more space at beg of every row and at each side of center v sp. **Row 23:** Work in same manner as Row 14, working 1 tr in each tr, 3 tr in each space and 1 tr-ch 5-1 tr in center v sp, ch 6, turn. **Rows 24 through 28:** Repeat Rows 17 through 22. **Row 29:** 3 tr in first sp, 1 tr in next tr, now work in same manner as Row 24, ending 3 tr in last sp, 1 tr in 3rd st of turning ch, ch 6, turn. **Rows 30 and 31:** Following new pattern, repeat Row 24. **Row 32:** Work in same manner as Row 23, ending ch 7, turn. **Row 33:** * 1 dtr in next tr, ch 3, skip 3 tr ,* repeat between *'s to 2 sts before center v sp, 1 dtr in next tr, ch 3, skip 1 tr, 1 dtr-ch 5-1 dtr in center v sp, ch 3, skip 1 tr, ** 1 dtr in next tr, ch 3, skip 3 tr ;** repeat between **'s to end of row, ending 1 dtr in 3rd st of turning ch, ch 7 turn. **Row 34:** Repeat Row 33. **Row 35:** * 1 d c, ch 2, 1 d c in next space, 1 d c in next dtr *; repeat between *'s to center v sp, 1 d c-ch 5-1 d c in same space, 1 d c in next dtr; repeat between *'s to end of row, ending 1 d c in 3rd st of turning ch, ch 6, turn. **Row 36:** (In next ch 2 sp, work a cluster as follows: * wrap yarn around hook 3 times, (yo, draw through 2 loops on hook) twice *; repeat between *'s 4

times more; yo, draw through all loops on hook, ch 1, in next ch 2 sp, work 1 dtr-ch 4-1 dtr (V st), continue to work in this manner across row to center v sp, 1 V st, ch 6, 1 V st in same space, work in cluster and V st pattern across row, ending 1 cluster in last space, 1 dtr in top of turning ch, ch 8, turn. **Row 37:** 1 V st in top of cluster, 1 cluster in ch 4 sp of V st, work in this manner to center v sp, 1 V st-ch 6-1 V st in same sp, work in cluster and V st pattern across row, ending 1 V st in last cluster, 1 dtr in top of turning ch, ch 6, turn. **Row 38:** * 1 dtr in next dtr, ch 4, 1 dtr in next dtr, ch 2 ;* repeat between *'s to center v sp, 1 dtr, ch 6, in same sp, work in dtr pattern across row, ending ch 4, 1 dtr in 4th st of turning ch, ch 6, turn. **Row 39:** Repeat Row 38, ending ch 4, turn. **Row 40:** 1 dtr in each dtr, 4 dtr in each ch 4 sp, 2 dtr in each ch 2 sp, continue to work in this manner across row to center v sp, 2 dtr-ch 6-2 dtr in same space, work in pattern to end of row, ch 7, turn. **Row 41:** * 1 dtr in next dtr, ch 3, skip 3 dtr ;* repeat between *'s to 2 dtr before center v sp, ch 3, skip 2 dtr, 1 dtr-ch 6-1 dtr in center v sp, ch 3, skip 2 dtr, work in pattern to end of row, ending ch 3, 1 dtr in top of turning ch, **Do Not Fasten Off.** Keeping work flat, work in s c across neck edge. Fasten off. Fringe: Cut strands of yarn 16 inches long. Knot 6 strands in every space across shaped edges of shawl. Trim ends. Steam lightly.

23 0
South American striping

SIZE: 48 inches measured through the center.

MATERIALS: Columbia-Minerva Nantuk® 4-ply, a knitting worsted weight yarn (4 oz. skein), 2 each colors A, C and F; Nantuk® Sweater and Afghan Yarn, a sport weight yarn, (2 oz. skein), 3 color E; Reverie, a mohair mixture yarn, (1 oz. skein), 8 color B, 6 color D, 4 color G. Aluminum Crochet Hook, Size J.

GAUGE: 3 dc/sc = 1 inch;
3 dc rows = 2 inches.

Note: Fasten off colors at end of a row. All dc, sc and chs will be referred to as **sts**. Beg and end of rows form top edge. **Row 1 (right side):** Beg at top edge with A, ch 4, in 4th ch from hook work 4 dc (counting chs at beg, 5 dc). Fasten off A; join B, turn. **Row 2:** 3 sc in first st, sc in next st, in next st work 5 sc, sc in next st, 3 sc in top of turning ch (2 sts inc at each end). Fasten off B; join C, turn. **Row 3:** Ch 3 (counts as 1 dc), 2 dc in first st, dc in each st to within center st of 5 st-grp, in next st work 5 dc, dc in each st across, ending 3 dc in last st. Fasten off C; join B, turn. **Row 4:** 3 sc in first st, sc in each st to within center-st, in next st work 5 sc, sc in each st across, ending 3 sc in top of ch-3. Fasten off B; join D, turn. **Row 5:** Ch 3, 2 dc in first st, dc in each st to within center-st, in next st work 5 dc, dc in each st across, ending 3 dc in last st. Join to D 1 strand B (1 each B and D), turn. Always increasing 2 sts at beg and end of row, work center-st inc as follows: * 3 rows with 3 sts in center-st, 1 row with 5 sts in center-st, repeat from * to end. **And at the same time,** work in stripe as follows: in dc work 1 strand each BD; in sc work 1 row B; in dc work 1 row F, 1 row DE, 1 row G; in sc work 1 row B; in dc work 1 row A; in sc work 1 row C, 1 row B; * in dc work 1 row F, 1 row DE, 1 row G; in sc work 1 row A, 1 row B; in dc work 1 row C; in sc work 1 row B; in dc work 1 row D, 1 row F, 1 row DE, 1 row G; in sc work 1 row B; in dc work 1 row A; in sc work 1 row C, 1 row B *, repeat between *'s 3 times, then in sc work 1 row B.

Edging: With B, ch 4, * skip 1 st, dc in next st, ch 1, repeat from * across, ending dc in last st omitting ch-1. Fasten off.
FINISHING: Border—Row 1 (wrong side): With F ch 6, dc in 3rd ch from hook and in next 2 chs (4 dc), turn. **Row 2:** Ch 3, (yo, insert hook in next st, yo and through 2 lps on hook) twice, yo and through 3 lps on hook (1 st dec), 2 dc in top of turning ch (1 st inc), turn. **Row 3:** Ch 3, dc in next 2 sts, dc in top of ch-3, turn. **Row 4:** Ch 3, dec 1 st, 2 dc in top of ch-3, turn. Repeat Rows 3 and 4 until piece measures evenly along top edge. Fasten off. With right side of border facing, fold in half and sew to top edge of shawl. **Fringe:** Cut 1 strand of each Color 14 inches long. Using 1 of each Color for fringe, fold in half and knot fringe in every other ch-1 sp of edging.

24 ⊗
Celtic warmth

By the North Sea, afghans and shawls are almost interchangeable. These intricate oblongs lie over beds and chairs, are flung on to wear outside.

SIZE: Approximately 52 x 68 inches.

MATERIALS: Spinnerin Irish Fisherman Yarn or Germantown Deluxe or Marvel Twist Deluxe or Spinloft or other knitting worsted weight yarn (4 oz. skein), 12 skeins.
Knitting Needles, 1 pair No. 10 and 1 double-pointed needle or cable needle.
Tapestry needle.

GAUGE: Each motif = 8½ inches square.

Afghan is worked in 48 squares.
STITCHES:
BACK CABLE (BC): Sl next 2 sts to dp needle and hold at *back*, k next 2 sts, k 2 from dp needle.
FRONT CABLE (FC): Sl next 2 sts to dp needle and hold at *front*, k next 2 sts, k 2 from dp needle.
TWIST 2 (T2): Skip 1 st, k next st through *front* loop and leave on left needle, k skipped st, drop 2 sts from left needle.
LEFT TWIST (LT): Skip 1 st, p next st through *back* loop and leave on left needle, k skipped st, drop 2 sts from left needle.
RIGHT TWIST (RT): Skip 1 st, k next st, p the skipped st.
BOBBLE (BO): K next st, leave on left needle, yo, pass last st on right needle over the yo, (k the worked st on left needle, leave on left needle, yo, pass last st on right needle over yo) twice; k in back loop of worked st on left needle, drop st from left needle, pass 3 sts on right needle over the last st on right needle.
MOTIF (Make 48): Cast on 41 sts. K 2 rows. **Row 1 (right side):** K 1, p 1, k 8, p 2, T2, p 3, k 1, p 5, k 1, p 3, p 12, k 2. **Row 2:** K 2, place a marker on needle; (on front loop of next st k 1, p 1, k 1; p next 3 sts tog) 3 times; place a marker on needle, k 3, p 1, k 5, p 1, k 3, p 2, k 2, p 8, k 2. Sl markers every row. **Row 3:** K 1, p 1, (BC) twice; p 2, T2, p 3, k 1, p 5, k 1, p 3, p 12, k 2. **Row 4:** K 2, (p 3 tog, work 3 sts in next st) 3 times; k 3, p 1, k 5, p 1, k 3, p 2, k 2, p 8, k 2. **Row 5:** K 1, p 1, k 8, p 2, T2, p 3, LT, p 3, RT, p 3, p 12, k 2. **Row 6:** K 2; repeat between markers of Row 2, k 4, p 1, k 3, p 1, k 4, p 2, k 2, p 8, k 2. **Row 7:** K 1, p 1, k 2, FC, k 2, p 2, T2, p 4, LT, p 1, RT, p 4, p 12, k 2. **Row 8:** K 2, repeat between markers of Row 4, k 5, p 1, k 1, p 1, k 5, p 2, k 2, p 8, k 2. **Row 9:** K 1, p 1, k 8, p 2, T2, p 2, BO, p 2, sl next st to dp needle, hold at *front*, RT, k st from dp, p 2, BO, p 14, k 2. **Row 10:** K 2; repeat

between markers of Row 2, k 2, p 1, k 2, p 3, k 2, p 1, k 2, p 2, k 2, p 8, k 2. Repeat these 10 rows (taking care to alternate sts between markers on every wrong side row) until there are 40 rows in pattern. P 1 row on right side. Bind off. **FINISHING:** Block each square lightly to measure 8½ inches square. Check photograph for the position of squares, and weave together from the right side. Join 6 squares in width, 8 squares in length. On side edges, from right side, work 1 row sc, ch 1; do not turn. Work 2nd row from left to right (backward crochet) and fasten off. **KNITTED FRINGE (Make 2 strips):** With 2 strands of yarn held tog, cast on 8 sts. **Row 1:** Yo (wrap yarn around right needle), p 2 tog, (yo, p 2 tog) 3 times. Repeat Row 1 until same length as lower edge of afghan. **Next Row:** Work 6 sts and drop last 2 sts from left needle without working (to form loops when raveled). Turn and bind off 6 sts loosely. Pin long side (opposite fringe) to edge of afghan and weave in same manner as with squares. Ravel fringe and steam lightly. Do not cut.

25 ⊗
Haltered, sexy

SIZES: 8, 10, 12, 14.

MATERIALS: American Thread Dawn Wintuk® Sport Yarn (2 oz. skeins) 3 (4, 4, 4) skeins
Knitting Needles, 1 pair each No. 4 and No. 6.
1 Crochet Hook, Size C.
1 yd elastic ½ inch wide.
4 small buttons.

GAUGE: Pattern on Size 6 Needles:
  6 sts = 1 inch;
  7 rows = 1 inch.

Blocking Measurements

Sizes	8	10	12	14
Actual Knitting Measurements (In Inches)				
Bust				
	31½	32½	34	36
Waist				
	23	24	25½	27
Hips				
	33½	34½	36	38

PATTERN STITCH: Sizes 8 (10, 12)—Multiple of 4 plus 4 sts. Size 14—Multiple of 4 plus 2 sts.
Row 1: (Wrong side): K 1 (1, 1, 2) * p 2, k 2; repeat from * across row ending p 2, k 1 (1, 1, 2). **Row 2:** P 1 (1, 1, 2) * k second st on left needle then k first st on left needle, sl both sts off needle, p 2, repeat from * across row, ending p 1 (1, 1, 2). **Row 3:** Repeat Row 1. **Row 4:** P 1 (1, 1, 2) * k into the back of second st on left needle (on wrong side) then k first st on left needle, sl both sts off needle, p 2. Repeat from * across row, ending p 1 (1, 1, 2).
NOTE: When increasing and decreasing always keep in pattern.
HALTER FRONT: With number 6 needles, cast on 100 (104, 108, 114) sts. (Row 1 is wrong side.) **Rows 1 through 20 (23, 26, 30):** Work in pattern st. (Approximately 3, 3¼, 3¾, 4¼ inches). **Row 21 (24, 27, 31):** Dec 1 st at beginning and end of row. **Rows 22 through 42 (25 through 45, 28 through 48, 32 through 52):** Repeat dec row every 7th row three more times. (Approximately 6, 6½, 7, 7½ inches.) **Rows 43 through 62 (46 through 65, 49

through 68, 53 through 72): Repeat dec row every fifth row four times (84, 88, 92, 98) sts. **Rows 63 through 82 (66 through 85, 69 through 88, 73 through 92):** Work even in pattern. (Approximately 3 inches). **Row 83 (86, 89, 93):** Inc 1 st at beg and end of row. **Rows 84 through 113 (87 through 116, 90 through 119, 94 through 123):** Repeat inc every tenth row 3 times (92, 96, 100, 106) sts. **Rows 114 through 119 (117 through 122, 120 through 125, 124 through 128):** Work even in pattern. (Approximately 17, 17½, 18 18¼ inches or desired length to armhole.) **HALTER SHAPING: Rows 120 through 123 (123 through 126, 126 through 129, 129 through 132):** Bind off two sts at the beg of each row. **Rows 124 through 127 (127 through 130, 130 through 133, 133 through 136):** Dec 1 st at the beg and end of each row. 76 (80, 84, 90) sts on needle. **Rows 128 through 159 (131 through 163, 134 through 168, 137 through 173):** Dec 1 st at beg and end of every other row—44 (46, 48, 52) sts on needle. End with Row 1 or 3. **SHAPE NECK: Row 160 (164, 169, 174):** Keeping in pattern, work 13 (14, 15, 16) sts. Attach another ball of yarn. Bind off center 18 (18, 18, 20) sts. Work 13 (14, 15, 16) sts. **Rows 161 through 170 (165 through 175, 170 through 180, 175 through 185):** Continue to dec 1 st every other row at armhole edge and **at the same time** at each neck edge, bind off 2 (2, 3, 4) sts once; then at this same edge, dec 1 st every other row 4 times. Bind off 2 (3, 3, 3) remaining sts. **BACK:** Work same as the front. **Rows 1 through 81 (83, 85, 87)**—(Approximately 11⅝, 11⅞, 12⅛, 12⅜ inches) ending with Row 1 or 3. (84, 88, 92, 98 sts). **Row 82 (84, 86, 88):** Work 36 (38, 39, 41) sts. Attach another ball of yarn. Bind off center back 12 (12, 14, 16) sts. Work remaining 36 (38, 39, 41) sts. **Rows 83 through 119 (85 through 122, 87 through 125, 89 through 129):** Working on both sides at once, matching 4 more inc at side seam to correspond to front (Rows: 83, 93, 103, 113—86, 96, 106, 116—89, 99, 109, 119—93, 103, 113, 123) and **at the same time** on both back sections, bind off 3 st every other row twice. Then dec 1 st every row until all remaining sts are worked off. **COLLAR:** With No. 4 needles, cast on 84 (84, 88, 88) sts. **Rows 1 through 32 (Approximately 4½ inches):** Work in k 2, p 2 ribbing. Bind off loosely. **FINISHING:** Weave side seams together matching incs and decs. Steam seams very lightly. Starting at right shoulder with size C hook work 1 row of sc down right side, all across back opening, up to left side shoulder and around neck holding in to desired fit. Using back loops of sc of previous row, work one row of sl st around back opening and neck. Sew collar to front neck of halter matching centers. With wrong side facing, on right side of collar, work 1 row sc, sew on 4 little buttons evenly spaced. On left side of collar work 1 row sc (22 st) ch 1, turn. 1 sc in same space, * ch 3, skip next 2 sc, 1 sc in each of the next 4 sc, repeat from * 2 more times. Ch 3, sc in last sc. (4 button loops made). Work 1 row sc around bottom of collar.

26 ⊗ Basic, sporting

SIZES: 8, 10, 12, 14, 16, 18.

MATERIALS: Spinnerin Corky (50 gram ball), 5 (6, 7, 8, 9, 10) balls.
Knitting Needles, 1 pair No. 5 and 1 set dp No. 5.

GAUGE: 6 sts = 1 inch;
        8 rows = 1 inch.

Blocking Measurements

Sizes	8	10	12	14	16	18
Actual Knitting Measurements (In Inches)						
Bust						
	32	34	36	38	40	42
Back at shoulders						
	12	12½	13	13½	14	14½
Sleeves at underarm						
	12	12	13	13	14	14

BACK: Cast on 97 (103, 109, 115, 121, 127) sts. Rib in k 1, p 1 for 3 rows. Work in St st to 16 inches from beg or desired length to underarm. **ARMHOLES:** Bind off 7 (7, 8, 8, 9, 9) at beg of next 2 rows. Dec 1 st each side every 2nd row 5 (7, 7, 9, 9, 11) times. Work on 73 (75, 79, 81, 85, 87) until armholes are 7 (7, 7½, 7½, 8, 8) inches. **SHOULDERS:** Bind off 5 (5, 5, 6, 6, 6) at beg of next 6 rows, 5 (6, 7, 5, 6, 7) at beg of next 2 rows. Place 33 (33, 35, 35, 37, 37) sts on holder. **FRONT:** Work same as back until armholes are 5 (5, 5½, 5½, 6, 6) inches. **NECK:** Work 25 (26, 27, 28, 29, 30), place center 23 (23, 25, 25, 27, 27) on holder, join 2nd ball, work to end. Working each side with separate yarn, dec 1 st at neck edges every 2nd row 5 times, shaping shoulders as on back when armholes are same length. **SLEEVES:** Cast on 48 (48, 52, 52, 56, 56) sts. Rib in k 2, p 2 for 6 inches for double cuff. Change to St st, inc 1 st each side every 6 rows 12 (12, 13, 13, 14, 14) times. Work on 72 (72, 78, 78, 84, 84) to 20 inches from beg, or 3 inches longer than desired length. **SHAPE CAP:** Bind off 7 (7, 8, 8, 9, 9) at beg of next 2 rows. Dec 1 st each side every 4th row 4 times, every 2nd row 10 (10, 12, 12, 14, 14) times. Bind off 3 sts at beg of next 2 rows. Bind off 24 sts. **FINISHING:** Block pieces to measurements and assemble (be sure to reverse seam for turnback cuff). **NECKBAND:** With dp needles from right side, beg at right shoulder seam, pick up 96 (96, 100, 100, 104, 104) sts around neck, including sts on holders. Join. Rib in k 2, p 2 for 7 inches. Bind off loosely in rib.

27 ⊗ Hooded, kangaroo pocketed

SIZES: 6-8, 10-12, 14-16.

MATERIALS: Columbia-Minerva Nantuk® Denim 4 ply, a knitting worsted weight yarn, (4 oz. skein), 5 (5, 6) skeins. Talon Riri 20 inch separating zipper.
Knitting Needles, 1 pair each No. 5 and No. 6.

GAUGE: 6 sts = 1 inch;
        13 rows = 2 inches.

Blocking Measurements

Sizes	6-8	10-12	14-16
Actual Knitting Measurements (In Inches)			
Back at underarms			
	16½	18	19½
Each front at underarms			
	8¼	9	9¾
Sleeves at upperarms			
	12	13	14

BACK: With No. 5 needles, cast on 89 (95, 103) sts. **Row 1:** K 1, * p 1, k 1; repeat from * across. **Row 2:** P 1, * k 1, p 1; repeat from * across. Repeat these two rows for 3 inches and in last row inc

10 (10, 12) sts evenly spaced—99 (105, 115) sts. Change to No. 6 needles. Work in st st (k 1 row, p 1 row) until 14 inches from beg or desired length to underarms. **ARMHOLES:** Bind off 6 (6, 8) sts at beg of next 2 rows. Dec 1 st each side every other row 8 times—71 (77, 83) sts. Work even until 7¼ (7¾, 8¼) inches above underarms. **SHOULDERS:** Bind off 7 (8, 9) sts at beg of next 4 rows; 9 sts at beg of next 2 rows. Bind off remaining 25 (27, 29) sts. **LEFT FRONT:** With No. 5 needles cast on 45 (51, 55) sts. Work ribbing as back and on last row inc 4 sts evenly spaced—49 (55, 59) sts. Change to No. 6 needles. **Row 1:** K to last 4 sts, (p 1, k 1) twice. **Row 2:** (P 1, k 1) twice, p across. Repeat these two rows until same length as back to underarm, ending with a p row. **ARMHOLES:** Keeping front border sts as established, bind off 6 (7, 8) sts at beg of next row. Dec 1 st at same edge every other row 8 times—35 (40, 43) sts. Work even until 4¼ (4¾, 5¼) inches above underarm, at front edge. **NECK AND SHOULDER:** Bind off 6 sts at front edge once; 2 (3, 3) sts once. Dec 1 st at same edge every other row 4 (6, 7) times—23 (25, 27) sts. Work even until armhole measures same as back. At armhole edge bind off 7 (8, 9 sts twice; 9 sts once. **RIGHT FRONT:** Work to correspond to left front, reversing all shaping. **SLEEVES:** With No. 5 needles cast on 41 (45, 49) sts. Work in ribbing as for back for 3 inches and on last row inc 10 sts evenly spaced-51 (55, 59) sts. Change to No. 6 needles. Work in st st and inc 1 st each side every 6th row 10 (11, 12) times—71 (77, 83) sts. Work even until sleeve measures 17 (17½, 18) inches or desired length. **SHAPING:** Bind off 6 (7, 8) sts at beg of next 2 rows. Dec 1 st each side every row 11 (12, 13) times. Bind off 3 sts at beg of next 6 rows. Bind off remaining 19 (21, 23) sts. **LEFT POCKET:** With No. 6 needles cast on 21 sts. Work in ribbing for 1 row. **Inc. Row:** Work 2 sts, inc in next st, rib to end. Keeping continuity of ribbing, repeat inc row every other row until there are 33 (35, 37) sts. Work 3 rows even. **Dec Row:** Work 2 sts, sl 1, k 1, psso, rib to end. Continue to dec 1 st every other row until 21 sts remain. Bind off in ribbing. **RIGHT POCKET:** Work to correspond to left pocket, reversing all shaping by having incs and decs at end of rows. **HOOD:** Cast on 7 sts on No. 6 needle, with same needle pick up and k 77 (83, 89) sts all around neck edge, cast on 7 sts on end of needle. **Row 1:** P 8, * k 1, p 1; repeat from * to last 9 sts, k 1, p 8. **Row 2: right side:** K 8, k 1, * p 1, k 1; repeat from * to last 8 sts, k 8. Repeat these 2 rows until 8½ (9, 9½) inches from beg, ending on wrong side. Mark center st. **Dec row:** Rib to within 4 sts of center marker st, k 2 tog, p 2 tog, k center st, p 2 tog, k 2 tog, finish row. Keeping continuity of ribbing, dec 2 sts each side of center st every other row until 37 (39, 43) sts remain. Bind off in ribbing. **FINISHING:** Sew shoulder, side and sleeve seams. Sew in sleeves. Sew straight edge of pockets to fronts along first st after ribbed edge, having pockets along top of lower ribbing. Sew increased and top edge in place. Seam top of hood. Fold 7 sts to wrong side and hem. **CORD:** On No. 5 needles cast on 5 sts. Work in st st until piece measures 1½ yards. Bind off. Pull piece tight to form cord. Insert cord between hood and turned-back facing. Knot at both ends. Sew zipper to fronts.

28 ⊗
Tennis warm-up

SIZES: Small (6-8), Medium (10-12), Large (14).

MATERIALS: Coats & Clark's Red Heart Wintuk® Sport Yarn, Art. E. 281, 2 ply (2 oz. skeins): 8 (10, 10) ounces No. 1 White; 2 ounces No. 905 Red for each size.
Knitting Needles, 1 pair each No. 5 and No. 6.
Separating Metal Zipper, 14 inches long, White.

GAUGE: 5 sts = 1 inch;
      15 rows = 2 inches.

Blocking Measurements

Sizes	Small (6-8)	Medium (10-12)	Large (14)
Body Bust Size (In Inches)	30½-31½	32½-34	36
Actual Knitting Measurements			
Bust	32	35	37
Width across back at underarm	16	17½	18½
Width across each front at underarm	8	8¾	9¼
Length from back of neck to lower edge	21	22	22½
Length of side seam	14	14½	15
Length of sleeve seam	17	17½	17½
Width across sleeve at upper arm	12	12¾	13½

BACK: Starting at lower edge with No. 5 needles and white, cast on 70 (78, 82) sts. **1st row:** P 2, * k 2, p 2. Repeat from * across. **2nd row:** K 2, * p 2, k 2. Repeat from * across. **3rd through 6th rows:** Repeat first and 2nd rows. **7th row:** Repeat first row. Break off white, attach red. **8th row:** K across. **9th and 10th rows:** Repeat first and 2nd rows. Break off red, attach white. **11th row:** P across. Continue in ribbing until total length is 4½ inches, ending with first row. Change to No. 6 needles. **Next row:** K across, increasing 10 sts evenly spaced. Now work in stockinette st (p 1 row, k 1 row) over the 80 (88, 92) sts until total length is 14 (14½, 15) inches, ending with a p row. **Raglan Shaping: 1st and 2nd rows:** Bind off 5 (6, 6) sts at beg of row, work across. **3rd row:** K 1, k 2 tog, k across to last 3 sts, sl 1, k 1, psso, k 1. **4th row:** P across. Repeat 3rd and 4th rows alternately until 20 (22, 24) sts remain. Place sts on stitch holder to be worked later for Collar. **LEFT FRONT:** Starting at lower edge with No. 5 needles and white, cast on 35 (39, 41) sts. Work as for Back until total length is 4½ inches, ending with first row. Change to No. 6 needles. **Next row:** K across, increasing 5 sts evenly across. Now work in stockinette st over the 40 (44, 46) sts until total length is 14 (14½, 15) inches, ending with a p row. **Raglan Shaping: Note:** Mark decreases at neck edge for easy counting. **1st row:** Bind off 5 (6, 6) sts, k across to last 3 sts, k 2 tog, k 1. **2nd row:** P across. **3rd row:** K 1, k 2 tog, k across. **4th row:** P across. **5th row:** K 1, k 2 tog, k across to last 3 sts, k 2 tog, k 1. Repeat 2nd through 5th rows until 10 (11, 12) sts in all have been decreased at neck edge. Continue to decrease as before at armhole edge only until all sts have been decreased. Break off. **RIGHT FRONT:** Work as for Left Front until total length is 14 (14½, 15) inches, ending with a k row. **Raglan Shaping: 1st row:** Bind off 5 (6, 6) sts, p across. **2nd row:** K 1, sl 1, k 1, psso, k across to last 3 sts, k 2 tog, k 1. **3rd row:** P across. **4th row:** K across to last 3 sts, k 2 tog, k 1. **5th row:** P across. Repeat 2nd through 5th rows until 10 (11, 12) sts in all have been decreased at neck edge. Continue to decrease as before at armhole edge only until all sts have been decreased. Break off. **SLEEVES:** Starting at lower edge with No. 5 needles and white, cast on 40 (44, 48) sts. Work as for Back until total length is 3½ inches, ending with first row. Change to No. 6 needles. **Next row:** K across, increasing 10 sts evenly across. Work in stockinette st, increasing one st at both ends of every 8th row until there are 70 (76, 78) sts. Work even until total length is 17 (17½, 17½) inches, ending with a p row. **Raglan Shaping: 1st and 2nd rows:** Bind off 5 (6, 6) sts, work across. **3rd row:** K 1, k 2 tog, k across to last 3 sts, sl 1, k 1, psso, k 1. **4th row:** P across. Repeat 3rd and 4th rows alternately until 10 sts remain. Place sts on stitch holder to be worked later for Collar. Pin pieces out to measurements, dampen and leave to dry. **COLLAR:** With wrong side facing, No. 5 needles and white, pick up and k 43 (44, 47) sts along left front

GOLF DESIGN

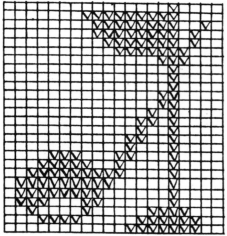

NAVAL DESIGN

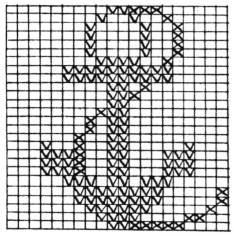

TENNIS DESIGN

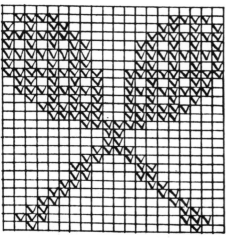

neck edge, k the 10 sts from one sleeve stitch holder; k the 20 (22, 24) sts from back stitch holder, place a marker, k the 10 sts from other sleeve stitch holder, pick up and k 43 (44, 47) sts along right front neck edge—126 (130, 138) sts. **Next row:** (P 2, k 2) 13 times; place a marker, * p 2, k 2. Repeat from * 4 (5, 7) more times; p 2. Place a marker, (k 2, p 2) 13 times. **Note:** Be careful to keep continuity of rib pattern. Now work in short rows as follows: **1st short row:** Work in pattern across to second marker. Turn. **Do not work over remaining sts. 2nd short row:** Work in pattern across 26 (30, 38) sts. Turn. **3rd short row:** Work in pattern across 30 (34, 42) sts. Turn. **4th short row:** Work in pattern across 34 (38, 46) sts. Continue in this manner, working 4 sts more at end of each short row until the 26th short row has been worked—all stitches have been worked. Work in pattern over the 126 (130, 138) sts for ½ inch, ending with a wrong-side row of Collar. Break off white, attach red. **Next row:** K across. Work 2 more rows of ribbing with red. Break off red. Attach white and p 1 row. Continue in ribbing for 1 inch. Bind off in ribbing. **POCKET:** With No. 6 needles and white, cast on 22 sts. Work in stockinette st for 27 rows. Bind off. With a crochet hook and white, work sc around pocket, making 3 sc in each corner. With red and using duplicate stitch, embroider chosen emblem on pocket, centering design. Sew side and sleeve seams. Sew pocket in place on left breast. Sew in zipper.

29ΦΦ
Color-rimmed singlet & babybag

SIZES: Petite (5-6), Small (7-8), Medium (9-10).

MATERIALS: Columbia-Minerva Nantuk® Sweater and Afghan Yarn (2 oz. skein); 4 skeins main color (MC), 1 skein contrasting color (CC).
Aluminum Crochet Hook, Size I.

GAUGE: 10 sc = 3 inches;
    4 rnds = 1 inch.

Blocking Measurements Sizes	Petite	Small	Medium
Actual Knitting Measurements Bust (In Inches)			
	32½	33½	34½

BODY: With CC, ch 109 (113, 115) to measure approximately 32½ (33½, 34½) inches. Join with a slip st to first ch (taking care not to twist ch) to form a ring. Ch 1. **Rnd 1:** Sc in same ch with joining (mark for beg of rnd), sc in each ch, join with a slip st to first sc—109 (113, 115) sc. Draw MC through loop on hook, drop CC. Mark beg of every rnd. **Rnd 2:** Working through back loops only, sc in same st with joining and in each sc around. Draw CC through loop, drop MC. **Rnd 3:** Repeat rnd 2. Join (do not drop CC), ch 1. **Rnds 4 and 5:** Working through both loops sc around, draw MC through loop at end of rnd 5, do not ch 1. **Rnd 6:** Repeat rnd 2, ch 1. **Rnd 7:** Repeat rnd 4. Draw CC through loop. **Rnd 8:** Repeat rnd 2. Draw MC through loop. Fasten off CC. **Rnd 9:** Repeat rnd 2. Ch 1. Continue to work sc rnds, join and ch 1 at end of every rnd until piece measures 18½ inches from beg, or desired length to beg of yoke. Ch 1, turn. **YOKE: Back: Row 1** (wrong side): Sc in each of 55 (57, 58) sts, ch 1, turn. Repeat this row 24 (26, 28) times, ending on wrong side, ch 1, turn. **SHOULDERS AND NECK: Row 1:** Sc in each of 16 (17, 17) sts, ch 1, turn. Repeat last row twice, fasten off. Skip 23 (23, 24) sc at center of last complete row for neck, join yarn in next st. Work 2nd shoulder to correspond to first shoulder. **YOKE: Front: Row 1** (wrong side): Join yarn from wrong side at end of first row of back, sc in each of 54 (56, 57) sc. Ch 1, turn. Repeat last row 16 (18, 20) times. **SHOULDERS AND NECK: Row 1:** Same as Row 1 of back shoulder. Repeat this row 7 more times: fasten off. Skip 22 (22, 23) sc for neck, work 2nd shoulder to correspond. Join shoulders as follows: with wrong side of back and front tog, front facing you; with CC, sc tog matching sts of back and front. **SLEEVES:** From right side, join CC at center underarm (space between front and back). **Rnd 1:** Sc in same place joining and in every 2nd row around armhole. Join as before, ch 1, do not turn. **Rnd 2:** Sc in same sc with joining and each sc around. Join, ch 1, draw MC through. Cut CC. **Rnd 3:** * Work sc in each of 2 sc, 2 sc in next sc, (1 sc inc); repeat from * around. Join, ch 1. **Rnds 4 through 9:** Sc in each sc, join, ch 1, do not ch at end of rnd 9, draw CC through loop, drop MC. **Rnd 10:** Through both loops, work sc rnd. Draw MC through loop, drop CC. **Rnd 11:** Through back loops only, work sc rnd. **Rnd 12:** With MC, repeat rnd 10. Draw CC through loop, drop MC. **Rnd 13:** With CC repeat rnd 11: **Rnds 14 and 15:** Repeat rnd 10, draw MC through loop, drop CC. **Rnd 16:** Repeat rnd 11. Draw CC through loop. Cut MC. **Rnd 17:** Repeat rnd 11. **Rnd 18:** Repeat rnd 10; join and fasten off. Work other sleeve in same way. **NECK EDGE:** Join CC at right shoulder seam. **Rnd 1:** (right side): Sc in end of each row and in each sc around. Join. Ch 1, do not turn. **Rnd 2:** Sc in each sc around and across back neck, dec 3 sts evenly spaced. Join and fasten off.

Babybag

MATERIALS: Columbia-Minerva Nantuk® Sweater and Afghan Yarn (2 oz. skein), small amounts Main Color (MC) and Contrasting Color (CC).
Aluminum Crochet Hook, Size I.

BACK: With MC, ch 4. Join with sl st to first ch to form ring. **Rnd 1:** Ch 1, work 8 sc in ring. Join with sl st to first sc. Draw CC through lp on hook, drop MC. Mark end of each rnd. **Note:** All rnds are worked from right side through BACK LPS ONLY. **Rnd 2:** Work 2 sc in each sc. Join with sl st to first sc (16 sc), ch 1. **Rnd 3:** * Sc in next sc, 2 sc in next sc; repeat from * around. Join as before, do not ch 1 (24 sc). Draw MC through lp on hook, drop CC. **Rnd 4:** * Sc in each of 3 sc, 2 sc in next sc; repeat from * around, join (30 sc). Draw CC through lp, drop MC. **Rnd 5:** Sc in each sc, join (30 sc). Draw MC through lp, drop CC. **Rnd 6:** Sc in each of 2 sc, * 2 sc in next sc, sc in each of 4 sc, repeat from * around, ending last repeat, sc in each of 2 sc, join (36 sc). Draw CC through lp. **Rnd 7:** Sl st in each of 6 sc, hdc in each of 2 sc, (2 hdc in next sc, hdc in each of 3 sc) 5 times, 2 hdc in next sc, hdc in next sc, sl st in each of last 6 sc. Join, fasten off. **FLAP:** Join CC in 6th sl st to right of last joining. **Row 1:** Sc in same st with joining and in next 11 sl sts (12 sc). Ch 1, turn. **Row 2:** Through both lps, sc in each sc. Ch 1, turn. **Rows 3 and 4:** Repeat Row 2, do not ch at end of Row 4, draw MC through lp, cut CC. Ch 1, turn. **Row 5:** Through both lps work sc, inc 1 st in first and last st (14 sc). Draw CC through, cut MC. Ch 1, turn. **Row 6:** Through front lps only, repeat Row 2. Draw MC through, cut CC. Ch 1, turn. Repeat last 2 rows once. **Row 9:** Through both lps work sc, dec 1 st each side. Draw CC through lp, cut MC. Ch 1, turn. **Row 10:** Through front lps, repeat Row 9. Draw MC through lp, cut CC. Ch 1, turn. **Row 11:** Skip first st, sl st in next st, sc in each st to last 2 sts, sl st in next st, fasten off. **FRONT:** With MC only and working all rnds through both lps work same as back. **STRAP:** With MC, chain for 30 inches or desired length, sc in 2nd ch from hook and in each ch to end. Working on other side of foundation ch, sl st at base of each sc. Fasten off. **FINISHING:**

Hold wrong side of front and back tog, with sts of last rnd of pieces matching. With front of bag facing you, join MC in first hdc at left at center top (sl st edge). Through double thickness work sc in matching hdc's (do not work across front opening) continue sc around flap, working 1 sc in each row and st, 3 sc at corners. Join with a sl st to first st. Fasten off. Attach strap at each side of bag near flap.

30 ⊗ Striped boatneck

SIZES: 6, 8, 10, 12, 14, 16.

MATERIALS: Lion Brand Charmette, (40 gram balls), 6 (7, 8, 9, 9, 10) balls White (Color A), 4 (5, 6, 7, 7, 8) balls Navy (Color B). Knitting Needles, 1 pair each No. 3 and No. 4.

GAUGE: St st on No. 4 needles
    7 sts = 1 inch;
    9 rows = 1 inch.

Blocking Measurements					
Sizes	6	8	10	12	14	16

Actual Knitting Measurements					
Bust (In Inches)					
30	32	34	36	38	40
Width of back or front at underarms					
15	16	17	18	19	20
Width of sleeve at upperarm					
14½	15	15½	16½	16½	17

STRIPE PATTERN: Rows 1 through 6: With B work in garter st (k each row). **Rows 7 through 18:** With A work in stockinette st (k on right side, p on wrong side). Repeat these 18 rows for stripe pattern. **BACK:** With A and No. 3 needles, cast on 100 (106, 114, 120, 128, 134) sts. Work in k 1, p 1, ribbing for 2½ (2½, 3, 3, 3½, 3½) inches, ending on right side. **Next Row:** (wrong side): P, inc 6 sts evenly spaced across row—106 (112, 120, 126, 134, 140) sts. Change to No. 4 needles and stripe pattern. Work even until 15 (15¼, 15¾, 16, 16¼, 16½) inches from beg or desired length to underarm. Place a marker on each end of last row to indicate armholes. Continue in stripe pattern until about 7¼ (7½, 7¾, 8, 8¼, 8½) inches above markers, ending on an A stripe **SHOULDERS AND NECK:** With B work in garter st, binding off 9 (10, 11, 12, 13, 14) sts at beg of next 6 rows—52 (52, 54, 54, 56, 56) sts. Change to No. 3 needles and stockinette st. Continue with B for 4 rows in stockinette st, inc 1 st each edge of each row for facing—60 (60, 62, 62, 64, 64) sts. Bind off loosely. **FRONT:** Work same as back. **SLEEVES:** With No. 3 needles and B, cast on 66 (68, 70, 72, 74, 76) sts. Work in stockinette for 5 rows. Change to No. 4 needles and work in garter st for 5 rows. Starting with row 7 work in stripe pattern, inc 1 st each edge of next row, then every 1 inch 17 (18, 19, 19, 20, 21) times more—102 (106, 110, 112, 116, 120) sts. Work even until 19½ (20, 20½, 21, 21½, 22) inches from beg or desired length to shoulder. Bind off loosely. **FINISHING:** Sew shoulder, side and sleeve seams. Sew in sleeves from marker to marker. Turn hem on sleeves to wrong side and sew in place. Turn facing at neck to wrong side and sew in place.

31 ⊗
A long & lacy smock

SIZES: Small, Medium, Large.

MATERIALS: Spinnerin Pippin, (50 gram ball) 13 (15, 16) balls.
Knitting Needles, 1 pair No. 4.
⅜ inch elastic.

GAUGE: 6 sts = 1 inch;
8 rows = 1 inch.

Blocking Measurements

Sizes	Small	Medium	Large
Bust (In Inches)			
	34	36	38

PATTERN 1—Row 1: K 2, * yo, sl 1, k 1, psso; repeat from * ending k 2. Row 2: Purl. PATTERN 2—Row 1: K 11, yo, sl 1, k 1, psso, * k 10, yo, sl 1, k 1, psso; repeat from * ending k 11. Rows 2, 4, 6, 8, 10 and 12: Purl. Rows 3, 5, 9 and 11: Knit. Row 7: K 5, yo, sl 1, k 1, psso, * k 10, yo, sl 1, k 1, psso; repeat from * ending k 5. Repeat these 12 rows for pattern. PATTERN 3—Row 1: K 9 (12, 15), yo, (sl 1, k 1, psso) 2 times; yo, * k 10, yo, (sl 1, k 1, psso) 2 times; yo; repeat from * ending k 9 (12, 15) sts. Rows 2, 4, 6, 8, 10, 14, 16, 18 and 20: Purl. Row 3: K 8 (11, 14), yo, sl 1, k 1, psso, k 2, sl 1, k 1, psso, yo, * k 8, yo, sl 1, k 1, psso, k 2, sl 1, k 1, psso, yo; repeat from * ending k 8 (11, 14). Row 5: K 7 (10, 13), yo, sl 1, k 1, psso, k 4, sl 1, k 1, psso, yo, * k 6, yo, sl 1, k 1, psso, k 4, sl 1, k 1, psso, yo; repeat from * ending k 7 (10, 13). Row 7: K 6 (9, 12), yo, sl 1, k 1, psso, k 6, sl 1, k 1, psso, yo, * k 4, yo, sl 1, k 1, psso, k 6, sl 1, k 1, psso, yo; repeat from * ending k 6 (9, 12). Row 9: K 5 (8, 11), yo, sl 1, k 1, psso, k 8, sl 1, k 1, psso, yo, * k 2, yo, sl 1, k 1, psso, k 8, sl 1, k 1, psso, yo; repeat from * ending k 5 (8, 11). Row 11: K 4 (7, 10), sl 1, k 1, psso, yo, k 3, sl 1, k 1, psso, yo needle 2 times; sl 1, k 1, psso, k 3, * sl 1, k 1, psso, yo needle 2 times; sl 1, k 1, psso, k 3, sl 1, k 1, psso, yo needle 2 times; sl 1, k 1, psso, k 3; repeat from * ending yo, sl 1, k 1, psso, k 4 (7, 10). Row 12: Purl first in front then in back where 2 yo's fall tog. Row 13: K 5 (8, 11), sl 1, k 1, psso, yo, k 8, yo, sl 1, k 1, psso, * k 2, sl 1, k 1, psso, yo, k 8, yo, sl 1, k 1, psso; repeat from * ending k 5 (8, 11). Row 15: K 6 (9, 12), sl 1, k 1, psso, yo, k 6, yo, sl 1, k 1, psso, * k 4, sl 1, k 1, psso, yo, k 6, yo, sl 1, k 1, psso; repeat from * ending k 6 (9, 12). Row 17: K 7 (10, 13), sl 1, k 1, psso, yo, k 4, yo, sl 1, k 1, psso, * k 6, sl 1, k 1, psso, yo, k 4, yo, sl 1, k 1, psso; repeat from * ending k 7 (10, 13). Row 19: K 8 (11, 14), sl 1, k 1, psso, yo, k 2, yo, sl 1, k 1, psso, * k 8, sl 1, k 1, psso, yo, k 2, yo, sl 1, k 1, psso; repeat from * ending k 8 (11, 14). Row 21: K 9 (12, 15), sl 1, k 1, psso, yo needle 2 times; sl 1, k 1, psso, * k 10, sl 1, k 1, psso, yo needle 2 times; sl 1, k 1, psso; repeat from * ending k 9 (12, 15). Row 22: Knit, knitting first in front then in back where 2 yo's fall tog. PATTERN 4—Rows 1 and 5: K 2 (4, 6), p 3, * k 5, p 3; repeat from * ending k 1 (3, 5). Rows 2 and 4: P 1 (3, 5), k 3, * p 5, k 3; repeat from * ending p 2 (4, 6). Row 3: K 2 (4, 6), p 1, yo, p 2 tog, * k 5, p 1, yo, p 2 tog; repeat from * ending k 1 (3, 5). Rows 6 and 12: Purl. Rows 7 and 11: K 6 (8, 10), p 3, * k 5, p 3; repeat from * ending k 5 (7, 9). Rows 8 and 10: P 5 (7, 9), k 3, * p 5, k 3; repeat from * ending p 6 (8, 10). Row 9: K 6 (8, 10), p 1, yo, p 2 tog, * k 5, p 1, yo, p 2 tog; repeat from * ending k 5 (7, 9). Repeat these 12 rows for pattern. BACK: Cast on 204 (216, 228) sts. Work in garter st (k every row) for 3 inches. Row 1 (wrong side): Purl. Rows 2 and 3: Knit. Row 4: Work Row 1 of Pattern 1. Row 5: Knit. Beg with Row 1, work Pattern 2 until 20

inches from beg, ending ready for a right side row. YOKE AND ARMHOLE—Row 1: * K 2 tog, p 2 tog; repeat from * to end-102 (108, 114) sts. Row 2: * K 1, p 1; repeat from * to end. Working in rib pattern, bind off 6 sts beg of next 2 rows. Dec 1 st each and every row 6 times-78 (84, 90) sts and 10 rows rib. Rows 11 and 12: Purl. Row 13: Knit. Row 14: Purl. Rows 15 and 16: Knit. Row 17: Work Row 1 of Pattern 1. Row 18: Knit. Beg with Row 1 work 22 rows of Pattern 3. Row 41: Repeat Row 17. Rows 42 and 43: Knit. Row 44 (wrong side): P 12 (14, 16), k 54 (56, 58) for garter st center panel, p 12 (14, 16). Repeat Rows 43 and 44, 3 times more. NECK—Row 1: K 24 (26, 28) sts, attach a 2nd ball yarn, bind off center 30 (32, 34) sts, k 24 (26, 28). Row 2: P 12 (14, 16), k 12, with 2nd ball k 12, p 12 (14, 16). Row 3: K 24 (26, 28), with 2nd ball k 24 (26, 28). Repeat Rows 2 and 3 until armholes measure 7½ (8, 8½) inches. SHOULDERS: Bind off 6 sts at beg of next 4 rows, then 6 (7, 8) sts beg of next 4 rows. FRONT: Work same as back. Sew shoulder seams. SLEEVES: From right side beg at side edge of underarm, pick up 102 (106, 110) sts along entire armhole edge to other side edge. Row 1 (wrong side): Purl. Rows 2 and 3: Knit. Row 4: Work Row 1 of Pattern 1. Row 5: Knit. Beg with Row 1, work Pattern 1 for 43 rows ending with Pattern Row 1. Rows 49 through 51: Repeat Rows 3 through 5. Rows 52 through 58: Beg with a k row, work in st st. Rows 59 through 61: Knit. Rows 62 through 68: Beg with a k row, work in st st. Row 69: Knit. Rows 70 through 94: Beg with Row 1, work Pattern 4 working 12 rows repeat 2 times (24 rows). Row 95: Knit. Rows 96 through 101: Beg with a p row, work in st st. Rows 102 through 108: Repeat Rows 52 through 58. Rows 109 through 111: Repeat Rows 3 through 5. Beg with Row 1, work Pattern 3 working k 7 (10, 13) instead of k 9 (12, 15) sts beg and end of row. Complete pattern having 2 sts less at each end. Row 133: Work Row 1 of Pattern 1. Row 134: Knit. Repeat Rows 52 through 94 once more. Beg with a k row, work in st st for 3 rows. Work in garter st (k every row) for 2 inches, ending on right side. Beg with a p row, work in st st for 3 rows. Bind off. FINISHING: Sew side and sleeve seams. Fold garter st band at lower edge of smock in half to inside and sew down. Fold under garter st band at sleeve edge to inside so garter st row lines up with bottom row of last row of Pattern 1. Sew bind off to edge leaving a small opening. Cut elastic to desired wrist size and draw through. Sew ends tog. Sew opening.

32 ⊗
Tiny tie-on halter

SIZES: 6, 8, 10, 12, 14.

MATERIALS: Brunswick Sparkletwist (2 oz. skein), No. 700 White 3 (3, 3, 4, 4) skeins.
Knitting Needles, 1 pair each No. 3 and No. 5.
Aluminum Crochet Hook, Size C.

GAUGE: 6 sts = 1 inch.

Measurements

Sizes	6	8	10	12	14
Body Bust Measurement (In Inches)					
	30½	31½	32½	34	36

BACK: With smaller needles cast on 84 (86, 90, 92, 96) sts and work k 1, p 1 ribbing for 2 inches. Change to larger needles and stockinette st, and inc 1 st each side every 2 inches, 3 times. When piece measures from beg 11 (11, 11¼, 11½, 12) inches, bind off remaining 90 (92, 96, 98, 102) sts. **FRONT:** Work same as back until piece measures 10 (10, 10½, 10½, 11) inches, ending on purl side. **Begin Pointelle: SHAPE ARMHOLE, NECK: Row 1:** K 3 (4, 6, 7, 9) sts, yo, sl 1, k 2 tog, psso, k to last 6 (7, 9, 10, 12) sts, yo, sl 1 k 2 tog, psso, yo, knit to end. **Row 2 and all wrong side rows:** Purl. **Row 3:** K 4 (5, 7, 8, 10) sts, k 2 tog through back loop (TBL), k to end. **Row 5:** K 10 (11, 13, 14, 16) sts, yo, sl 1, k 2 tog, psso, yo, knit to last 11 (12, 14, 15, 17) sts, yo, sl 1, k 2 tog, psso, yo, knit to end. **Row 7:** K 11 (12, 14, 15, 17) sts, yo, k 2 tog TBL, k to last 13 (14, 16, 17, 19) sts, yo, k 2 tog TBL, k to end. **Rows 9 and 10:** Bind off 7 (8, 10, 11, 13) sts at beg (next) 2 rows. **Row 11:** K 1, k 2 tog, k 7, yo, sl 1, k 2 tog, psso, yo, k to last 14 sts, yo, sl 1, k 2 tog, psso, yo, k to last 3 sts, k 2 tog, k 1. **Rows 12, 14, 16, 18, 20, 22, 24, 26 and 28:** P 1, p 2 tog, p to last 3 sts, p 2 tog, p 1. **Row 13:** K 1, k 2 tog, k 6, yo, k 2 tog TBL, k to last 12 sts, yo, k 2 tog TBL, k to last 3 sts, k 2 tog, k 1. **Row 15:** K 1, k 2 tog, k to last 3 sts, k 2 tog, k 1, k 2 tog, k 1. **Row 17:** K 1, k 2 tog, k 5, yo, sl 1, k 2 tog, psso, yo, k to last 12 sts, yo, sl 1, k 2 tog, psso, yo, k to last 3 sts, k 2 tog, k 1. **Row 19:** K 1, k 2 tog, k 4, yo, k 2 tog TBL, k to last 9 sts, yo, k 2 tog TBL, k to last 3 sts, k 2 tog, k 1. **Row 21:** K 1, k 2 tog, k to last 3 sts, k 2 tog, k 1. **Row 23:** K 1, k 2 tog, k 10, yo, sl 1, k 2 tog, psso, yo, k next 7 sts, yo, sl 1, k 2 tog, psso, yo, k to last 3 sts, k 2 tog, k 1. **Row 25:** K 1, k 2 tog, k 9, yo, sl 1, k 2 tog TBL, k 8, yo, k 2 tog TBL, k 8, yo, k 2 tog TBL, k to last 3 sts, k 2 tog, k 1. **Row 27:** K 1, k 2 tog, k to last 3 sts, k 2 tog, k 1. **Row 29:** K 1, k 2 tog, k 10, bind off next 16 sts, k to last 3 sts, k 2 tog, k 1. Working back and forth on 1 strap only, dec 1 st on inside edge only every other row 5 times. Work even until strap measures about 15 inches. Bind off. Work other strap the same. Weave or sew side seams. Work 2 rows sc around entire top and straps easing in to fit.

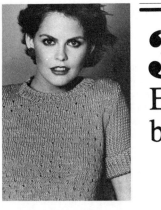

33 ⊗ Eyeletted baby-pull

SIZES: Small (6), Medium (8-10), Large (12-14).

MATERIALS: J. & P. Coats "KNIT-CRO-SHEEN": Art A 64: 12 (12, 13) balls (175 yds. each) No 4-A Medium Blue. Knitting Needles, 1 pair each No. 3 and No. 5.

GAUGE: Pattern St: 5 sts = 1 inch
7 rows = 1 inch.
Ribbing on No. 5 needles (slightly stretched):
5 sts = 1 inch
7 rows = 1 inch.
Use 3 strands held together throughout.

Blocking Measurements

Sizes	Small (6)	Medium (8-10)	Large (12-14)
Body Bust Size (In Inches)	30½	31½-32½	34-36
Actual Knitting Measurements Bust	31	33½	36½
Width across back or front at underarm	15½	16¾	18¼

Length from shoulder to lower edge	17½	19	20
Length of side seam	11	11½	12
Length of sleeve seam	8	8½	9
Width across sleeve at upper arm (slightly stretched)	12	12½	13

Wind any single ball into 3 equal parts. BACK: Starting at lower edge with 3 strands held together and No. 3 needles, cast on 70 (78, 86) sts. Working in back loop of each knit st on ribbing only, work in k 1, p 1 ribbing for 2½ inches, increasing 6 sts evenly spaced across last row—76 (84, 92) sts. Change to No. 5 needles and work in pattern as follows. **Row 1 (right side):** K across. **Row 2:** P across. **Row 3:** K 5, yo, k 2 tog, * k 6, yo, k 2 tog. Repeat from * 7 (8, 9) more times; k 5. **Row 4:** P across. **Row 5:** K across. **Row 6:** P across. **Row 7:** K 1, * yo, k 2 tog, k 6. Repeat from * across, ending last repeat with k 1 instead of k 6. **Row 8:** P across. Repeat last 8 rows for pattern. Work in pattern until total length is 11 (11½, 12) inches, ending with a p row. **Armhole Shaping:** Continuing in pattern throughout, bind off 5 (5, 6) sts at beg of next 2 rows, dec one st at each end every other row 3 (5, 6) times—60 (64, 68) sts. Work even in pattern (no more decs) until length is 6½ (7½, 8) inches, from first row of armhole shaping, ending with a p row. **Shoulder Shaping:** Continuing in pattern, bind off 5 (5, 6) sts at beg of next 4 rows. Bind off 5 (6, 6) sts at beg of following 2 rows. Place remaining 30 (32, 32) sts on a stitch holder to be worked later for neckband. **FRONT:** Work same as Back until length is 4 (5, 5½) inches from first row of armhole shaping, ending with a p row. **Neck Shaping:** Continue in pattern until there are 21 (22, 24) sts on right-hand needle. Slip remaining sts onto another stitch holder. Continuing in pattern over sts on needle only, bind off 2 sts at neck edge every other row 3 times. Work in pattern over remaining 15 (16, 18) sts until length of armhole is same as on Back, ending at armhole edge. **Shoulder Shaping: Row 1:** Bind off 5 (5, 6) sts, complete row. **Row 2:** Work in pattern across. **Rows 3 and 4:** Repeat Rows 1 and 2. **Row 5:** Bind off remaining 5 (6, 6) sts. Leaving center 18 (20, 20) sts on stitch holder, slip remaining sts onto a No. 5 needle, attach yarn at neck edge and work to correspond with opposite side, reversing shaping. **SLEEVES:** Starting at lower edge with 3 strands held together and No. 5 needles, cast on 60 (62, 64) sts. Knitting in back loop of each k st, work in k 1, p 1 ribbing until total length is 8 (8½, 9) inches. **Top Shaping:** Bind off 5 (5, 6) sts at beg of next 2 rows. Dec one st at each end every other row until 20 (22, 24) sts remain. Dec one st at each end every 4th row 0 (2, 3) times. Bind off 2 sts at beg of next 4 rows. Bind off remaining sts. Block to measurements. Sew left shoulder seam. **NECKBAND:** With 3 strands held together and No. 3 needles, k across sts on back stitch holder, pick up and k 21 (21, 22) sts along left front neck edge, k across sts on front stitch holder, pick up and k 21 (21, 22) sts along right front neck edge—90 (94, 96) sts. Knitting into back loop of each k st, work in k 1, p 1 ribbing for 1 inch. Bind off loosely in ribbing. Sew right shoulder seam including neckband. Sew side and sleeve seams. Sew in sleeves. Turn up a 2 inch cuff.

34 ⊗ Tiny tank

SIZE: One size fits 8-12.

MATERIALS: Lion Brand Charmette, (40 gram balls), 3 balls.

Knitting Needles, 1 pair No. 3.
Aluminum Crochet Hook, Size C.

GAUGE: St st: 7 sts = 1 inch.

BACK: Cast on 97 sts, and work in k 1, p 1, ribbing, increasing 1 st at both ends every 12th row, 8 times. Work on 113 sts until piece measures 11½ inches. **ARMHOLE AND NECK SHAP—ING:** Bind off 6 sts at the beg of next row, work across next 19 sts, bind off center 63 sts, work across last 25 sts. Turn. Bind off 6 sts at the beg of next row, work across next 19 sts. Work on these sts only, dec 1 st at both ends of the following row and every other row 6 times, ending with wrong side facing. Next row: P 1, k 1, p 3, k 1, p 1. Following row: K 1, p 1, k 3, p 1, k 1. Repeat last 2 rows until armhole measures 7 inches. Leave on needle. Work other side to correspond. **FRONT:** Cast on 97 sts, and work in ribbing as for back, increasing 1 st at both ends, every 12th row 4 times. Work on 105 sts until piece measures 7 inches. Work as follows: **Row 1:** K 43, rib 19, k 43. **Row 2:** P 44, rib 17, p 44. **Row 3:** K 45, rib 15, k 45. **Row 4:** P 46, rib 13, p 46. **Row 5:** K 47, rib 11, k 47. **Row 6:** P 48, rib 9, p 48. **Row 7:** K 49, rib 7, k 49. **Row 8:** P 50, rib 5, p 50. **Row 9:** K 51, rib 3, k 51. **Row 10:** Purl. **Row 11:** K 13, yo, k 2 tog, k 12, yo, k 2 tog, k 12, yo, k 2 tog, k 19, yo, k 2 tog, k 12, yo, k 2 tog, k 12, k 2 tog, k 13. **Row 12:** Purl. Work 16 rows in stockinette st. Repeat rows 11 and 12 and then work 8 rows in stockinette st. **Neckshaping: Row 1:** K 50, p 1, k 1. Slip remaining 53 sts on holder. Turn and work over the first set 52 sts only as follows: **Row 2:** P 1, k 1, p 50. **Row 3:** K 48, k 2 tog (dec), p 1, k 1. **Row 4:** P 1, k 1, p to end of row. **Row 5:** K to 2 sts before p st, k 2 tog, p 1, k 1. **Row 6:** Repeat row 4. **Rows 7 and 8:** Repeat rows 5 and 6. **Row 9:** K 13, yo, k 2 tog, k 12, yo, k 2 tog, k 12, yo, k 2 tog, k 2, k 2 tog, p 1, k 1. **Row 10:** P 1, k 1, p across. **Armhole shaping: Row 11:** Bind off 6 sts at beg of row, work across, dec 1 st at front edge as before. **Row 12:** Repeat row 10. **Row 13:** K 1, p 1, sl 1, k 1, psso, k to last 4 sts, k 2 tog, p 1, k 1. **Row 14:** P 1, k 1, p to last 2 sts, k 1, p 1. Repeat last 2 rows 5 times. Now dec 1 st at neck edge once, ending with a purl row. Next row: K 1, p 1, k to last 5 sts, k 3 tog, p 1, k 1, (2 sts decreased at neck edge). Work in this manner, dec 2 sts at front edge as before every other row until 7 sts remain, ending with right side facing. Work strap as follows: **Row 1:** K 1, p 1, k 3, p 1, k 1. **Row 2:** P 1, k 1, p 3, k 1, p 1. Repeat last 2 rows until armhole measures 7 inches. Leave on needle. Attach yarn to 53 sts from holder, bind off center st and work other side to correspond, reversing shapings. **FINISHING:** Sew side seams. Work a row of sl sts along back shaping. Weave sts of straps together.

35 ⊗
Barebacked, with a shrug of shawl

SIZES: Small (6-10), Medium (12-16).

MATERIALS: Columbia-Minerva Glimmer Yarn, sports yarn weight, (2 oz. skein), Halter 3 (4) skeins, Shawl 3 skeins. Knitting Needles, Circular needle (29 inch) No. 10½ and 1 pair straight needles No. 10½ and 1 set double-pointed needles No. 10½. Aluminum Crochet Hook, Size J.

GAUGE: 3 sts = 1 inch; 4 rnds = 1 inch.

Measurements
Sizes	6-10	12-16

Body Bust Size (In Inches)
31½-35	36-38

Note: Work with 2 strands held together throughout. Use a plastic ring to mark rnds. Wind single skein into 2 equal balls.

Halter:

BODY: Beg at lower edge, cast on 75 (83) sts on circular needle, join, being careful not to twist sts. Work in st st (k each rnd) until 4 inches from beg. Beg working pattern as follows: **Rnd 1:** K next 36 (44) sts, k 2 tog, yo, k 1, yo, SKP, k remaining sts. **Rnds 2 and all Even Rnds to 42:** Knit. **Rnd 3:** K to within 1 st before previous yo, k 2 tog, yo, k 1, yo, SKP, k remaining sts. **Rnd 5:** Repeat Rnd 3. **Rnd 7:** K to within 2 sts before previous yo, k 2 tog, yo, k 3, yo, SKP, k remaining sts. **Note:** Always k to within 2 sts before previous yo, work sts as stated on following rnds, then k remaining sts to end of that rnd. **Rnd 9:** K 2 tog, yo, k 5, yo, SKP. **Rnd 11:** K 2 tog, yo, k 7, yo, SKP. **Rnd 13:** K 2 tog, yo, k 9, yo, SKP. **Rnd 15:** K 2 tog, yo, k 11, yo, SKP. **Rnd 17:** K 2 tog, yo, k 13, yo, SKP. **Rnd 19:** K 2 tog, yo, k 5, k 2 tog, yo, k 1, yo, SKP, k 5, yo, SKP. **Rnd 21:** K 2 tog, yo, k 5, k 2 tog, yo, k 3, yo, SKP, k 5, yo, SKP. **Rnd 23:** K 2 tog, yo, k 5, k 2 tog, yo, k 5, yo, SKP, k 5, yo, SKP. **Rnd 25:** K 2 tog, yo, k 5, k 2 tog, yo, k 7, yo, SKP, k 5, yo, SKP. **Rnd 27:** K 2 tog, yo, k 5, k 2 tog, yo, k 9, yo, SKP, k 5, yo, SKP. **Rnd 29:** K 2 tog, yo, k 5, k 2 tog, yo, k 11, yo, SKP, k 5, yo, SKP. **Rnd 31:** K2 tog, yo, k 5, k 2 tog, yo, k 13, yo, SKP, k 5, yo, SKP. **Rnd 33:** K 2 tog, yo, k 5, k 2 tog, yo, k 15, yo, SKP, k 5, yo, SKP. **Rnd 35:** K 2 tog, yo, k 5, k 2 tog, yo, k 17, yo, SKP, k 5, yo, SKP. **Rnd 37:** K 2 tog, yo, k 5, k 2 tog, yo, k 19, yo, SKP, k 5, yo, SKP. **Rnd 39:** K 2 tog, yo, k 5, k 2 tog, yo, k 21, yo, SKP, k 5, yo, SKP. **Rnd 41:** K 2 tog, yo, k 5, k 2 tog, yo, k 23, yo, SKP, k 5, yo, SKP. **Rnd 43:** K 2 tog, yo, k 5, k 2 tog, yo, k 25, yo, SKP, k 5, yo, SKP. **Rnd 44:** K to 3 sts after last SKP of previous rnd, bind off loosely next 26 (34) sts for Back. **DIVIDE FOR FRONTS (left side) — Row 1:** With straight needles and 1 st on right-hand needle, K 1, k 2 tog, yo, k 5, k 2 tog, yo, k 11, k 2 tog, place remaining sts on holder. **Row 2 and All Even Rows:** Purl. **Row 3:** K 1, k 2 tog, yo, k 5, k 2 tog, yo, k 13. **Row 5:** K 2 tog, yo, k 5, k 2 tog, yo, k 12, k 2 tog. **Row 7:** K 2 tog, k 4, k 2 tog, yo, k 12, k 2 tog. **Row 9:** K 2 tog, k 2, k 2 tog, yo, k 12, k 2 tog. **Row 11:** K 2 tog, k 2 tog, yo, k 12, k 2 tog. **Row 13:** K 2 tog, yo, k 12, k 2 tog. **Rows 15, 17, 19, 21 and 23:** In st st dec 1 st at each end. **STRAP:** Working on 5 sts work in st st (k 1 row, p 1 row) until piece measures evenly to center back neck. Bind off. **Right Side — Row 1:** With right side facing and 2 strands, join to next st, k 2 tog, k 12, yo, SKP, k 5, yo, SKP, k 2. **Row 2 And All Even Rows:** Purl. **Row 3:** K 14, yo, SKP, k 5, yo, SKP, k 1. **Row 5:** K 2 tog, k 13, yo, SKP, k 5, yo, k 2 tog. **Row 7:** K 2 tog, k 13, yo, SKP, k 4, k 2 tog. **Row 9:** K 2 tog, k 13, yo, SKP, k 2, k 2 tog. **Row 11:** K 2 tog, k 13, yo, SKP, k 2 tog. **Row 13:** K 2 tog, k 13, k 2 tog. **Rows 15, 17, 19, 21, 23 and Strap:** Work to correspond to left side. Bind off. **FINISHING:** Weave straps at center back. With 2 strands work sc evenly around lower edge of halter, armholes, back and neck edges.

Shawl:

Working with 1 strand beg at center, cast on 2 sts on each of 4 dpn (8 sts). Use marker to mark rnds. **Rnd 1:** K in back lp in each st around. **Rnd 2:** Inc 1 st (**To Inc:** K in front and back of st) in each st around. Place marker between center sts in each panel. **Rnd 3 And All Odd Rnds:** Knit. **Rnd 4:** K around, inc 1 st before and after marker. Repeat last 2 rnds 12 times-(28 sts in each panel). Place sts on circular needle. **Eyelet Rnd:** * Yo, SKP, repeat from * around. **Next Rnd:** Being careful not to lose yo on previous rnd, K each st and yo, inc'ing 1 st before and after marker-(30 sts in each panel). **Next Rnd:** Knit. Repeat Eyelet Rnd, then repeat 2nd Inc Rnd every other rnd 18 times-(66 sts in each panel). **Next Rnd:** Repeat Eyelet Rnd. **Next Rnd:** K each st and yo, inc'ing 1 st before and after marker. **Next Rnd:** Knit. Repeat last 3 rnds twice, then repeat Inc Rnd every other rnd 5 times-(84 sts in each panel). Bind off, working corners as follows: Inc 1 st (3 sts on needle), (bind off 2) twice. **Edging:** Working in back lp only, sc evenly around working 3 sc in corners, join with sl st to first sc. **Rnd 2:** Working in back lp, hdc in each sc around, join with sl st to first hdc. **Rnd 3:** Working from left to right, sc in each st around. Fasten off.

36 ◐
Small sexies: halter

SIZES: Small (30½-31½ inch bust), Medium (32½-35 inch bust), Large (36 inch bust).

MATERIALS: J. & P. Coats "KNIT-CRO-SHEEN", Art. A.64: 4 (5, 6) balls (175 yards each).
Steel Crochet Hook, Size 1.

GAUGE: Pattern
    13 sts (including ch sts) = 2 inches;
    3 rows = 1 inch.
Use 2 strands held together throughout.

Blocking Measurements

Sizes	Small	Medium	Large
Body Bust Size (In Inches)			
	30½-31½	32½-34	36
Actual Crocheting Measurements			
Width across lower edge (excluding bottom band)			
	19½	20½	21½
Length up center (excluding neck and bottom bands)			
	12¼	13	13¾

Wind any single ball into 2 equal parts.
HALTER: Starting at lower edge (excluding bottom band) with 2 strands held together, ch 134 (140, 146) to measure 20½ (21½, 22½) inches. **Row 1 (wrong side):** Dc in 8th ch from hook, * *ch 2, skip next 2 ch, dc in next ch*—**sp made.** Repeat from * across chain—43 (45, 47) sps, including sp formed by first dc at beg of row. Ch 3, turn. **Row 2:** Skip first dc, dc in next dc, * *2 dc in next sp, dc in next dc*—**block over sp made;** *ch 2, dc in next dc*—**sp over sp made.** Repeat from * across to within last 2 sps, 2 dc in next sp, dc in next dc, skip next 2 ch sts, dc in next ch—dec made at each end. Ch 3, turn. **Row 3:** Skip first dc, dc in next dc, * ch 2, skip next 2 dc, dc in next dc, ch 2, dc in next dc. Repeat from * across to last block, ch 2, skip next 2 dc, dc in next dc, dc in top of turning ch-3. Ch 3, turn. **Row 4:** Skip first 2 dc, 2 dc in first sp, dc in next dc, * ch 2, dc in next sp, dc in next dc. Repeat from * across, ending with 2 dc in last ch-2 sp, skip next dc, dc in top of turning ch-3. Ch 3, turn. **Row 5:** Skip first 3 dc, dc in next dc, * ch 2, dc in next dc, ch 2, skip next 2 dc, dc in next dc. Repeat from * across, ending last repeat with ch 2, dc in next dc, skip last 2 dc, dc in top of ch-3—another dec made at each end. Ch 3, turn. **Row 6:** Skip first dc, dc in next dc, * ch 2, dc in next dc, 2 dc in next sp, dc in next dc. Repeat from * across to within last ch-2 sp, ch 2, dc in next dc, dc in top of ch-3. Ch 5, turn. **Row 7:** Skip first 2 dc, dc in next dc, * ch 2, skip next 2 dc, dc in next dc, ch 2, dc in next dc. Repeat from * across, ending last repeat with ch 2, skip last dc, dc in top of ch-3—39 (41, 43) sps. Ch 3, turn. **Rows 8 through 19:** Repeat last 6 rows (Rows 2 through 7) 2 more times—31 (33, 35) sps on last row. Ch 3, turn. **Row 20:** Skip first dc, dc in next dc, * make block over next sp, sp over next sp. Repeat from * across to within last 2 sps, block over next sp, skip next 2 ch, dc in next ch. Ch 3, turn. **Row 21:** Skip first dc, dc in next dc, * ch 2, skip next 2 dc, dc in next dc, ch 2, dc in next dc. Repeat from * across to last block, ch 2, skip next 2 dc, dc in next dc, dc in top of ch-3. Ch 3, turn. **Row 22:** Skip first 2 dc, dc in next dc, * sp over next sp, block over next sp. Repeat from * across to within last sp, skip last sp and following

dc, dc in top of ch-3. Ch 5, turn. **Row 23:** Skip first 2 dc, dc in next dc, work sps across as before, ending with ch 2, skip last dc, dc in top of ch-3—27 (29, 31) sps. Ch 3, turn. Repeat last 4 rows (Rows 20 through 23) 3 (4, 4) more times; then repeat Rows 20-21, 1 (0, 1) more time. There are 13 sps on last row on all sizes. Break off and fasten. **NECKBAND AND TIES: Row 1:** With 2 strands held together, ch 75 (80, 85); with right side of halter facing, sc in first st on last row, make 2 sc in first sp, (3 sc in next sp, 2 sc in next sp) 6 times; sc in top of last st. Ch 76 (81, 86), turn. **Row 2:** Sc in 2nd ch from hook, sc in each ch to within last ch of turning chain, *draw up a loop in last ch, draw up a loop in next sc, thread over hook and draw through all 3 loops on hook*—**dec made;** sc in each of next 32 sc, dec over next sc and following ch st, sc in each remaining ch. Ch 1, turn. **Row 3:** * Sc in each sc across to within next dec, dec over next 2 sts. Repeat from * once more; sc in each remaining sc. Ch 1, turn. **Row 4:** Repeat last row. Ch 1, turn. **Row 5:** Sc in each sc across. Break off and fasten. **BOTTOM BAND AND TIES:** With 2 strands held together, ch 105 (110, 115); with right side of halter facing and working along opposite side of starting chain of halter, make 3 sc in each sp across lower edge. Ch 106 (111, 116), turn. **Row 2:** Sc in 2nd ch from hook, sc in each ch and in each sc across to end of first long chain. Ch 1, turn. **Rows 3, 4 and 5:** Sc in each sc across. Ch 1, turn. At end of last row, do not turn. **EDGING:** From right side, sc in top of last sc made, *ch 3, sl st in top of sc just made*—**picot made;** along end of tie make sc in end st of each row, ch 3, complete picot; working along opposite side of long chain, make (sc in each of next 5 ch, picot in top of last sc) 21 (22, 23) times; being careful to keep work flat, along side edge continue to work 5 sc and a picot across ends of rows to within neckband; along opposite side of starting chain of neck tie, work (sc in next 5 ch and a picot) 15 (16, 17) times; work along end of tie as before and continue in this manner to work 5 sc and a picot edging along entire outer edge (including ties), ending with sc in each remaining st after last picot. Join to first sc at beg of this rnd. Break off and fasten. Block to measurements.

37 ⊗
Small sexies: skivvy

SIZES: Small (6-8), Medium (10-12), Large (14-16).

MATERIALS: J. & P. Coats "KNIT-CRO-SHEEN", Art. A.64: 7 (9, 10) balls (175 yards each).
Knitting Needles, 1 pair each No. 3 and No. 5.
Crochet Hook, Size G.

GAUGE: Rib pattern on No. 5 needles (slightly stretched)
    6 sts = 1 inch;
    7 rows = 1 inch.
Use 3 strands held together throughout.

Blocking Measurements

Sizes	Small (6-8)	Medium (10-12)	Large (14-16)
Body Bust Size (In Inches)			
	30½-31½	32½-34	36-38
Actual Knitting Measurements			
Bust (slightly stretched)			
	32	34	38
Width across back or front at underarm			
	16	17	19
Length from shoulder to lower edge			
	18½	19½	20½

Length of side seam			
	12	12	12½

Wind any extra ball into 3 equal parts.

BACK: Starting at lower edge with 3 strands held together and No. 3 needles, cast on 87 (93, 105) sts. **Row 1 (wrong side):** P in back of first st, * k 1, p in back of next st. Repeat from * across. **Row 2:** K in back of first st, * p 1, k in back of next st. Repeat from * across. Repeat Rows 1-2 alternately for Twisted Rib pattern. Work in Twisted Rib pattern for 2 inches. Change to No. 5 needles and continue in Twisted Rib pattern until total length is 4 (4, 4½) inches, ending with a row on wrong side. Keeping continuity of Twisted Rib pattern throughout, and working inc sts in pattern, inc one st at each end of next row and every 10th row thereafter 4 times in all—95 (101, 113) sts. Work even in pattern until total length is 12 (12, 12½) inches, ending with a row on wrong side. **Armhole and Neck Shaping: Rows 1-2:** Keeping continuity of pattern throughout, bind off in ribbing 6 (6, 8) sts at beg of each row. **Row 3:** Dec one st at beg of row, work in pattern until there are 29 (31, 34) sts on right-hand needle, work next 2 sts tog, place these 30 (32, 35) sts on a stitch holder; bind off in ribbing next 19 (21, 23) sts; keeping in pattern, dec over next 2 sts, work in pattern across, decreasing one st at end of row. Working over 30 (32, 35) sts on needle only, shape both edges as follows: **Row 4:** Work in pattern across, decreasing one st at end of row—neck edge. **Row 5:** Decreasing one st at each end, work in pattern across. Repeat last 2 rows alternately 6 (6, 7) more times —9 (11, 11) sts. Keeping armhole edge straight, work in pattern, continuing to dec one st at neck edge every row until 7 (7, 9) sts remain. Work even in pattern until length is 6½ (7½, 8) inches from first row of armhole shaping, ending at armhole edge. Bind off all sts in ribbing. With right side facing, slip sts from stitch holder onto a No. 5 needle, attach triple strand to neck edge and work to correspond with opposite side, reversing shaping. **FRONT:** Starting at lower edge with 3 strands held together and No. 3 needles, cast on 91 (99, 111) sts. **Row 1 (wrong side):** P in back of first st, (k 1, p in back of next st) 17 (19, 22) times; place a marker on needle; k 2, p 3, (k 4, p 3) twice; k 2—**center panel;** place a marker on needle; p in back of next st, (k 1, p in back of next st) 17 (19, 22) times. **Row 2:** K in back of first st, (p 1, k in back of next st) 17 (19, 22) times; slip marker, p 2, (yo, sl 1, k 2 tog, psso, yo, p 4) twice; yo, sl 1, k 2 tog, psso, yo, p 2, slip marker; k in back of next st, (p 1, k in back of next st) 17 (19, 22) times. **Slip markers on every row. Row 3:** Work in Twisted Rib pattern same as for Row 1 to next marker, slip marker; k 2, (p 2 tog through back of sts, yo, p 1, k 4) twice; p 2 tog through back of sts, yo, p 1, k 2; complete row in Twisted Rib pattern as established. **Row 4:** Work in Twisted Rib pattern same as Row 2 to marker; p 2, (k 3, p 4) twice; k 3, p 2; complete row in Twisted Rib pattern. **Hereafter work all sts before and after center panel in Twisted Rib pattern. Row 5:** Work to marker; k 2 (p 3, k 4) twice; p 3, k 2; complete row. Repeat last 4 rows (Rows 2 through 5) for Front pattern. Work in pattern until total length is 2 inches. Change to No. 5 needles and continue in pattern until total length is 4 (4, 4½) inches, ending with a row on wrong side. Keeping continuity of pattern and working increased sts in Twisted Rib pattern, inc one st at each end on next row and every 10th row thereafter 4 times in all—99 (107, 119) sts. Work even in pattern until total length is 12 (12, 12½) inches, ending with a wrong-side row. **Armhole and Neck Shaping: Rows 1-2:** Bind off in ribbing 6 (6, 8) sts, work in pattern across. **Row 3:** Dec one st at beg of row, work in pattern until there are 29 (31, 34) sts on right-hand needle, work next 2 sts tog, place these 30 (32, 35) sts on a stitch holder; bind off in pattern next 23 (27, 29) sts, dec over next 2 sts, work in pattern across, decreasing one st at end of row—30 (32, 35) sts. Starting with Row 4 of Armhole and Neck Shaping, complete same as for Back. Block to measurements. Sew side and shoulder seams. **NECK EDGING: Rnd 1:** With right side facing, using crochet hook, attach triple strand to end of left shoulder seam at neck edge; easing in edge slightly, sc evenly along entire neck edge. Join with sl st to first sc. **Rnd 2:** Sl st in each sc around. Break off and fasten. **ARMHOLE EDGING:** Starting at top end of side seam, work same as for Neck Edging along each armhole edge.

380

Shoulder-buttoned, slouchy

SIZES: Small (6), Medium (8-10), Large (12-14).

MATERIALS: J. & P. Coats "KNIT-CRO-SHEEN", Art. A. 64: 16 (16, 18) balls (175 yards each) No. 103 Pongee. Steel Crochet Hook, Size 1. 4 buttons, ½ inch in diameter.

GAUGE: Pattern Stitch (including ch sts)—
8 sts = 1 inch;
4 rows = 1 inch.
Use 2 strands held together throughout.

Blocking Measurements Sizes	Small (6)	Medium (8-10)	Large (12-14)
Body Bust Size (In Inches)	30½	31½-32½	34-36
Actual Crocheting Measurements Bust	31½	33½	37
Width across back or front at underarm	15¾	16¾	18½
Length from shoulder to lower edge (excluding ribbing)	17	18½	19½
Length of side seam (excluding ribbing)	10½	11	11½
Length of sleeve seam (excluding ribbing)	14	14½	15
Width across sleeve at upper arm	11	11½	12

WAISTBAND: Starting at side edge with 2 strands held together, ch 15 for all sizes to measure 2½ inches. **Row 1:** Sc in 2nd ch from hook and in each ch across—14 sc. Ch 1, turn. **Row 2:** Working in the back loop of each sc, sc in each sc across—14 sc. Ch 1, turn. Repeat Row 2 until piece measures (slightly stretched) 31½ (33½, 37) inches. Break off and fasten. Picking up back loop of sts only, sew last row to starting chain for side seam. **BACK:** Starting at lower edge, above waistband, with 2 strands of thread held together ch 128 (136, 150) to measure 16¾ (17¾, 19½) inches. **Row 1 (right side):** H dc in 4th ch from hook, * ch 1, skip 1 ch, h dc in next ch. Repeat from * across—64 (68, 75) h dc, 63 (67, 74) ch-1 sps counting turning ch at beg of row as 1 h dc and 1 ch. Ch 2, turn. **Row 2:** Skip first h dc, h dc in next ch-1 sp, * ch 1, skip next h dc, h dc in next ch-1 sp. Repeat from * across to within last h dc and turning chain, ch 1, h dc in turning chain sp, h dc in 2nd chain of turning chain—there are 2 h dc at each end, counting ch-2 at beg of row as 1 h dc. Ch 3, turn. **Row 3:** Skip first 2 h dc, * h dc in next ch-1 sp, ch 1, skip next h dc. Repeat from * to within turning chain, h dc in top of turning chain. Ch 2, turn. Repeat Rows 2 and 3 alternately for pattern. Work in pattern until total length is 10½ (11, 11½) inches, ending with a wrong-side row. (Do not ch 3 at end of last row). **ARMHOLE SHAPING: Row 1:** Sl st in first 2 h dc, (sl st in next ch-1 sp, sl st in next h dc) 3 (4, 4) times; sl st in next ch-1 sp, ch 3, skip next h dc, h dc in next ch-1 sp, * ch 1, h dc in next ch-1 sp. Repeat from * across to within last 8 (10, 10) sts (including ch sts), do not work over remaining sts. Ch 3, turn. **Row 2:** Skip first 2 h dc, h dc in next ch-1 sp, * ch 1, skip next h dc, h dc in next ch-1 sp. Repeat from * across to

within last h dc and turning chain, ch 1, h dc in top of turning chain—one st decreased at each end. Ch 3, turn. **Row 3:** Skip first 2 h dc, h dc in next sp, * ch 1, skip next h dc, h dc in next ch-1 sp. Repeat from * across to within last h dc and turning chain, ch 1, h dc in sp formed by turning chain—another st decreased at each end. Ch 3, turn. **Rows 4 through 7:** Repeat Rows 2 and 3 alternately twice—there are 99 (103, 107) sts (including ch sts) across last row. At end of last row ch 2, turn. **Next Row:** Skip first h dc, h dc in next ch-1 sp, * ch 2, skip next h dc, h dc in next ch-1 sp. Repeat from * across to within last h dc and turning chain, ch 1, h dc in turning chain sp, h dc in 3rd ch of turning chain. Ch 3, turn. Starting with Row 3 of pattern, work in pattern (no more dec) until length is 4½ (5½, 6) inches from first row of Armhole Shaping, ending with Row 2 of pattern, ch 3, turn. **NECK SHAPING: Row 1:** Skip first 2 h dc, h dc in next ch-1 sp, (ch 1, h dc in next sp) 14 (16, 17) times; h dc in next h dc. Do not work over remaining sts. Ch 3, turn. **Row 2:** Skip first 2 h dc, h dc in next ch-1 sp, work in pattern across same as for Row 3 of pattern. Ch 2, turn. **Row 3:** Work in pattern across same as for Row 2 of pattern to within last h dc and turning chain. Ch 1, h dc in top of turning chain. Ch 3, turn. **Rows 4 through 8:** Repeat Rows 2 and 3 of Neck Shaping alternately twice and Row 2 once more—25 (27, 29) sts (including ch sts), thus ending at armhole edge. Turn. **SHOULDER SHAPING: Row 1:** Sl st across first 8 (10, 12) sts including ch sts, ch 2, skip next h dc, h dc in next ch-1 sp, * ch 1, h dc in next sp. Repeat from * across to within last h dc and turning chain, ch 1, h dc in top of turning chain. Ch 3, turn. **Row 2:** Skip first 2 h dc, h dc in next sp, (ch 1, h dc in next sp) 3 times; sc in next h dc. Break off and fasten. Turn. Skip next 35 sts on last long row made before Neck Shaping; attach double strand of thread to next h dc, ch 2, h dc in next sp and complete to correspond with opposite side, reversing shaping. **EDGING:** With right side facing, attach double strand to lower right side edge, sc evenly around outer edges of back excluding lower edge, making 3 sc in same st at each corner and being careful to keep work flat. Break off and fasten. **FRONT:** Work same as for Back. **SLEEVES: CUFF:** Starting at seam edge, with double strand, ch 16. Having 15 sc, work same as for Waistband until total length is 6 (6½, 7) inches. Break off and fasten. Sew back loop of each sc on last row to starting chain. Starting at lower edge, with double strand, ch 62 (64, 68) to measure 8½ (9, 9½) inches. **Row 1:** Work same as for Row 1 of Back having 31 (32, 34) h dc and 30 (31, 33) ch-1 sps, counting turning chain at beg of row as 1 h dc and 1 sp. **Rows 2 through 8:** Repeat Rows 2 and 3 of Back alternately 3 times and Row 2 once more. Ch 3, turn. **Row 9 (inc row):** *H dc in first h dc—2 st inc made;* * ch 1, skip next h dc, h dc in next ch-1 sp. Repeat from * across to within last h dc and turning chain, *(ch 1, h dc in next st) twice;—2 st inc made at end of row.* Ch 2, turn. **Rows 10 through 14:** Repeat Rows 2 and 3 of Back alternately twice and Row 2 once more. Ch 3, turn. Repeat last 6 rows (Rows 9 through 14) 7 more times—89 (93, 97) sts (including ch-1 sps). Work even (no more incs) in pattern until total length is 14 (14½, 15) inches, ending with a wrong-side row. Turn. **TOP SHAPING:** Work same as for Back Armhole Shaping until 7 rows of Armhole Shaping have been completed. Repeat Rows 2 and 3 of Armhole Shaping until 41 (35, 35) sts remain (including ch sts). At end of last row, ch 2, turn. **Next Row:** *Skip first 2 h dc, holding back on hook last loop of each h dc, h dc in each of next 2 sps, thread over and draw through all 3 loops on hook—3 sts* **decreased at beg of row;** ch 1, work in pattern across *to within last 3 h dc and turning chain, dec over next 2 sps, do not ch 1, h dc in top of turning chain—3* **sts decreased at end of row.** Ch 2, turn. Repeat last row 3 (2, 2) more times. Break off and fasten. Work edging along outer edge of sleeve same as on Back. Block to measurements. Picking up back loop of each sc, sew side, sleeve and right shoulder seam. Starting at armhole edge, sew about ½ inch of left shoulder seam together. Adjusting lower edge of sleeve to fit, sew a cuff to each sleeve, matching underarm seam. Adjusting lower edge to fit, sew waistband to lower edge, allowing for stretching. Picking up back loop of each sc, sew in sleeves. **NECKBAND:** With double strand, ch 6. Working over 5 sc work same as for Waistband until piece when slightly stretched fits around entire neck edge. Break off and fasten. Sew neckband

to neck edge easing in to fit. **BUTTON LOOPS:** With pins, mark the position of 4 button loops evenly spaced along left front shoulder edge and neckband. With right side facing, attach double strand to first free sc at shoulder edge, (sc in each sc to within next pin, ch 4, skip next 3 sc) 4 times; sc in each remaining sc. Break off and fasten. Sew on buttons.

39 ⓒ
Stringy carry-all

SIZE: 15 inches from center bottom to top edge.

MATERIALS: Jute Twine (45 yard balls) 12 balls from variety or hardware store. NOTE: Since jute twine comes in various size balls and cones, buy enough at one time.
Aluminum Crochet Hook, Size K.

GAUGE: 2 dc = 1 inch; 1 rnd = 1 inch.

Starting at center bottom, ch 6; join with sl st to form ring. **Rnd 1:** Ch 3, 13 dc in ring; join with sl st to top of ch 3 (14 dc counting ch-3 as 1 dc). **Rnd 2:** Ch 3, dc in base of ch, 2 dc in each dc around; join (28 dc). **Rnd 3:** Repeat Rnd 2 (56 dc). Continue working rnds in dc, adding as many extra dcs evenly spaced in each rnd as needed to keep work flat. When piece measures 18 inches in diameter, work 5 rnds even without inc'ing. **Next (dec) rnd:** Ch 3, dc around, skipping 1 dc 5 times evenly spaced in rnd. Turn. Now working in **rows,** ch 3, dc in dc **halfway** around edge, skipping 10 dc evenly spaced across. Turn. **Next row:** Ch 3, dc in dc across, skipping 10 dc evenly spaced across. Turn. **Next row:** Ch 3, dc in dc across, skipping 6 dc evenly spaced across. Turn. **Next row:** Ch 3, dc in dc across, skipping 4 dc evenly spaced across. Turn. **Next row:** Ch 3, dc in dc across, skipping 3 dc evenly spaced across. Turn. **Next row:** Ch 3, dc in dc across, skipping enough sts so that 6 dc remain (counting turning ch as 1 dc). Working over 6 dc, continue in rows of dc until 5 rows more are completed. Fasten off. Attach twine to opposite halfway mark on top edge. Complete opposite side and handle as for first side and handle. Whip ends of 2 handle pieces together.

40 ⓒ
Stringy tote

SIZE: 11 x 15 inches.

MATERIALS: Jute Twine (45 yard balls) 6 balls (from variety or hardware store). NOTE: Since jute twine comes in various size balls and cones, buy enough at one time.
Aluminum crochet hook, size K.

GAUGE: 2 tr = 1 inch; 1 row = 1 inch.

Ch 36 for foundation ch. In 4th ch from hook tr and make 1 tr in each ch across; ch 4, turn. **Row 1:** In first st work tr in back loop and strand just below it; repeat across row. Repeat Row 1 for 21 more rows. Fasten off. Fold piece in half crosswise and sew sides of bag together. **STRAPS:** On top edge of bag mark a point 3 inches in from each side. Fasten 2 strands of jute to right-hand mark and make 32 inch chain. Fasten end to opposite mark. Repeat on back of bag.

41 ◑
Long pull & scarf

SIZES: Pull: 8, 10, 12, 14, 16;
     Scarf: 4 x 60 inches without fringe.

MATERIALS: Reynolds Rosalie, a slubbed yarn, (40 gram balls), 8 (9, 10, 11, 12) balls.
Aluminum Crochet Hooks, Sizes G and H.
Matching sewing thread.

GAUGE: With size H hook 4 hdc = 1 inch; 7 rows = 2 inches.

Blocking Measurements					
Sizes	8	10	12	14	16
Body Bust Size (In Inches)					
	31½	32½	34	36	38
Actual Knitting Measurements					
	32	34	36	38	40
Width across back or front at underarm					
	16	17	18	19	20
Width of sleeve at upperarm					
	12	12½	13	13½	14

STITCH: Half double crochet (hdc): Chain specified number of sts. Row 1: Hdc in 3rd ch from hook and in each ch across, ch 2, turn. Row 2: Skip first hdc, counts as 1 hdc, hdc in each hdc across, hdc in top of turning ch. Ch 2, turn. Repeat row 2 for pattern. TO BIND OFF: At beg of a row, sl st across number of sts specified, then sl st in next st, ch 2 and work in pattern across. At end of row, simply work across row to within number of sts to be bound off. Turn. To dec 1 hdc: Yo, draw up a lp in each of next 2 sts, yo and draw through all 4 lps on hook. To inc 1 hdc: Work 2 hdc in one hdc.

Pull

BACK: With size H hook ch loosely 64 (68, 72, 76, 80) to measure 16 (17, 18, 19, 20) inches; ch 2 more for turning ch. Work hdc on 64 (68, 72, 76, 80) sts until piece measures 6 inches from beg. Change to size G hook, continue even in hdc until piece measures 10 inches from beg. Change back to size H hook and continue even in hdc until piece measures 16 (16½, 17, 17, 17) inches from beg or desired length to underarm. SHAPE ARMHOLES: Bind off 3 (4, 4, 5, 5) sts at each end of next row. Continue in hdc and dec 1 st each end of every row 3 (3, 4, 4, 5) times—52 (54, 56, 58, 60) sts. Work even until armholes measure 7 (7½, 7½, 8, 8) inches above first bound-off sts. SHAPE SHOULDERS: Bind off 7 sts at each end of next row. Bind off 7 (7, 8, 8, 9) sts at each end of next row. Fasten off—24 (26, 26, 28, 28) sts remain for back neck. FRONT: Work same as back until armholes measure 3½ (4, 4, 4½, 4½) inches. SHAPE SQUARE NECK: Next Row: Work across 14 (14, 15, 15, 16) sts. Ch 2, turn. Working on this side only, continue even in hdc until armhole measures same as back. SHAPE SHOULDER: Next Row: Bind off 7 sts at beg of armhole edge, finish row. Bind off 7 (7, 8, 8, 9) sts at end of next row. Fasten off. Leave center 24 (26, 26, 28, 28) sts unworked for center front neck, attach yarn to remaining sts and work other side to correspond. SLEEVES: With size H hook ch loosely 38 (38, 40, 40, 42) to measure 9½ (9½, 10, 10, 10½) inches; ch 2 more. Work hdc on 38 (38, 40, 40, 42) hdc for 3 inches. Continue in hdc, inc 1 st each end every 8th (7, 7, 6, 6)th row 5 (6, 6, 7, 7) times—48 (50, 52, 54, 56) sts. Work even until sleeve measures 17 inches from beg or desired length to underarm. SHAPE CAP: Bind off 4

sts at each end of next row. Continue in hdc and dec 1 st each end of every other row 9 (10, 11, 12, 13) times. Bind off 3 sts at each end of next 2 rows. Fasten off—10 sts remain. FINISHING: With matching sewing thread, sew side, shoulder and sleeve seams. Sew sleeves in place. Using size G hook work 1 rnd hdc around neck, each sleeve and lower edge of blouse. Press garment carefully on wrong side through a damp cloth with a medium hot iron. Do not press down hard on garment. Press seams open flat on wrong side. Run in all yarn ends on wrong side.

Scarf

With size H hook ch loosely 16 to measure 4 inches; ch 2 more. Work even in hdc on 16 sts until piece measures 60 inches or desired length. Crochet 1 rnd hdc all around scarf working (hdc, ch 1 and hdc) in each corner. Fasten off. FRINGE: Cut strands of yarn 10 inches long. For each fringe fold 3 strands in half to form a loop. Insert hook through first st at one end of scarf, draw folded loops through, then draw loose ends through loop. Pull up to fasten. Work a fringe in every other st across each end of scarf. Trim fringe evenly.

42 ⊗
Boat-necked, easy

SIZES: Small, Medium, Large.

MATERIALS: Spinnerin Sabrina, (50 gram ball), 6 (7, 8) balls OR Sports Yarn (2 oz. balls), 5 (6, 6) balls.
Knitting Needles, 1 pair each No. 4 and No. 5.

GAUGE: St st: 6 sts = 1 inch; 8 rows = 1 inch.
     Pattern st: 4½ sts = 1 inch; 8 rows = 1 inch.

Blocking Measurements			
Sizes	Small	Medium	Large
Bust (In Inches)			
	34	37½	41

PATTERN STITCH: Row 1: K 3, p 2, k 1, * k 2 tog, yo; repeat from * ending k 3, p 2, k 3. Rows 2, 4 and 6: K 1, p 2, k 2, p to last 5 sts, k 2, p 2, k 1. Row 3: K 3, p 2, k 2, * yo, k 2 tog; repeat from * ending yo, k 2, p 2, k 3. Row 5: K 3, p 2, k 2, * k 2 tog, yo; repeat from * ending k 2 tog, k 3, p 2, k 3. Repeat these 6 rows for body pattern. BACK: With smaller needles cast on 96 (106, 116) sts. Row 1: * K 1, p 1; repeat from * to end. Repeat Row 1 until 4 inches from beg. Change to larger needles. On right side of work p 1 row dec 20 (22, 24) sts evenly across. K 1 row on 76 (84, 92) sts. Beg Pattern. Work until about 20 (20¾, 20¾) inches from beg, ending with Row 6 of pattern. Neck and Shoulder Band: Row 1 (right side): K 3, p to last 3 sts, k 3. Row 2: K 1, p 2, k to last 3 sts, p 2, k 1. Row 3: K 3, p 2, k to last 5 sts, p 2, k 3. Row 4: K 1, p 2, k 2, p to last 5 sts, k 2, p 2, k 1. Repeat Rows 3 and 4, 9 times more. Bind off loosely. FRONT: Work same as back. SLEEVES: With smaller needles cast on 48 (52, 56) sts. Work in rib pattern as back for 3 inches. Change to larger needles. P 1 row, inc 4 sts evenly across. K 1 row on 52 (56, 60) sts. Row 1: K 1, * k 2 tog, yo; repeat from * ending k 1. Rows 2, 4, and 6: Purl. Row 3: K 2, * yo, k 2 tog; repeat from * to end. Row 5: K 2, * k 2 tog, yo; repeat from * ending k 2. Repeat these 6 rows for pattern. Work until about 19 inches from beg, ending with Row 6. P 1 row, k 1 row. Bind off very loosely. FINISHING: Fold top K bands in half to inside and sew down. Sew or weave 3 (3¼, 3½) inches tog at each side of top for shoulders. Sew side seams leaving a 7 (7½, 8) inch opening to shoulder edge for sleeves. Sew sleeve seams. Set in sleeves easing into armhole.